LESSONS FROM THE LION'S DEN

LESSONS FROM THE LION'S DEN

 Jossey-Bass Publishers
San Francisco

Therapeutic Management of Children in Psychiatric Hospitals and Treatment Centers

by Nancy S. Cotton

foreword by
Robert Coles, M.D.

Substantial discounts on bulk quantities of Jossey-Bass books
are available to corporations, professional associations, and other
organizations. For details and discount information, contact the
special sales department at Jossey-Bass Inc., Publishers.
(415) 433-1740; Fax (415) 433-0499.

For sales outside the United States, contact Maxwell Macmillan
International Publishing Group, 866 Third Avenue, New York,
New York 10022.

Manufactured in the United States of America

The paper used in this book is acid-free and meets the
State of California requirements for recycled paper
(50 percent recycled waste, including 10 percent
postconsumer waste), which are the strictest guidelines
for recycled paper currently in use in the United States.

10% POST
CONSUMER
WASTE

Drawing on title page spread copyright © 1993 by Mary Cotton.

Library of Congress Cataloging-in-Publication Data

Cotton, Nancy S., date.
 Lessons from the lion's den : therapeutic management of children
in psychiatric hospitals and treatment centers / Nancy S. Cotton.
 — 1st ed.
  p. cm. — (The Jossey-Bass social and behavioral science
series)
 Includes bibliographical references and index.
 ISBN 1-55542-575-5
 1. Behavior disorders in children — Treatment. 2. Temper tantrums
in children — Treatment. 3. Discipline of children. 4. Problem
children — Behavior modification. 5. Mentally ill children — Care.
I. Title. II. Series.
RJ506.B44C67 1993
618.92'891 — dc20   93-3623
                                                      CIP

FIRST EDITION
HB Printing   10 9 8 7 6 5 4 3 2 1   *Code 9374*

The Jossey-Bass
Social and Behavioral Science Series

CONTENTS

Part One:
Designing the Framework of Treatment

TABLES, FIGURES, AND EXHIBITS

Figures

Exhibits

FOREWORD

I well remember working with children such as those described so compellingly in this book — quite troubled boys and girls who had to be confined in a state facility outside of Boston, now closed. I was a resident in child psychiatry, and I regret to say that I thought I knew a lot more than I really did know. One day, as I told an enraged, temper-ridden boy that he would be denied various "privileges" because of his verbal outbursts and his physical assaults on other children, he turned on me — hit me hard with a comment I would never forget: "You think you're such a big shot, but I can see right through you — you're just as scared as I am!"

I had, of course, just finished telling him how "scared" he was. So doing, I had pretended to be calm, self-assured, and knowledgeable — confident of myself as an observer of others, an interpreter of the psychological truths that lay buried within their minds. But that boy knew otherwise — knew that a young, inexperienced doctor was hiding *his* anxiety and apprehension behind a mask of professional "cool," a posture of detachment interrupted, now and then, by wordy psychological assertions meant to assert authority and power.

And needless to say, I wasn't immediately privy to the kind of self-awareness that boy was trying to press on me. I pretended to ignore his comment, insisting to him that *his* troubles were the issue: *his* worries and his unrealistic expectations of others. Only later, as I struggled hard and long to forget his words, did I realize how shrewdly he'd sized me up. A child in many ways trapped by life, with diminished prospects of having a reasonably happy existence, had at least asserted a desperate capacity to provoke one of his "keepers": he got the doctor's mind going (and going) no matter how hard the doctor tried to concentrate exclusively on the patient's problems.

That boy came back to me as I read this instructive and poignant book — a powerful evocation of what happens when earnest and well-meaning (and, not rarely, frustrated and stymied) doctors, nurses, psychologists, and social workers try to take on the roar, the rage, the ferocity of impulse implied in the title. Again and again, the author connects us not only to theory but the lived particulars of certain young lives — boys and girls whose words, deeds, confusions, and confrontations challenged a whole world before they entered the hospital "den" and whose struggles continued, even became more hard-fought, when they had become confined. We meet these children, read about them, and attend their spoken remarks, even their written words — cries of the heart, exclamations offered in response to all sorts of worries. These are children who have already had a terrible time of it, who have suffered an assortment of emotional disasters, who have been treated badly, indeed, at the hands of fate. The hospital, often enough, is their last chance: a place where they finally may be able to face down the various demons that already have tormented them to the point of ruin. Theirs are lives constantly, mercilessly disrupted — lives vulnerable and fragile, hurt and sad, at times disorganized to the point of seeming chaotic. We are told, in the pages that follow, how those who want to help such children, want to lead them, eventually, out of the "den," go about their work, trying to offer hope and purpose as well as a reliable and predictable rhythm of daily activity.

In a sense, then, this book offers a documentary rendering of a certain world — a place where reason and compassion struggle with raw instinct, with a history of violation, of pain so deep and strong that it has become a most formidable antagonist. All those who want to know how such pain can slowly be understood, confronted, and challenged, be made to yield its tenacious hold on some children at least, will want to attend the pages that follow with care, with respect. Soon enough, I suspect such readers will feel the gratitude that students show an intelligent, conscientious teacher—in this instance, one whose story as a brave and determined and knowing healer began, one suspects, during her own childhood, as her sister, to whom the book is dedicated, challenged those near her in many ways. The rest, so to speak, is one able clinician's, now lucid, open-hearted writer's, personal history.

June 1993   Robert Coles
                               Professor of Psychiatry
                               and Medical Humanities
                               Harvard Medical School
                               and Pulitzer Prize–winning author
                               of *The Children of Crisis*

In Memory of My Sister
Virginia Clare Shea
February 8, 1947–June 12, 1976

Ginny was funny, intelligent, and loving.
She was also the bravest person I ever
knew. Her struggle with schizophrenia is
the inspiration for my work. Every
patient I ever knew was better off
because she lived.

Children loved Ginny's conversation and
sense of occasion. She knew how to
bring out the best in a child. Ask Moira.

PREFACE

This is the book I wish I had when I became the director of a child psychiatric inpatient unit in 1977. As the unit director, I was expected to oversee decisions about the practical management of disturbed children during the course of an average day. I could find no single theory or resource that presented developmentally and clinically useful guidelines for the therapeutic basis of management decisions for children during periods of either normal emotional and behavioral distress or serious and dangerous behavioral crises. Instead, I listened to frequent conflicts over which path was more therapeutic: limit setting or permissiveness; emotional expressiveness or behavioral change; insight or conformity.

Lessons from the Lion's Den: Therapeutic Management of Children in Psychiatric Hospitals and Treatment Centers presents a comprehensive developmental-clinical model for decision making in therapeutic management that does not choose one extreme of action over another. This model prescribes therapeutic action based on what a patient needs in different phases of treatment. The model integrates theory and practical treatment interventions from multiple theoretical perspectives and varied treatment settings. It incorporates restrictive treatment interventions from the clinical literature for the child in severe psychological crisis; clinical psychotherapeutic techniques from the treatment of less disturbed children; and strategies from the normal child-rearing literature for the same child during healthier phases of treatment.

Our model integrates ideas from a wide range of perspectives: normal developmental, psychodynamic, social-learning, psychiatric, educational, and parent training. Therapeutic management is described in terms of practical, creative solutions to the common situations encountered in clinical work with disturbed children and their families. These situations include aggression, vandalism, running away, sexual acting out, poor listening and disobedience, low self-esteem, self-abuse, peer problems, bizarre thinking and behavior, and despair and hopelessness.

This model developed out of a collaborative effort of nurses, counselors, social workers, psychologists, psychiatrists, pediatricians, educators, occupational therapists, therapeutic recreationalists, and expressive therapists to treat emotionally disturbed children in a psychiatric inpatient setting and in residential treatment settings. However, the model describes clinical strategies that are relevant for children with developmental, behavioral, and emotional difficulties in outpatient and day treatments, as well as in school settings. This book should be of value to clinicians and special educators who work with hard-to-reach children in need of special help to develop more adaptive ways of coping with problems and stress.

I hope that clinicians from the fields of nursing, child care, psychology, social work, counseling, psychiatry, special education, and recreational, expressive, and occupational therapy will turn to this book during the training, program development, and clinical phases of their work with children.

Overview of the Contents

This volume consists of two parts. Part One outlines the first phase of the model, or designing the framework of treatment.

The framework of treatment consists of the environmental and interpersonal aspects of the holding environment for therapeutic management. Part Two describes the second phase of the model, which presents techniques for the overwhelmed child who needs control from without. We then outline the techniques that help the child transition back into the program following a behavioral crisis.

Future writings will focus on the work of the third and fourth phases of therapeutic management that teach children new skills and new meanings and then help them carry these treatment gains out of the treatment setting. Although this work begins during the inpatient phases we describe in this book, the third and final phases of therapeutic management usually become the focus of treatment that occurs outside of hospital and residential settings. Many of our techniques developed for later-phase work can "travel" to the newly developed components of the system of care for severely disturbed children.

Chapter One outlines the environmental context of treatment, which sets the stage for the interpersonal interactions between patients, families, and staff members. Culture, space, people, and time are designed to protect, engage, and teach patients and their families. The environmental context of treatment is particularly important for relationship-resistant patients who are unable to form adult-child relationships or use them when they are feeling overwhelmed by negative feelings or experiences.

Chapter Two describes the interpersonal holding environment, which is made up of the triad of empathy, communication, and discipline. These interdependent processes are the bases of socialization in both healthy childrearing and therapeutic management. Empathy consists of our efforts to feel and understand the child's point of view. It leads to genuine communication, which is the only basis for an effective discipline system. Chapter Two reviews the steps in the socialization process and focuses on the practical skills needed to create empathic connections. It concludes with a discussion of the empathic formulation: our translation of what the child's behavior means for the child and what it is trying to say and do for the child.

Chapter Three is devoted to an extensive description of

the skills of good listening and helpful talking, as well as the problems with not helpful or destructive talk. We outline and illustrate specific skills for helpful communication that can bring out the best in the child. The chapter concludes with a discussion of nonverbal therapeutic communication, the characteristics of not helpful and destructive touching, and the prevention of institutional abuse of children.

Chapter Four outlines the eight steps of a growth-promoting discipline system. This system is geared to each child's developmental level of functioning, encourages children to experience and express feelings in adaptive ways, restricts maladaptive behavior, sets reasonable standards and values, models adaptive functioning and self-control, uses a lot of encouragement and praise, and imposes kind and firm negative consequences when children make mistakes and cannot live up to adult expectations. The chapter emphasizes that discipline is one step in the adult's efforts to teach self-control and adaptive coping with feelings, daily challenges, and stress. The foundation of the discipline process is the two-part adult response to children: adults respond to all feelings with understanding and acceptance; they respond to some behavior with approval and other behavior with disapproval and limits. Special attention is given to the therapeutic design of the penalty step (punishment), which delivers negative consequences following misbehavior.

Chapter Five describes the modifications that need to be made to the normal discipline process to allow the emotionally disturbed child to complete the discipline step. More specifically, we focus on time-out and privilege systems as examples of therapeutic discipline. The chapter concludes with a summary of the guiding principles for therapeutic discipline.

Chapter Six introduces the active containing interventions that are designed for the relationship-resistant, undersocialized, and ego-deficit child who is unable or only partially able to respond to therapeutically designed structure, empathy, communication, and discipline. The action-oriented techniques are designed to stop and contain a child's maladaptive and dangerous behaviors: quiet rooms, physical holding, seclusion, mechanical restraints, and psychopharmacotherapy (including chemical restraints). Clinical vignettes illustrate the ways of using these control techniques with empathy, respect, and attention to the full range of a child's psychological needs.

Chapter Seven describes the techniques to transition the child back into the milieu program and relationships, focusing on the reactive contract. The components of the reactive contract translate the separate psychological steps needed for the "return journey" into required actions for the child and staff. We emphasize that the postbehavioral crisis period provides a unique therapeutic opportunity to help children profit from their mistakes and learn how to repair relationships.

We conclude with an epilogue that addresses the impact of this work on the staff who care for these children. We use a metaphorical story to illustrate the ways we all meet our own inner lions when we try to help others tame theirs. Our lives are changed profoundly by the opportunity to help these children as well as their parents and siblings.

The People in This Book

I was not alone in the work described in this book. For this reason, I talk of "we" throughout the book, emphasizing the essential collaborative role of the interdisciplinary team in the delivery of therapeutic management: nurses, counselors, occupational therapists, recreational therapists, expressive therapists, educators, social workers, psychiatrists, pediatricians, psychologists, unit secretaries, and hospital administrators. The treatment approach is a synthesis of the work of many creative, caring, and hard-working clinicians who listened and responded to many creative, caring, and hard-working children, parents, and siblings. The staff were called on to think creatively, care deeply, and respond imaginatively during stressful times. At the end of this volume, I have listed the people who worked with me from 1977 through 1987 at New England Memorial Hospital. They created the clinical "stuff" from which the book was written.

The "we" also includes the 600 children and their families treated during this period. To respect their privacy, I will not name them. However, they are all present in the spirit of this book as well as in the clinical vignettes and their drawings. For purposes of illustration, the book introduces twelve children who appear throughout the phases of treatment. The children represent composites of actual children, with multiple changes of pertinent details to fully conceal their identities. Any similarity to actual persons is purely accidental. A more detailed description of the book's children is provided at the end of the volume. The clinical vignettes actually happened, but again I have changed pertinent facts to make them unrecognizable, including the identities of staff members involved. The vignettes present an accurate picture of what we say and do with the children and their parents. I thank them for all they have taught us.

Writing the stories of the children, parents, and staff brought them back into my life. Working alone in my study, I was suddenly surrounded by people. My memories included intense remembrances of love, learning, anger, frustration, sadness, curiosity, and laughter. It was hard and painful work, but I was reminded of how much we laughed and clapped. As I sifted through my notes and memories, I chuckled at the children's ingenuity in defying us and at our resourcefulness as we tried to join them. I recalled meeting discouraged and defensive parents who initially repelled us with hostility, then broke our hearts with the weight of their own maimed childhoods and difficult lives.

I realized again why I do this work and why I wanted to write a book — for my colleagues who also love this work, for my fellow parents who love their children, and for the children themselves. In the writing and the reading we are connected across time and place. We form the net that hopefully will catch falling children and their families before they hit the ground. I also realized (as you will read in the concluding chapter) that through the children and families, we developed our humanity as we faced our own inner lions in the course of helping them tame theirs.

Acknowledgments

The book is based primarily on my experience as director of the Child Psychiatry Inpatient Unit at New England Memorial

Hospital in Stoneham, Massachusetts, and on my consultation experiences since I left the unit in 1987. I would like to thank the following colleagues and mentors who supported and taught me through the years. Ron Geraty hired me, developed the vision with me, mentored me, joined with me, and allowed the program to blossom through his remarkable administrative talents and love of children and family life. Dr. Mirna Aeschlimann, the late Dr. Herb Siegert, and Fredda Zuckerman-Match had the humanistic and clinical vision to start Massachusetts's first psychiatric inpatient service for children in a general hospital. I thank the administration of the hospital for creating such an exceptionally caring environment for this work: Henry Wall, Jim Boyle, Wolfgang Von Mack, Landon Kite, and Jim Bruer, who encouraged this program for children even when it cost them money or when the kids tried to destroy the place. We had a wonderful time! The Children's Unit has continued to develop and change under the leadership of Dr. David Binder and his new staff.

I am personally indebted to Fredda Zuckerman-Match, Helen Finch, Barbara Stephens, Sue Ayers, Gino DeSalvatore, Clare deZengotita, Deborah Rosenman, Suzanne Vienneau, and Sam Rofman for all they taught me and put up with in me. My wonderful colleague and friend, David Fassler, has helped me to create this work, write it, and then name it (he knew about the lions). In writing this book I met a new colleague and valued friend, Barbara Okun, who generously spent a lot of time encouraging and instructing me on how to write a book. She ended up editing most of it and making it possible for me to finish it. Thank you, Barbara.

I am very grateful for encouragement and critical reviews of this work given to me by my colleagues and friends Gordon Harper, Lyn Sanford, Joseph Woolston, Jackie Scarbrough, and Rick Barth (Jossey-Bass introduced us). Alan Rinzler, my editor at Jossey-Bass, has been extremely helpful, wearing both editorial and clinical hats. I would also like to thank Gracia A. Alkema and Mary White, who were my first connections at Jossey-Bass.

I want to thank my friends and family, who've helped me write this book even when it interfered with their lives. My friends have fed me, listened to me, prodded me, amused me, and believed in me. It was my husband Paul's idea for me to write a book. I now can thank him for the idea and his belief in my capacity to do it, as well as for his editorial assistance and clinical insights. My sister, Moira Shea, made me feel good about what I was doing and helped with the final preparation of the manuscript. Anna, Mary, and Billy Cotton have been wonderfully understanding and helpful. They made suggestions along the way, sharing their wise and considerate philosophies of how to help children: Anna was always caring and practical, Billy stressed listening and talking to the kids, and Mary told me to make them laugh. Mary also assured me if she could learn to read, I could write a book. We did it, Mary!

Gay Head, Massachusetts   Nancy S. Cotton
June 1993

THE AUTHOR

Nancy S. Cotton is an instructor in psychology in the Department of Psychiatry, Harvard Medical School at Massachusetts General Hospital. She received her B.A. degree (1967) in psychology from Newton College of the Sacred Heart and both her M.S. degree (1973) and Ph.D. degree (1976) in developmental psychology from Tufts University in the Department of Psychology. She completed her clinical internship at McLean Hospital and a child and adolescent postdoctoral fellowship at Beth Israel Hospital in the Department of Psychology.

Cotton has been a principal teacher and supervisor in Harvard Medical School child psychiatry and child psychology training programs since 1977, first at Cambridge Hospital and now at Massachusetts General Hospital. She teaches the core child development course in the Harvard Medical School Consolidated Department of Psychiatry. Cotton was director of the Child Psychiatry Inpatient Unit at New England Memorial Hospital in Stoneham, Massachusetts, a Harvard Medical School teaching affiliate, from 1977 through 1987. She supervises child psychiatrists and consults to child and adolescent treatment programs in the Pembroke/Westwood Health System. She has been a consultant to the Division of Child and Adolescent Services in the Massachusetts Department of Mental Health since 1987. In addition to her teaching and consulting, Cotton has a private practice in psychotherapy and parent guidance. She is a member of several professional associations, including the American and Massachusetts Psychological Associations, the Society of Research in Child Development, the American Orthopsychiatric Association, and the National Registry of Health Service Providers.

Cotton's principal clinical, teaching, and writing interest has been the development of creative treatment programs and individual treatment solutions for severely disturbed children and their families, based on her academic background in developmental psychology and training in clinical psychopathology. She presents frequently at professional conferences and consults nationally on the organization, design, and evaluation of therapeutic treatment settings. She conducts workshops and lectures nationally on various aspects of developmental psychopathology and the treatment of severely disturbed children and adolescents: milieu treatment, therapeutic management, the therapeutic use of seclusion and restraint, the development and treatment of self-esteem, and the therapeutic design of physical treatment spaces. She has written articles and book chapters on these subjects. Among the journals she has contributed to are *American Journal of Orthopsychiatry, Journal of the American Academy of Child and Adolescent Psychiatry, Child Psychiatry and Human Development, Journal of Studies on Alcohol,* and *Hospital and Community Psychiatry.*

LESSONS FROM THE LION'S DEN

Introduction: What Is Therapeutic Management?

Ralph (age twelve) was admitted to our inpatient unit because he attacked the principal of his school while the principal was lecturing him on his disruptive behavior in science class. He had been disciplined and suspended frequently in the last six months. His biological father wondered whether Ralph could still live with him, his new wife, and his new baby. Ralph is coarse, very fat, wears ill-fitting clothes, and loves to "gross out" girls and adults. When he is angry, he completely loses control and strikes out at whoever is in the way.

> Ralph was in the quiet room after he had disrupted our community meeting with lewd remarks about another patient, Maria, and a counselor, Richard. He had also punched and kicked two counselors, Fran and Steve, on the way to the quiet room. He screamed and punched the walls for almost a half hour. I approached him after the door was unlocked. Ralph was lying down on the bench when I came in.
>
> "I heard your roaring and talked to Fran about your clawing," I said matter-of-factly.
>
> "He's a fuckin' liar! I didn't claw him. I don't roar either. What do ya think I am, a fuckin' lion?"

"Yes . . . You remind me of a lion . . . not a very well-behaved lion. I've never actually met a real lion, only children who remind me of lions. Well-behaved lions are handsome and strong."

"I'm fat, not handsome. I don't want to talk about this. Talk to those little brats about your lion stuff."

"You said yesterday you weren't going to get angry anymore. You were going to be good. But I told you it wouldn't work."

"I tried. Don't rub it in."

"You need your anger."

Ralph thought for a minute and replied with some bitterness, "Oh sure! Tell that one to my dad's wife."

I was quiet for a moment. "Your anger is like the lion inside. It gives you the kind of guts you need to get what you want and get through the hard times in your life."

"I'm always in trouble."

"I'd rather see you tame your lion and make it your friend. Then you'd know there was something strong and handsome inside to help you when things get tough. You could even introduce him to people, when you learn to like and trust someone." Ralph was listening.

"Would you like us to help you train and make friends with your lion?"

Ralph had been curled up, listening carefully to my words. His arm was covering his face. He began to smile as he spoke. "No. I can bite! I can scratch! What a stupid thing to say," he giggled, then made an imitation roar and a fake scratch in the air. "You're weird."

I laughed at his imitation. "You're not. You do a good imitation of a lion. Can I bring you a glass of water, before you go back to your group?"

"Sure."

Our patients are the discontented, sad, and angry lions in the playing fields and classrooms of childhood. We want them to keep their lion strength, passion, and aggression, within the treatment settings and strategies we create for them. We don't want them to abandon the inner lion but to befriend and tame it.

Taming lions starts with respect for the lion. It requires skill, patience, and love. We offer ourselves to our patients as teachers and temporary lion keepers, until they can become their own. That is the essence of therapeutic management.

Therapeutic management is to the care of disturbed children what normal socialization is to childrearing. The socialization process describes how children's relationships to adults help children develop effective and acceptable ways of

- Getting needs met and wishes granted
- Adaptively coping with stress
- Expressing feelings
- Controlling internal impulses and feelings
- Maintaining a positive self-concept
- Acting responsibly and ethically
- Creating satisfying relationships with adults and peers

The socialization process incorporates the notion that raising healthy children requires adult-child interactions that balance adult modeling of positive behavior, nurturance, discipline, and child participation in problem solving according to the children's developmental stage, temperament, parental values, and personal style.

Although our theory of therapeutic management is modeled on how adults need to interact with normal children to promote healthy development, the process looks different with our patients. Socialization on an inpatient unit incorporates "corrective steps" in the normal socialization process in order to address the consequences of pathological development. Therapeutic management creates a "corrective experience" (Kalogjera, Bedi, Watson, and Meyer, 1989, p. 280). The painful reality of working with disturbed children is that they are often incapable of making use of adult-child relationships due to past distortions in relationships or their own cognitive and ego deficits. Thus, our work starts with the problem behavior and the internal damage caused by pathological development.

The process of therapeutic management is based on what all children need to grow and develop (the components of normal childrearing or socialization) plus the corrective steps needed for emotionally disturbed children who have to get back on the path of positive development. The corrective steps are culled from the history of institutional care of children and child psychotherapies.

A Brief History of Child Treatment

The history of institutional care of children provides the basis of current therapeutic management practices in hospitals or residential treatment centers (Alt, 1960; Mayer, Richman, and Balcerzak, 1978; Noshpitz, 1982; Harper and Geraty, 1987; Whittaker, 1979). Historically, treatment was categorized as having two distinct components: psychotherapy and milieu management. Management tasks were linked to the physical and protective needs of the child, as opposed to the psychological treatment needs of the child. Management in this sense took place in the almshouses of the seventeenth century and in the orphanages, reform schools, and penal institutions that developed in the eighteenth and nineteenth centuries. The patient care in these institutions was guided by the following concerns: religious principles, the need for protection and corrective discipline, an emphasis on constructive work, and a desire for educational reform.

In the late nineteenth century, these institutions began to be transformed into residential treatment settings with a new purpose: to treat the unique psychological and developmental needs of children. Early programs recognized the importance of regimentation, routines, predictable scheduling, and discipline systems. Psychoanalytic theory shaped the design of the residential treatment centers in the early twentieth century. These institutions emphasized that the children's living situation or *milieu* should be protectively benign and separate from the "real" treatment that took place in the psychotherapy office.

Psychoanalytic treatment was based on the centrality of regression and transference as principles of treatment. Thus, programs continued to espouse the separateness of management and psychotherapy. Theorists believed that involving the psychotherapist in the practical realities of the children's lives would dilute the therapeutic relationship. Also, patients would feel freer to regress during psychotherapy without fear that the treatment would influence decisions about privileges on the unit. Adult psychiatric inpatient treatment developed the "administrator-therapist" split to separate administrative (management) tasks from therapeutic tasks performed by different people (Stanton and Schwartz, 1954). Accordingly, the assumed value of psychotherapy over milieu treatment was incorporated into the education and training of doctors and social workers until recently.

Defining psychotherapy as the definitive treatment and keeping it separate from the work in the children's milieu was questioned and modified when:

* Residential clients and inpatients were more severely disturbed and their problems proved less amenable to change from psychotherapy alone (Noshpitz, 1962, 1971).
* The administrator-therapist split was creating confusion and dubious treatment results (Gutheil, 1982a, 1982b, 1982c; Beck, Macht, Levinson, and Strauss, 1967; Caudill, Redlich, Gilmore, and Brody, 1952; Caudill, 1958).
* Psychotherapists became directors of residential treatment centers (for example, Bettelheim and Sylvester, 1948; Cohen and Grinspoon, 1963; Redl and Wineman, 1951, 1952; Noshpitz, 1962).
* The therapeutic potential in the systematic design of the children's living environment became more obvious.

In the mid-twentieth century, a new model of milieu treatment evolved that specifies an integrated relationship between the milieu experience and psychotherapy. This approach emphasizes the therapeutic manipulation of time and space and of individual and group experiences in order to make the children's living situation itself a comprehensive therapeutic intervention. In this model, the goals and work of milieu treatment overlap in part with the therapeutic goals and work of psychotherapy. Milieu treatment and individual psychotherapy are both "real treatment" working in a complementary relationship with each other.

To summarize, milieu treatment is the therapeutic manipulation of all aspects of the children's living situation. Therapeutic management is one component of milieu treatment.

What Is Therapeutic Management?

Therapeutic management consists of adult-child interactions and interventions that take place in the children's living situation and that are designed to protect, engage, and teach the children. The goal of therapeutic management is to heal suffering, contain and modify maladaptive behavior, promote development of greater competence, and build a stronger and more valued sense of self for emotionally troubled children.

Therapeutic management integrates therapeutic and management values and functions. The word *therapeutic* implies values such as healing, understanding, permissiveness, expression of feelings, insight, individualized treatment, and the primacy of developing therapist-patient relationships. The word *management* means actively doing something for the patient, such as providing shelter and food, monitoring self-care, providing protection, containing dangerous or unacceptable behavior, establishing and maintaining schedules, routines, and rules, and teaching moral development and the development of self-control through the discipline process.

The concept of therapeutic management respects the therapeutic potential in children's behavioral interactions with their environment. The therapeutic interpersonal environment is designed to value the apparently mundane as well as more emotionally significant interactions between children and adults in the course of their daily lives. The process of therapeutic management is made up of even the "little" interpersonal moments when one says "yes," "please," "thank you," or "no," and the moments when one nonverbally communicates pleasure (smile), disapproval (frown), distress (wince), or sadness (tears).

The way a child is handled, protected, controlled, guided, or managed can teach, model, and convey emotional messages that can be therapeutic or nontherapeutic. Consider the situation with a recently admitted patient on our inpatient unit.

Lisa (age eleven) started making lewd remarks during the Friday night movie. A new counselor, Susan, asked her to stop or leave the group. Lisa blew up, hitting walls, kicking furniture, and swearing at kids and staff. Susan was injured when she tried to get Lisa to the quiet room.

In our attempt to understand what happened and why, we learned that Susan had felt badly for Lisa and had made an exception to the unit rules for her. Lisa had received her fourth check on a "movie star chart," which meant that she would not be able to go to the Friday night movie. Our routine specified that a child who received nine stars and less than three checks (we do not expect perfection) was invited to movie night.

Contrary to unit routine, Susan gave Lisa another chance, rationalizing that she "didn't know the rules yet." Susan had felt that it was unfair to punish Lisa, who had been through many unsuccessful foster placements and had not seen her mother for over a year. Susan had hoped that her leniency would convey her sympathy and undo some of Lisa's past pain.

This is "untherapeutic management." Lisa learned that she could change the rules and steal the good time. Causing trouble had become her way of easing inner tension, diffusing her sorrow, and ensuring predictable reactions. Susan learned that what you need to give a patient is not always the total acceptance that it feels right to give. Let's rewrite the scenario.

A half hour before the movies were to start, Lisa earned her fourth check by teasing a younger patient. She knew that if she earned four checks, she would be unable to go to movie night. She was given a choice of spending the time in her room or in the quiet room. Choosing to be in her room, Lisa lay down on her bed and started to sing lewd songs about Susan and a male counselor.

She was asked to stop. When she continued in a louder voice, she was asked to move to the quiet room, where she was told that she could say whatever she wanted with the door shut.

When Lisa refused to move from her bed, Susan was one of the four staff members who tried to walk her to the quiet room. Lisa fought them and needed physical holding and locked-door seclusion. During this struggle, Susan was injured.

Susan observed Lisa every five minutes from the window in the seclusion room door. When Lisa started to cry, Susan unlocked the door and entered the quiet room and comforted her. Lisa uttered a few weak swears through her sobs. Soon she was curled up in Susan's arms and cried softly for about half an hour. Susan said very little. She told Lisa that she was a brave child who had had terrible luck and a lot of unfair things happen to her.

She said that she hoped that Lisa did not blame herself for all of it.
The evening ended with Lisa and Susan having hot chocolate in Lisa's room before Lisa fell asleep.

Why is this scenario therapeutic management? The answer to
this question is the central theme of this book. *Susan's response
to Lisa included ingredients of structure (aimed at containment), followed
by nurturance, empathic listening, and talking.* The important point
in Susan's encounter with Lisa is the sequence of interventions,
which Lisa determined.

How do we give children what they can take in, at a particular moment, to cope with that moment in the best way they
can? The star chart was a way to structure and protect those
children who would need to ruin the movie time because they
did not feel that they deserved the special event or were unable
to follow the rules of group living during the event. Allowing
children to fail by ruining the movie time is not therapeutic.
It becomes yet another failure for children whose lives are already full of failures. The star chart routine gives children an
opportunity to weed themselves out of the good time, putting
them in control of their lives. The star chart is part of the unit
structure that creates a safe adult protective boundary to test
and oppose, acting like parental limits in the home. When Susan circumvented this for Lisa, she weakened the unit structure and made the environment less predictable for her, and
therefore less safe.

These children and their families take a while to show
us what they can take and use. This often means saving our
empathy, our praise, our humor, our listening, and our affection while we focus on providing the supportive controls and
boundaries that our patients don't have the psychological resources to construct or sustain for themselves.

Our model of therapeutic management is based on the
principles of milieu treatment — the therapeutic manipulation
of time and space and of individual and group relationships.
The model also draws on other concepts borrowed from newer
child treatments that focus on family involvement, pediatric psychopharmacology, social-cognitive competence building, and

well-articulated behavior management approaches. Therapeutic management includes:

- *Dynamic* therapies, which offer strategies for developing insight, expressing and regulating intense feelings, changing self-concepts, reworking trauma, and creating healthier relationship capacities.
- *Behavioral and social-cognitive* therapies, which provide techniques and practical programs for building interpersonal, prosocial, and psychological coping skills.
- *Biomedical* treatments, which address anxiety, hyperactivity, attention deficits, depression, and distorted thought processes. In particular, psychopharmacological treatment can increase the child's capacity to make use of milieu treatment by minimizing and buffering the cognitive, affective, and attention deficits that disrupt and distort the child's interactions with people and environmental demands.
- *Systems or family* therapy approaches, which help understand what interactional patterns have been used pathologically in families, sometimes through multiple generations, and why. These same patterns of interaction are reenacted in the relationships children forge with us during treatment.

Therapeutic management is ambitious and imaginative; it effectively reaches children who have profound and pervasive problems. When possible, we will bring the children's families into the hospital living situation so that they can participate in and contribute to milieu treatment. Parents and siblings are the natural models and teachers for our patients.

Some of the most important work in the milieu occurs when we can enhance the parents' capacity to understand, communicate with, and discipline their children. The concept of therapeutic management allows us to talk about the therapeutic potential in the daily interpersonal exchanges between children and their peers, family, and staff. When these exchanges are shaped to be therapeutic, children have the opportunity to develop hope, change behavior, build competence, and gain insight.

Some children, because of their history of conflict and suffering, cannot depend on, relate to, or communicate with other people. Even kindness and generosity stimulate hostility or indifference, as we saw with Lisa. For these "relationship-resistant" children (Trieschman, Whittaker, and Brendtro, 1969, p. 52), we use environmental or less interpersonal aspects of the milieu to soothe and care for their needs, before healing relationships can be developed. These children cannot rely on their fragile capacity to trust or depend on what an adult will do or say.

The practice of therapeutic management harnesses the therapeutic potential of personal relationships for those who can form them as well as the potential of contextual components of the environment. We pay special attention to the therapeutic potential of unit culture, space, and programming of time to create a therapeutic "holding environment" in which children can begin the process of treatment. Work at this level often precedes motivation for or interest in treatment. The systematic design of more protective and growth-promoting environments creates new frameworks for treatment and development.

A Four-Phase Model of Therapeutic Management

We propose a comprehensive model of therapeutic management that organizes diverse management and treatment skills and values into a sequence of four phases. Each phase has a primary goal of treatment. The model is prescriptive in the sense that we act according to what children and their families need, can use, and understand. *Protection and containment of pathology precede interventions to initiate new behaviors and new meanings.*

- *Phase I or Designing the Framework for Treatment* focuses on designing a welcoming environmental and an interpersonal framework of treatment.
- *Phase II or Responding to Trouble* provides "controls from without" for the child who has not developed internal controls.
- *Phase III or Introducing New Ways* helps children learn adaptive skills and understand their lives in new ways.

- *Phase IV or Leaving and Taking It All Home* describes the work of leaving the treatment setting and taking it all home.

All phases simultaneously attempt to protect, engage, and teach children and their families according to their current resources and problems. Table 1 outlines the four-phase model. In this book, we elaborate on Phases I and II and give a brief overview of Phases III and IV.

This model describes the total process of treatment from troubled start to more adaptive finish. Therapeutic management moves from our more unilateral actions during the early phases of treatment to more equal participation by staff, parents, and patients in the process of change and healing in the later phases of treatment.

Table 1. Four-Phase Model of Therapeutic Management.

I. Designing the framework for treatment
  A. The environmental context of the holding environment: culture, space, people, and time
  B. The interpersonal context of the holding environment: empathy, communication, and discipline
II. Responding to trouble
  A. Techniques for the overwhelmed child: controls from without
    1. Quiet room
    2. Physical holding
    3. Seclusion
    4. Mechanical restraints
    5. Psychopharmacotherapy, including chemical restraints
  B. Techniques for the child in transition: picking up the pieces and moving on
    1. Reactive contracts
    2. Child-oriented interventions
    3. Staff-oriented interventions
III. Introducing new ways
  A. New skills: preventive contracts
  B. New meanings: the stories children tell about themselves
IV. Leaving and taking it all home
  A. Saying goodbye
  B. Taking it all home

Thus the shape of the model is developmental. The adult-child relationship becomes the arena for treatment and development. As in development itself, there is no linear path from pathology to health; the course of treatment is uneven and reflects the role of regression in the service of growth and mastery (Siskind, 1982, p. 27).

Sequence of Phases

Our treatment approach starts with patients who lack verbal skills, trusting relationship capacities, and competency-building techniques. Therefore, we need to reorder the normal developmental process of discipline. In normal development, children develop attachments to their parents and learn to comply with parental expectations in order to maintain and strengthen those relationships. Children accept adult supervision and guidance to keep them safe until they can keep themselves safe.

We cannot assume that our patients have developed sufficient controls to keep themselves safe and to be safe with others. Nor can we assume that our patients will not run away from treatment. We cannot even assume patients' interest in changing their behavior in more adaptive directions. I remember an admission interview with Ralph:

> I asked him, "What are the things you don't like about yourself?"
> "I fight a lot," mumbled Ralph.
> "Do you want to change the fighting?"
> Ralph looked up and responded quickly, "Yeah, I want to fight better so that I can win more."

Ralph informed me that the "rules" were different in his town than on the unit. He came in fighting when things didn't go his way. It took some time to interest him in other ways of defending himself and proving that he is a "cool" kid without the use of physical violence.

Our experience with more extreme pathology and acute phases of mental illness requires us to emphasize a different sequence of events than in traditional treatment. *Extreme pathology requires immediate and effective attention to safety, protection, containment, and simplification of the environment.* It also means that children are unable to use relationships with others or internal resources to cope with stress or solve their problems.

When control of pathology is achieved, we can begin to help the child in other ways. The need to fit the treatment techniques to each child's current mixture of pathology and adaptation is emphasized. A basic position of this approach is that failure to find the right sequence and mixture of interventions indicates an inadequate treatment approach, not an inadequate child or untreatable family.

The sequence of phases also reflects a "one-step-ahead" approach, which leads to the use of active control techniques earlier in a potentially dangerous sequence. In crisis situations, we recommend the early use of interventions such as physical holding, seclusion, and restraints rather than using them as "last-resort" measures. While we recognize that the legislative and legal literature on managing emotionally disturbed children also recommends and in some cases mandates a last-resort (Tardiff, 1989) approach, we believe that stopping children before they hurt themselves or others is possible and desirable.

Phase I: Designing the Framework for Treatment

In Phase I we welcome, set the stage, and then design the framework of treatment, which includes environmental and interpersonal components.

The environmental context consists of:

- *Culture:* the values, philosophy, and atmosphere of treatment
- *Space:* the design and components of physical space
- *People:* the quantity, qualities, and organization of staff
- *Time:* the daily schedule and activity program

The environmental context of treatment is impersonal in the sense that it is designed to meet the needs of groups of children as well as of individual children. It does not depend on an individual child's capacity to relate to adults. All children

entering the hospital receive the same basic environment, which
does not depend on whether children are good or bad, motivated or unmotivated. The external structure needs to regulate,
protect, contain, encourage, and inspire.

Phase I also involves design of the interpersonal holding
environment. Organizational structure and staffing patterns determine how many people will be available for the children, when
they will be available, and what their role for the children will
be. The interpersonal holding environment defines how they
will relate to the children.

*The basis for the interpersonal framework is the triad of empathy,
communication, and discipline: genuine understanding leads to effective
communication and constructive discipline.* All children need to be
understood, talked to and listened to, and taught values and
acceptable behavior. Normal children need these kinds of adult-
child interactions to develop, and our patients also need them
with corrective modifications.

Our work assumes that without an empathic understanding of the child and family, treatment cannot proceed. Some
understanding of the meaning of the child's inner world must
precede our behavioral programming. We also need to appreciate the cultural context of the family's style.

In summary, Phase I brings a therapeutically designed
"rescue squad" to the patients and their families, who are derailed far away from the tracks of healthy growth and development. The unit's structure and our understanding surround the
stranded patients and their families and offer hope that change
can take place. This phase constructs the framework in which
the work of the next three phases can occur.

Phase II: Responding to Trouble

Phase II is our response to the patients' troublemaking. An effective treatment program for our patients needs to anticipate and
respond to the inevitable trouble that the patients will bring.
*This phase involves providing that measure of "control from without" that
children need to supplement and support the "controls from within"* (Redl
and Wineman, 1952). We use a lot of active control techniques

designed to stop or contain problem behaviors while we begin the process of redirecting feelings and conflicts. This phase appreciates the persistence, intensity, and pervasiveness of pathology. With aggressive or persistently suicidal and self-injurious children, this work is for survival of the children and the staff.

The strategies of Phase II can be divided into techniques for the overwhelmed child who is beyond (or below) treatment in the midst of a crisis and techniques for the child who is returning from troubling incidents. Active control techniques are the "external egos" of the overwhelmed child: physical holding, mechanical restraints, separating a child in a quiet room, seclusion (locked door), or psychopharmacotherapy and chemical restraint. After the trouble has occurred, the child needs help "picking up the pieces" and returning to the group and treatment program. The process of the *reactive contract* technique includes routines to help the child complete the process of making a mistake, taking a penalty, making amends, receiving forgiveness, and experiencing self-forgiveness. This process allows the child to return to the community and relationships in the community following a crisis.

The interventions in this phase sound extreme, but they keep the treatment environment safe and demonstrate to the children and their families that control is necessary and possible. Therapeutic work depends on the perceived safety of patients, staff, and family members. When we respond with limits to the children's need to cause trouble, we spare the patients the burden of more guilt and shame about their actions and the increasing anxiety that results from a sense of power in the face of no control.

Therapeutic management in Phase II must clearly distinguish between the legitimacy of all emotions and the necessary limits on "some" behavior. *We are "permissive" about wishes and feelings but we "set limits" on behaviors that violate the rights of others or jeopardize the patients' safety.* We continually make the point to our patients that we have never known a bad kid, but we have known a lot of kids who did bad things. *The problem for our patients is not the size of their anger (or any feeling), but the size of their controls.*

In summary, our work in this phase is focused on stopping the negative cycle of stress and conflict, followed by maladaptive coping, which produces more stress and conflict. Containing troublemaking can begin again the process of building internal control through the children's experience of external control from without and identification with adults who have and use their controls.

Phase III: Introducing New Ways

In previous phases, the child has learned what not to do. In Phase III, the child learns what to do instead. Once the "trouble" is contained, therapeutic management can move on to strengthen and teach positive responses that are in fact incompatible with the previous disrupting behaviors. Therapeutic change requires reciprocal development on both of these fronts: "To do one without the other, to provide new experiences without the opportunity to organize them internally, or to provide internal restructuring without the opportunity to learn more competent behaviors, is to fail to provide the balance of skill and understanding necessary to cope with challenging future experiences" (Hornik, 1987, p. 8).

Interventions in this phase include "life-space interviews" (Redl, 1966a), time-out procedures, staff praise and positive programs (star charts), and proactive contracts that anticipate trouble and program alternative behaviors. The child may have used these interventions in previous phases of treatment, but during phase III they become the focus of our work. By this time, the child has a "working ego," entailing some control of impulses, some capacity to regulate intense feelings, and some capacity to perceive accurately and make use of what we are saying and doing and why we are doing it. The child also has some motivation to learn and practice new skills, because there is now some hope that the old pattern of failure can be changed.

This is where our treatment begins to look more like what psychotherapy with children is "supposed" to look like. We look toward the behavioral and social-cognitive therapies for the guiding principles and practical strategies for skill building (Barth, 1986; Herbert, 1987; Hersen and Van Hasselt, 1987; Kendall and Braswell, 1985; Spivack, Platt, and Shure, 1976; Strayhorn, 1988; Werry and Wollersheim, 1989). We focus on programs that develop skills our patients need, such as anger control, problem solving, and social skills training. It's in this phase that dynamic therapies can provide guiding principles and treatment strategies for developing insight, expressing and regulating intense feelings, changing self-concepts, reworking trauma, and creating healthier relationship capacities.

Fostering insight is now a complementary process. It works hand in hand with limit setting and skill building. We listen to children's stories and help them understand the assumptions they have used to organize their life experiences and their enduring internal self-images. We encourage questioning old assumptions, using new ways of "researching" old concerns and considering new ways to understand old events.

Considering new answers often involves changing old story lines. For example, Lisa figured that she was a "rotten kid" and that is why she had had so many foster placements. We helped her to reexamine that notion. She began to believe that maybe her failures in all these homes were not all her fault. Maybe she was not a rotten kid. Maybe she did not know how to behave, because she had never had the experiences that children need to teach them how to live in families. Children cannot believe in their own worth unless we help them to understand that they neither caused nor deserved some of the badness that has happened to them. Their assumptions about themselves—how good or bad, how competent or incompetent, how effective or helpless—are the building blocks of their developing self-concept. It is this sense of self that filters what is happening and what will happen to them.

In summary, the work of Phase III helps children develop new skills and new meanings. This in turn leads to greater competence and the integration of these changes into a healthier sense of self. The purpose of this phase of work is to help children fashion a more accurate and benign self to carry wherever they go.

Phase IV: Leaving and Taking It All Home

How do we make the gains of hospitalization portable? Building a good bridge to home does not begin near the time of leaving. The framework of treatment has continuously brought the patient's outside world — family and agencies — into hospital treatment.

But therapeutic management at this phase involves even more contact with the world outside of the hospital. Children visit old and new schools to adjust to new schedules, new expectations, new rules. Visits home continue and visits to new homes start if placement outside of the family is needed.

Families make visits, too. If their children are not going home, we help parents learn about how to remain active participants in their children's treatment in new settings. They learn to transfer their newfound confidence in getting help to new people and new settings. We hope to help the children and their families "consolidate" their gains and "generalize" new, more adaptive ways of coping to home or outside hospital settings.

This involves a careful structuring of the "goodbye" experience to reduce regression and to provide models for handling the emotion-laden experience of leaving and losing. We acknowledge with the children and the families the mixed experience of positive and negative feelings that accompany change, fostered by the losing and gaining involved in all changes. For patients who have had frequent and often traumatic losses, this phase of treatment is as precarious as our initial work during the starting-out phase.

This is a sketch of the entire journey through treatment.

A brief description of the population is necessary before we proceed on our journey.

Who Are the Children and Their Families?

Our patients are similar to the seriously impaired group of children described in other samples of psychiatrically hospitalized children (Berlin, 1978; Hoffman, 1982; Kashani and Cantwell, 1983; Weinstein and others, 1989).

Our patients are commonly called "troublemakers," "psychiatric cases," and children with "adaptive or ego deficits." Each of these descriptions suggests a differing but overlapping perspective growing out of a particular treatment setting and treatment approach: juvenile detention and residential settings, psychiatric hospitals, foster homes and special schools.

Troublemakers

Our patients make trouble for others and for themselves. They have troubled feelings and thoughts that lead to very troubled behavior. Hospital intake forms often describe the trouble they make: physical and sexual assaultive behavior; vandalism; stealing; suicidal behavior; fire setting; alcohol and drug abuse; distorted and bizarre thought and behavior; severe depression and anxiety; and detailed accounts of how hard these children are to manage in families, schools, and communities due to extremes of noncompliant and oppositional behavior. Pervasive behavioral and psychological problems have caused them to fail in family, school, and community settings.

We need to anticipate and be prepared for such trouble in our treatment framework. We view these "bad behaviors" or "symptoms" as the best efforts of incompetent children to cope with the challenges of their lives.

Psychiatric Cases

Our patients can also be described by psychiatric diagnostic labels. The most common psychiatric diagnoses of our patients are:

- Disruptive behavior disorders, including conduct disorders, attention-deficit disorders, oppositional disorders
- Post-traumatic stress disorders
- Mood disorders, including bipolar and depressive disorders
- Psychotic disorders, including pervasive developmental disorders, schizophrenia
- Developmental disorders and personality disorders

Most of our patients carry more than one primary mental illness diagnosis and have moderate to severe developmental problems, neuropsychological diagnoses, histories of severe stress and trauma, and long-term problems in adjusting.

These labels are useful as guides in the choice of the biomedical components of therapeutic management, especially psychopharmacotherapy. Psychopharmacotherapy is an integral part of inpatient treatment of children with attentional problems, psychosis, aggressivity, agitation, anxiety, and affective disorders, primarily depression (Dalton and Forman, 1992; Popper, 1987). The more severe, complex, and acute the psychiatric diagnostic picture, the more likely patients will need and benefit from advances in pediatric psychopharmacology. On an acute inpatient unit, virtually all patients will be candidates for trials of psychotropic medications.

Psychiatric diagnoses can also be used to describe limiting factors in the design of therapeutic management programs. For example, when children have major language disorders, we will modify the use of language. When children have attention deficits, we will try to adjust rules and routines to provide the degree of structure these children find helpful. When we have hyperactive children, we can use active time-outs (for example, time on exercise bicycles), if sitting on a chair proves to be too demanding. Or if children continue to have psychotic symptoms, in spite of active psychopharmacological treatment, we modify our language and our structure to anticipate the more vulnerable world in which they live.

These children's pervasive behavioral problems are the product of a massive developmental failure and failures in socialization. Biomedically, these children often have neurological deficits in perception; impaired synthetic or integrative functions; severe attention problems, sometimes accompanied by hyperactivity; moderate to severe language disorders involving receptive, expressive, and processing deficits; learning disabilities; major mental illnesses like affective disorders and psychoses; and genetic vulnerabilities due to family histories of psychiatric illnesses, such as schizophrenia, affective disorders, alcoholism, or psychopathy. Psychologically, they have poor self-esteem, defective object relations, poor impulse control, maladaptive coping strategies, and immature defenses. Socially, they frequently have lived in poverty or with overstressed families in which loss, violence, neglect, and abuse have created chronically chaotic family environments.

Interactions of biological, psychological, and social factors have created childhoods that foster failure, incompetence, emotional emptiness, negative self-image, and low self-esteem. Many of the parents of these patients were also burdened by their own share of inadequate parenting, neglect, trauma, and poverty. They are caught in negative cycles of parent-child interactions, with emotional burdens of hatred and despair and ineffectual efforts to get out of all the trouble. Frequently, the children they need to parent are unusually difficult to parent from the beginning, due to difficult temperaments and biological vulnerabilities, such as neurological and cognitive limitations.

Children with Adaptive or Ego Deficits

These patients are children who cope poorly and have failed often at what they are trying to do. They don't like themselves. Their adaptive deficits invade every arena of their lives. They suffer frequent failures and setbacks in their efforts to negotiate the social, cognitive, physical, and psychological tasks of childhood. They don't trust or depend on adults to be helpful, and they often blame adults for their troubles. They hold pessimistic views of their current and future lives. They have ingrained negative self-images, inadequate capacities to relate to adults and peers, and vulnerable self-esteem.

Our patients have poor track records in less comprehensive and intensive treatment settings. Their problems are too severe and too pervasive. They have been described as "beyond the reach of education and below the grip of the psychiatric interview technique" and "as children who hate" or the "ego deficit or predelinquent child" (Redl, 1966b; Redl and Wineman, 1951, 1952). They have also been characterized as "relationship-resistant" (Trieschman, Whittaker, and Brendtro, 1969) and, more recently, as "abuse-reactive" (Small, Kennedy, and Bender, 1991).

Redl and Wineman's (1951) dam-and-lock metaphor captures the inner happenings of ego-deficit children. They compare the ego to a system of dam and locks on a water reservoir. When a flood occurs, the problem could be with the quality of construction of the dam and locks or the quantity and intensity of the water flowing through the system. Even a well-built dam cannot withstand the water flow of a hurricane, and a poorly built dam will collapse when a normal amount of water flows through at a normal speed.

The dam-and-lock system is like the child's system of ego capacities. This system includes the child's capacity to regulate emotions, maintain relationships with adults and peers, cope with stress, develop social skills, solve problems, master past trauma or hurt, and maintain an accurate and positive image of the self. Inner emotional turmoil and external stress and trauma can overwhelm this ego structure even if it is well made and well maintained. When the structure is weak and incomplete, it can easily crack under normal circumstances. Our patients have weakly constructed ego structures, and many of them have overwhelming histories of stress and trauma.

Conclusion

The four phases of therapeutic management described in this chapter have been designed to create an external and interpersonal treatment setting to heal the damage caused by the biological and social histories of our patients. Treatment interventions are borrowed from the history of institutional and psychological treatment of children and from the ingredients of the normal socialization process. The sequence of interventions follows the psychological capacities and needs of the patients and their families. We first act as the "external egos" that facilitate positive development and therapeutic repair. Then we help our patients rebuild the internal egos needed to live their lives with more competence, self-confidence, meaning, and fun.

Let the lion taming begin!

PART 1

Designing the Framework of Treatment

Lion sick in bed

weird
Lion

The Environmental Context of Therapeutic Management: Culture, Space, People, and Time

The framework of treatment includes both environmental and interpersonal components. The environmental features of treatment set the stage for interpersonal interactions. In residential and hospital work, we have a unique opportunity to design treatment that spans the child's whole environment.

Therapeutic management starts with the environmental context. The environmental context of treatment consists of the *culture,* which conveys the values and atmosphere of the treatment setting, the design of the physical *space,* the *people* or the treaters, and the programming of the *time* that the children and their families spend in the space. The environmental components of treatment are for all children and all groups of children regardless of the quality of their interpersonal interactions or therapeutic relationships. In this sense, the environmental components of the treatment framework play a special role in the therapeutic management of relationship-resistant children and families.

Culture

The treatment culture permeates the atmosphere that welcomes and surrounds the patients and their families. The World Health

Organization report on mental health (1951) cited the atmosphere of a program as the single most important factor in the efficacy of psychiatric hospital treatment. The treatment impact of any specific intervention or particular person will be mediated by the institutional culture in which it occurs. The culture of a program is the "glue" that binds the multiple components of the environment together. The values, aspirations, and emotional tone set by staff beliefs and actions determine the treatment culture.

When we first walk in the door of any institution, be it a school, business, or recreational club, we experience its culture. Our patients are on the lookout for our cultural messages: what we will give and what we will not give, what we will accept and what we will not accept, how we can help and how we are unable to help, and what we expect from them and what we will not expect.

The culture of a setting is guided by the values of the treatment program, which need to be explicitly communicated. Our primary treatment values are *hope, respect,* and *understanding.*

Hope

Hope breeds optimism and allows us to appreciate existing health, competence, and potential rather than focusing on pathology, conflict, deficits, and past failures. We live in the present, search the past, and believe in the future.

This requires "trained" eyes to look for small gains and potential for positive change in the midst of severe psychopathology, tragic histories, and a great deal of anger and discouragement. Our first treatment task, then, is to help our patients and their families live, search, and believe with us.

Banking on potential is essential to maintaining an optimistic attitude in the face of severe, multigenerational psychopathology. We assume that the pathology we see in our patients is their "best effort" to cope with life's demands, which means that if they could "do it better," they would do it better.

We believe that our patients and their families may be demoralized as well as unskilled. If we cannot rekindle their lost hope, we cannot engage them in the hard struggle to heal and to develop new competencies. An essential aspect of our treatment environment is to hold more positive and empathic expectations and attitudes for our patients and their families than they initially hold for themselves.

Our job is to communicate our sense of hope to them. This often means helping them lower the "protective shield" of hopelessness that has been forged to keep them from further discouragement and failure.

Respect and Understanding

Respect and understanding go hand in hand. Respect sets the stage for our efforts to understand children and their families. Genuine treatment does not require that we like every patient or family, but we will be unable to treat patients and families that we are unable to respect.

This means that we need extraordinary "professional" qualities to deliver respect to children who taunt, torture, or otherwise harm others and parents who neglect, abandon, or abuse their children. Some patients or their parents are outrageously egocentric or demanding. Some patients are painfully ineffectual or passive. We encounter repulsive cruelty. Treatment cannot proceed if we respond to such histories and personalities with moral indignation, rejection, or judgmental labeling. The "bad kids" and the "bad parents" know all about their "badness." A purpose of treatment is to help them find their goodness and their health in the midst of all this trouble.

We work with all parents regardless of their attitude toward us or their unwillingness to join the treatment team. Our outreach can redefine what we are willing to call a "participating" parent. We call and send letters to parents who are unable to come for appointments. We avoid judgmental or demeaning confrontations. Our job is to help parents explore all possible avenues for positive family changes. The value of respect translates directly into these interactions and attitudes, which will set the stage for treatment.

A fuller understanding of a child's and a parent's behavior

supports our respect for them. Parental neglect is so hard to bear when you know its impact on children. But when we get to know "neglecting" parents, we hear about their histories of similar neglect. Understanding parents or other family members is to see them in the context of their own history, which may be as impoverished and compromised as their children's.

In other situations, we meet families where a child's psychiatric impairment has derailed normal family functioning. We do not find overt neglect or trauma. Parents have become indifferent and hostile toward a child who has "ruined" the family.

Maggie's (age six) parents missed visiting days, rarely called ahead, and came late for treatment appointments. Milieu staff complained that they were being used as "baby sitters." Jill (a social worker) listened to their complaints and then spoke quietly about her last meeting with them.

"I know they seem callous, but Maggie was their first child after years of trying. She was a dream come true. But now she's turned into a nightmare. She was kicked out of four preschool programs. They were asked not to come to a family reunion, because the cousins were frightened she'd burn down the house they had rented on a lake."

"Maggie says they didn't want to go anyway. They don't like those cousins," said Brent, her counselor.

"After the last fire, her parents started sleeping in shifts. They were afraid she would kill the family with another fire," continued Jill.

"They were so ashamed of her. They didn't even get her any treatment," said Stacy (a counselor), who was very angry at them.

"They put off seeking psychiatric help, because they believed that seeing a 'shrink' could label her for life. When relatives pressed for them to send her to residential treatment, they refused to send her away," Jill responded.

"If they care so much, where are they?" asked Brent.

"I talked to them on the phone last night. They've missed their appointments with me, too. They feel very guilty about sending her to the hospital. Maggie calls them every night and cries about being here. They're embarrassed to face the staff, afraid that we may judge them the same way they've been judged by their own family. Her dad told me that whatever they have done has proved to be the wrong thing.

"They didn't come to visiting last week, because Maggie had screamed at them on the telephone. She said that they loved her younger brother too much to send him to a hospital."

Allyson (a nurse) hesitated and then responded, "I know it doesn't sound very empathic, but that's just the problem. They let her boss them around and run the family. No wonder Maggie has so much trouble obeying."

"Please bear with them, they are loving parents who are absolutely overwhelmed. The most poignant part of the interview was when her father asked me if they should give up and give her to someone or some place who could help her. He wanted to do what was best for Maggie."

Our respect and understanding is based on our belief that our patients are "troubled kids from troubled families." They are not "good kids from bad families," as suggested by certain theories and institutional practices.

It is a painful experience to bring your child, your family, and yourself to a hospital or treatment center with humiliating stories of personal failures, deficits, and mistakes. We try to maintain respect and understanding for the families, and especially the parents of our patients, by imagining how we would feel and handle the situation if we were in their place. Many staff have enhanced their own capacity to remember this when they imagine what it would be like to have their own parenting scrutinized in a treatment setting.

We search for solutions to problems, and we actively avoid blaming the children or their families. We often need to help the children and their families stop blaming themselves. Exhibit 1 is an example of the welcoming page from a parent handbook.

Welcoming words must be matched by welcoming actions. Every effort should be made to create admission procedures that convey the spirit of treatment as well as explain the multitude of practical details and protective steps necessary for legal and medical reasons. We put special emphasis on how telephone calls are handled and how visiting is conducted in order to continue our efforts at including parents and families. Every institution must be wary of nontherapeutic telephone or visiting procedures

Exhibit 1. Example of the Welcoming Page from a Parent Handbook.

WELCOME!
WE ARE GLAD THAT YOU ARE HERE. We know that it is hard to have
your child in a psychiatric hospital. We hope that we can make this a positive
experience for you and your family. Although children are here to work on their
problems, we believe that parents are central to any positive change in their children's lives. This is true even if your child no longer lives with you.

Some parents need help providing the special environment that a child, particularly an emotionally disturbed child, needs to grow and develop. We believe
your choice to allow your child to receive treatment was your way of providing
for your child's special needs.

We are here to help you provide that specialized environment that your child
needs right now. We are not here to substitute for your relationship with your
child. This would not be good for your child and no one can substitute for a parent in a child's eyes, anyway. We hope that we can work as a team with you
to help your child and your family during this stressful time. We hope that you
will let us support your continued parenting of your child.

We would like to clear up one thing. Sometimes parents feel they are to blame
for their children's problems. We don't believe that parents can cause major psychiatric prolems, therefore we will not blame you. We also do not think parents
intentionally hurt their children. We believe that most parents do the best they
can. Sometimes this is not enough for a particular child and sometimes this involves hurtful experiences when a parent's own problems cause them to be hurtful.

We believe that children's development depends upon more than one event
or problem. This means that parents can't take full credit for the "healthiest" child
or full blame for a "sick" child. Development depends upon the physical, psychological, and social aspects of a child. This means that solutions to serious problems require help in many areas. Your participation in your child's treatment
is one of the most important parts of his or her treatment in our hospital. You
can make a difference in the solutions to your child's problems.

We want to work with you and your child to understand the strengths and
problems in your child and family. We will try to help you identify and understand any negative patterns which are going on between you and your children.
We will also help you develop any special parenting skills required by your child's
special needs. Our efforts will be focused on how to help you stop negative cycles
from continuing and replace them with more positive patterns.

Your knowledge of your family and your child will be very important. We want
to help you identify what's good about your parenting, your family, and your
child. We want to help you preserve, regain, or begin to enjoy the goodness in
your family.

We hope that this will be a positive experience for you, your family, and your
child. We know that it may involve some difficult times and we want you to let
us know if we can be of any help during those times.

---

that develop in response to time constraints or other practical problems.

The explicitly stated values of a program should guide the development of all phases of the framework of treatment.

Space

The physical space of a treatment setting can contribute to treatment when it is designed to translate clinical philosophy into specific design details (Cotton and Geraty, 1984). Bettelheim (1950, 1955, 1974) reminds us that the physical environment is the "house of the spirit." This environment sends behavioral cues to children. Children are concrete thinkers, which means that they believe that things are the way they appear to be. This makes them more susceptible to the messages, both therapeutic and antitherapeutic, of the physical environment.

We can design spaces that encourage the hard work of healing and behavioral change and that also communicate our hope that our patients and their families have fun. Alternatively, we can aggravate a child's sense of guilt and poor self-esteem by providing prisonlike structures featuring stripped-down interiors with such highly visible protective features as bars, locks, safety screens, and warning bells. Facilities can be frightening "institutional" settings in big, impersonal buildings constructed of materials like tile, cement, cinder block, and metal, decorated in bland color schemes of washed-out pastels, muddy greens, and browns, and with long corridors, sleeping wards, and cafeterias.

Designing a therapeutic space requires a budget to support architectural expertise and specially designed spaces for the unique developmental and psychiatric needs of child patients. A specifically designed space is cost-effective over time because it reduces vandalism, promotes proper use of materials, provides secure spaces for behavioral crises, and offers alternative physical materials for tension discharge. It also reduces staff expenses with efficient layouts and reduces daily maintenance costs through vandalproof hardware.

We designed our physical environment to complement

our goals of therapeutic management (Figure 1). These goals are *protecting, engaging,* and *teaching.*

Features to Protect

Designing a place for disturbed children presents unique challenges. Consider the histories of our patients:

- Johnny had kicked so many holes in the walls of his special needs classroom that he was required to attend class barefoot.
- Raoul had set fires causing over $500,000 worth of damage and killing one horse.
- Donna burned down a three-family dwelling. Her family was forced to move to a new town, because landlords refused to rent to the family.
- Lisa was removed from a foster home because she tried to enlist her younger siblings in sexual activities she had learned from her uncle.
- Andrew wet his pants at least six times daily and pooped in his pants at least once a week.
- Michael sought out sharp edges and pointed objects to scrape, cut, and pick at himself to help define the boundaries of his own body.

Physical spaces need to be created to contain and discourage these activities. Safe physical environments balance protection and freedom during acute phases of treatment. Although design details for safety may convey punitive messages, these same visual images can be comforting to children with impulse control problems or children who live in frightening home environments. Locks keep children in a place, but they also keep people out of a place.

Units can be locked-door units, or else locks can be used within an open unit, as we use them. In this way, we are able to "close down" the unit when certain patients or groups of patients need such control and "open" the unit when we are treating a different profile of patients. Specific spaces are always locked, such as the oven switch, refrigerator, and drawers for sharp objects.

Figure 1. Diagram of Unit Space.

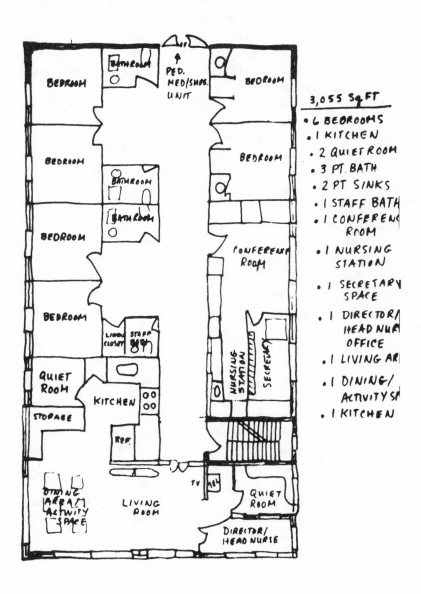

The following design features support our goals to protect the children from themselves and from each other and to contain their aggressive and self-destructive outbursts:

1. We use quarter-inch Plexiglas or shatterproof glass (required by fire codes). We avoid breakable glass, bars, or darkening safety screens.
2. Exterior-type vandalproof lighting fixtures are used in interior spaces.
3. The design incorporates open spaces with locked or lockable equipment, drawers, or cabinets. We use individual locks for the stove and refrigerator. Power cutoff switches are controlled by a special key and are checked at the change of every shift.
4. Tamperproof screws are used.
5. The design calls for low-pile, fireproof, indoor-outdoor carpeting specially treated for vomit and urine.
6. Observation windows are installed in all private spaces except the bathrooms.
7. No visible pipes, rods, wiring, plumbing, or removable vents are allowed in patient places.
8. Heavy (nonthrowable), durable, butcher-block furniture with rounded corners was purchased. It has no exposed springs, is easily upholstered, and has nonremovable casters.
9. We had large vinyl floor pillows made for flexible, comfortable sitting and fantasy play.
10. Floor-to-ceiling armoires are bolted to the wall, with air pockets, breakaway shelving (at thirty pounds), no hooks, and magnetic catches for closure.
11. We designed and built hardwood toy boxes with air vents, divided compartments, two-inch finger spaces between box and lids, and heavy-duty hinges. These storage boxes line the walls and double as window seats.
12. Tab curtains with Velcro closings and breakaway wooden poles (no complicated drapery hardware or curtain pins) provide attractive, safe, and durable window treatments.
13. We decided on framed Kydex bulletin boards that use tape and not tacks, staples, or magnetic pins. This material

cleans well; for example, ballpoint pen ink can easily be removed.

14. Unit layout includes two quiet rooms situated near the activity areas (see Chapter Five for description), multiple bathrooms for privacy during dressing, and one- or two-person bedrooms placed near staff areas. Public, supervised patient areas are at the closed end of the unit.

15. Washable, durable, nontoxic paint is applied throughout the unit for easy maintenance. Surfaces that could be permanently marked (cement, burlap, cork) are avoided.

16. Beds were designed with durable frames, tamperproof screws, rounded corners, handholds instead of handles, restraint capabilities, no springs, and heavy-duty vinyl mattress covers (can't be ripped once punctured).

17. Expensive equipment such as stereos, air conditioners, or television sets are housed in nonbreakable storage containers or suspended above the general field of activity.

18. Staff use lockable cubbies in the staff room to keep money and other valuables. Staff are required to lock up cigarettes, matches, or lighters.

19. Easy-to-destroy equipment and surfaces are painted neutral colors (beige curtains, gray shades, white rods), and relatively nondestructible surfaces are painted stimulating and individualizing colors.

Features to Engage

Design choices balance protective with welcoming features. The space that needs to contain violence also needs features to invite and communicate hope, love, and respect. We created small and simple spaces to be more homelike and less institutional.

The corridors contain framed blank bulletin boards that orient and inform children and their families about the program and staff. Wall displays encourage children to express their progress, opinions, interests, and complaints. For example, we display staff names and pictures, daily schedules, announcements about special activities, unit rule books, and educational materials.

Walls also include exhibits by individual patients or group

projects, such as Jimmy's art show, posters from the problem-solving group, recipes from community supper, "Hero of the Week," and awards for academic, athletic, or therapeutic progress. We avoid permanent murals that witness past staff-patient efforts or depict stereotypically cheerful images of childhood. Our wall decorations are constantly changing tributes to current treatment efforts of children and staff and future hopes for the time after the hospital.

Here are some other design features used to engage patients in treatment:

1. Single or double bedrooms (versus ward structures) contain furniture for storage and display of personal belongings brought from home. Each child has use of one long wall of bulletin board space for personal decoration.

2. Four small tables (heavy, oak, Formica) were provided; they can be joined for community dinners or group activities.

3. A unit kitchen looks like a home kitchen and is open to the living room (selected equipment and storage areas are locked).

4. Living areas include varied colors and textures with home-like butcher-block furniture, floor pillows, bookcases, toy boxes, and good lighting and air quality.

5. Carpeting and cloth upholstery are used in public patient spaces.

6. Reinforced plywood walls are used in quiet rooms and other areas determined to be more likely to be kicked or punched. Tile is used only in bathrooms.

7. Colors are inviting and interesting, but not intrusive. Public living spaces and bedroom door jambs are painted red to invite entrance and to define different spaces. Door jambs are not outlined when they frame nonpatient spaces (staff bath or conference room). Each bedroom is painted a different color scheme to emphasize individuality. We encourage children to decorate their bedrooms to express their interests, accomplishments, and attachments — with baseball cards, music posters, homework, art work, star charts, staff congratulatory notes, and family pictures.

8. The quiet room is painted a warm tone that allows the child to project the changing feelings that occur in such a room — for example, rage, sadness, relief, and eventual peace and pride with regained control. Cloth wall hangings of rainbow imagery or different weather states convey hope and validate different strong feelings.

9. Special attention was paid to choosing materials that can be easily and inexpensively maintained (wood-grained Formica in private patient areas, carpeting, vinyl floor covering in kitchen and activity area). A clean and tidy space is highly valued, and all staff are responsible for the maintenance of the unit.

10. Storage areas are assigned to family members for their personal belongings; bathroom facilities are available for use by family members.

11. Letters, cards, and pictures from patients and family members are posted on the corridor bulletin boards.

12. Inspiring quotations or posters are hung on the walls to emphasize our values and convey hope.

Features to Teach

Our setting is designed to encourage children to use new skills and more adaptive coping behaviors, as well as to have more fun. Our space reflects our belief that through play children can learn, express strong emotions, cope with stress and past trauma, develop skills, and enjoy themselves. This enjoyment is an essential antidote to the hard work of treatment. We also encourage families to play with and enjoy each other. The following list includes the areas and supplies we use to encourage fantasy and play for the patients and their families:

1. The living room bookcase contains a range of appealing picture, reading, and reference books that children can pick up and glance at or seek out to answer questions. We include a children's encyclopedia, dictionary, world atlas, *Guinness Book of World Records,* and book of maps. Comic books entertain children waiting for an activity to begin. Parents can read books to their children during visits.

2. Toy boxes contain basic toys that are always available to the children: blocks, cars and trucks, dolls, stuffed animals, and games.

3. Toy cabinets (closed or locked) contain activities that need more supervision: popular board games, Legos, computer games, arts and craft materials.

4. A cabinet for visiting time ("visiting time cabinet") contains materials just for visiting families. Selection is based on activities that could encourage interaction, yet are sufficiently simple for different ages and different abilities.

5. A cabinet for afternoon rest periods in bedrooms ("personal time cabinet") contains toys for quiet time in the patient rooms: construction toys, cars and road maps, dolls and doll clothes, puzzle and maze books, crafts, coloring books, electronic games.

6. A "fantasy trunk," for dramatic play, contains dress-up clothes, props for different adult roles, microphone, and masks. Toy cabinets contain doll houses, miniature people, puppets and a puppet theater, and materials for pretend play (store, kitchen, office, fire station, police, school).

7. Play spaces or private nooks have been created by indenting the spaces in the corridors at the entrance to the bedrooms for uninterrupted play. Children can play in visible but more protected and less busy small spaces.

8. "Fantasy boxes" (one- by two- by four-foot oak boxes with three sides, painted with stylized headlights and waves), are designed for children to play in or pretend with. These have become the children's favorite furniture.

9. The floor plan, furniture groupings, and play spaces are designed to balance social interaction and play with privacy and enjoyable time alone.

10. Educational materials are arranged on bulletin boards for subjects that relate to treatment goals: developmentally designed and attractive displays about drug and alcohol use, health care, good ways to express feelings, fire and water safety, and taking care of property.

11. Private spaces are provided for children who want to calm down, be alone, do a project, finish homework, think about

something, or "escape." Children can spend time in the quiet room, their bedrooms, or even their closets.

12. An athletic punching bag and batakas (soft bats) are made available for use in the quiet room or play spaces to encourage alternate ways of expressing anger and frustration. An exercise bicycle provides another avenue for release of energy and tension.

13. Sheets and blankets are used to create private, safe, and personal spaces. For example, runaway behavior is diverted into building private forts with fantasy boxes and sheets.

14. Mats in the corridors and play spaces provide opportunities for indoor roughhouse play.

15. Off-unit spaces (indoors and out of doors) are used for gross motor outlets and skill development: occupational therapy room, gym, tennis court, athletic field, therapeutically designed outdoor play space, wooded areas for walking, fishing, and cross-country skiing, and a nearby motel pool.

Attention to the initial design of a space needs to be matched by attention and budgeting to the special maintenance needs of spaces serving emotionally disturbed children. Our patients are active, destructive, and careless about their own and our possessions and space. Staff attention and programming for chores and inspections completed several times during the day can complement active hospital efforts to clean, repair, and pick up the space.

People

In addition to therapeutic culture and space, therapeutic management requires "therapeutic people." This means a sufficient *quantity* of people, selected for certain *qualities, trained* to deliver therapeutic management, and arranged in an *organizational structure.* At this point, we will describe the use of people primarily involved in the delivery of therapeutic management (milieu therapists), not the staffing pattern for the total diagnostic and treatment program.

Quantity

We determine the right number of milieu therapists according to a ratio that describes the number of staff members needed on a particular shift to the number of patients on the unit. On our unit, we calculate the staff-patient ratio based on an assumption of twelve patients.

Milieu therapists are people who work for predetermined eight-hour shifts (day, evening, and night) and who are assigned to cover the direct-care tasks for patients on a twenty-four-hour basis. Milieu therapy staffs are made up of nurses and counselors.

Nursing milieu therapists (the nurses) deliver biomedical treatment, assume medical supervision tasks, and take responsibility for decisions about the use of seclusion and restraint (this authority changes with local laws and regulations). They also perform the "counseling" tasks carried out by all milieu therapists.

Milieu counselors are high school or recent college graduates who may have had experience working with children in group settings or are interested in pursuing further education in a mental health discipline. In some cases, they may have had previous mental health care experience. They are supervised by professionally trained clinicians from nursing, psychiatric, psychological, or social work disciplines.

The children understand that the milieu therapist is a "special kind of friend" or a "special kind of teacher."

> Andrew (age seven) had just arrived on the unit. He asked Steve (a counselor) what he did on the unit.
> "I'm a counselor. I stay with you all day," answered Steve.
> "What's that?"
> "A counselor is like a special kind of friend or a special kind of teacher," answered Steve. "I'm like a friend because we play games, share things, go on trips together, and help each other out. I'm not like your other friends because I'm also in charge of you and have to get you to do things, like brush your teeth or follow the rules.
> "I'm like a teacher because my job is to help you learn new ways to do things. But I'm not like your school teacher, because the new things don't have to do with numbers and letters. They have to do with feelings and relationships with people.

"Sometimes we'll talk about the stuff that you and your social worker or your doctor talk about. We all are here to help you with your problems or help you like yourself better or help you get what you want without getting into trouble.

"Does that make sense to you?" concluded Steve.

"Can I go outside and play yet?" answered Andrew.

Although milieu therapists assume the responsibility for twenty-four-hour supervision of patients, all clinicians on the treatment team are active participants in therapeutic management. Professionally trained clinicians supervise milieu therapists and assist in groups and crisis management situations. Psychiatrists, psychologists, social workers, teachers, and occupational and recreational therapists are given training in management techniques and protocols (including techniques for seclusion, physical holding, and restraint) and a working knowledge of the unit discipline system and typical ways of handling the children.

This means that all unit staff are prepared to assist in behavioral crises and to "cover" for milieu therapists when they are attending clinical planning conferences, staff meetings, milieu program planning meetings, and individual or family therapy appointments when needed. Therapeutic activity groups are co-led by milieu and nonmilieu therapists, just as teachers and milieu therapists work together during programmed school times.

The number of milieu therapists needed is determined by job descriptions and program requirements for safety and individualized programming. The delivery of individualized, intense, and complex therapeutic management will require budgeting for enough people, with enough time to get to know, understand, and respond to patients and their families. Budgets should include resources for clinical supervision, program development, group leadership, and clinical professional availability during unit crises.

The "perfect" staff-patient ratio (the number of staff members needed to treat a specified number of patients) does not exist. It will vary according to the clinical status and needs of patients and the time frame and nature of work a treatment center is expected to perform.

We can discuss guidelines to select milieu staff-patient ratios for therapeutic management. We cannot give exact formulas because the milieu staffing needs vary greatly according to the availability of other clinicians working in the milieu or scheduling and program variables. A sufficient staff-patient ratio should be determined by (1) profiles of the setting's patients and staff, (2) medical assessment and treatment, (3) diagnostic/treatment mission, and (4) physical space.

Greater numbers of staff are required for the following patient profile:

- Greater numbers of patients
- Broader range of ages (for example, more staff for combined school-age and adolescent populations)
- Larger spans of levels of developmental functioning (for instance, combining cognitively impaired and/or psychotic children with brighter, behaviorally disordered children)
- Greater severity and pervasiveness of impairments (for example, language processing problems, neuropsychological deficits, learning disabilities, mood disorders, psychosis)
- More severe lethality of symptoms (such as suicidality, aggressiveness, sexual promiscuity)
- Lack of family or support systems outside of the hospital
- Patient's initial unwillingness to engage in treatment (court-referred children)
- Frequent staff turnover
- Shorter lengths of stays (more acute admissions and inability to develop routines and relationships)

When medical assessment and treatment are required, the staffing pattern needs to reflect nursing and physician expertise to observe, document, diagnose, and deliver treatment such as psychopharmacotherapy or the use of control techniques (seclusion and restraints) that require medical authorization. Most of the severely ill children profiled in this book have multiple psychiatric diagnoses (comorbidity) and both cognitive and physical deficits or delays, which require milieu as well as non-milieu medical and nursing expertise.

Inpatient and residential centers require special pediatric psychopharmacological expertise. Comorbidity, cognitive and attentional limitations, and medical problems create a need for frequent monitoring and experimental use of newly developing treatments. At least three-quarters of our patients were receiving psychopharmacological treatment at any point in time.

The diagnostic/treatment profile consists of the diagnostic and treatment goals for the setting. The diagnostic/treatment profile that requires the most extensive (and expensive) professional staffing consists of programs that deliver complete:

- Biopsychosocial diagnostic protocols
- Biopsychosocial treatment interventions
- Range, complexity, intensity of treatment interventions
- Availability of auxiliary staff (such as occupational, recreational, and special education training) to milieu staff
- Availability of other programs (for example, separate school, specialty groups)

The profile of the physical space design can also influence the number of people needed. If the physical space includes protective features to contain or limit vandalism, aggression, and self-injurious behavior, then the staff-patient ratio does not need to be increased dramatically to treat children who act in these ways. The number of milieu therapists can also be adjusted if the space provides engaging and distracting interiors, play materials, and audio-video equipment to be used during nonacute phases of treatment.

The staff-patient ratio for our unit was five or six milieu therapists (including two or three nurses) for twelve patients during the Monday to Friday day shift program. This pattern included the nurse manager, who worked in the milieu half time and performed her administrative tasks during the other half time of her forty-hour week. Four or five milieu therapists (including two nurses) worked the Monday to Friday evening shift program. Night coverage was done by one nurse and one counselor. On weekends, milieu coverage was reduced to three or four milieu therapists because patients spent time with their families at home or visiting on the unit when clinically indicated. Additional milieu therapists were used when patient acuity required them to stay on the unit.

This staff-patient ratio is similar to the current standards proposed by the American Academy of Child Psychiatry (1990), which suggest a minimum daytime staff-patient ratio of 1:3 for basic inpatient psychiatric milieu treatment. These standards recommend a higher staff-patient ratio when the patients require more intensive interventions. The range for residential treatment centers can be as low as 1:5 when the children are better known to the staff, when they stay for longer periods of time, and when those in crisis are transferred to more highly staffed areas within the institution or transferred to a hospital.

Qualities

We selected people with certain qualities to deliver therapeutic management as we defined it. I firmly believe that not every good clinician can be an effective milieu therapist. I also believe that not all good milieu therapists can work well in every kind of milieu setting. *The personal qualities of the milieu therapist need to fit compatibly with the values of the treatment setting.*

I learned about my strong beliefs from a young woman while I was firing her.

The counselor rode her bicycle to work. On the previous evening she had insisted on sleeping in the quiet room, because it was snowing heavily. She refused to leave when the nursing supervisor and doctor on call had explained that the quiet room was for patient emergencies and the hospital was not in a position to offer lodging to staff. In fact, I had discussed with her the need for alternative transportation when I hired her. She assured me that she was able to acquire rides from friends.

Her actions were consistent with a developing pattern of identifying with the patients. She seemed to be increasingly needy and irritable in her interactions with peers and patients. When a patient's parents had invited her to a college football game with them, she was visibly annoyed when I explained to her that she could not participate with patients and their families in nontreatment activities outside of the hospital.

She accused me of "requiring everyone to be the same." My first reaction was to disagree with her criticism of my leadership style and deny the accusation, proclaiming my tolerance for all kinds of people. I came to realize, however, that she was absolutely right. I did have standards of behavior and biases toward certain personality qualities. In this case, I was respecting the unique nature of the patient-therapist relationship. I also was alert to the need for adults working with emotionally disturbed children to maintain a boundary between their lives and the life of the unit and the lives of their patients. This meant that staff members needed to care for personal needs outside of the work environment.

I believe now that an essential quality of program leadership is the capacity to recruit people with identified qualities necessary to maintain the therapeutic milieu. This leadership focus contributes to a coherent treatment approach and a patient-focused milieu. The patients are allowed to be different and are supposed to be different. Staff are allowed to have different styles only if they share similar values and attitudes toward treatment.

To deliver therapeutic management as defined here, we require milieu therapists with certain skills and qualities. In most treatment settings, the qualities desired in staff are not clearly defined. But when qualities are made explicit, they can be used for recruitment, training, supervision, and performance appraisal. When things are running more or less smoothly, our staff members actually do begin to react in similar ways.

Respect for multicultural and ethnically different values, attitudes, and behavior is a guiding principle of our general treatment approach (Hendren and Berlin, 1991; McGoldrick, Pearce, and Giordano, 1982). When possible, we try to recruit staff who are either ethnically similar or sensitive to the different ethnic groups represented in our patient population. We are aware of the danger of imposing values, attitudes, and behaviors from our own cultural and socioeconomic backgrounds on patients and their families from different cultures and socioeconomic groups.

The following list of qualities is the collective description of the "person that we all hope to be." I should emphasize that none of us reflects all of these qualities all of the time in their most mature and creative form. But we assume a basic capacity for honesty, dependability, and commitment to the interests of the patients and their families.

The particular staff qualities that we encourage are:

- Respect and empathy
- Self-reflection and self-awareness
- Energy
- Resiliency
- Cooperation
- Intellectual curiosity
- Playfulness

Respect and Empathy. Our patients need our capacity to respect their lives, to appreciate what they are experiencing and feeling, and to help them bear those experiences and feelings. We cannot help these children if we are unwilling or unable to enter their worlds. Our patients need to know that we can meet them in their most unacceptable and unbearable moments, so that we can help them learn to bear these feelings and become open to other feelings when they are able. Children can sense whether we have met them in the depths of their inner worlds. Sometimes our empathy is never verbalized to the patient, but only felt during a physical hold or a silence shared from across a room. But some children are so vulnerable that they may never be able to share in our understanding of them.

Our empathic understanding of children and their parents creates the bridge from our world into theirs. Empathic connections with painful experiences are one of the most demanding aspects of therapeutic management. Working with our patients and their families is emotionally stimulating and challenging. Containing an abandoned child's rage or controlling the self-injurious actions of a child's self-hate are deeply emotional interactions not usually a part of most people's lives.

Self-Reflection and Self-Awareness. This work requires self-reflection and self-awareness. Milieu therapists need to be prepared to shape their ways of relating to people according to the needs of the patients, their families, and even their staff colleagues, who will require close working relationships. The interpersonal style of milieu therapists is always being challenged, usually in public. Staff need to tolerate the kind of patient and collegial scrutiny this kind of work involves.

We often question whether we are too warm or too cold, too strict or too permissive, too aggressive or too meek, too harsh or too diffuse, too distant or overly involved. Staff need to analyze their own management style and know what works for certain children and what triggers other children to be less capable.

Self-reflection leads to increased self-awareness. We are reminded of our childhoods as we help children cope with their own. Our patients' parents stimulate memories of our own parent-child interactions. Just as rearing children stimulates a parent's own experience of being a child, managing a child on a daily basis stimulates personal memories. In supervision, I have heard the ways in which milieu interactions reflect memories of past parent-child interactions. Staff listen to and soothe their patients as they were comforted and listened to. Or they give to these children what they wish they had received from their own parents.

In supervision, we also talk of the times when therapeutic management did not occur because the staff member was reenacting a painful parent-child interaction. Milieu therapists know that they are "too hard on" a child who is clingy when it evokes their own unwelcome memories of depending on their parents. Some of our patients are very angry and mean. Milieu therapists begin to recognize when they are too intolerant and judgmental because of their own past anger or sadistic urges, reawakened during their interactions with these troubled children.

Then there is fear. Milieu staff have to contend with fear for their physical safety when they try to contain children and family members who have histories of seriously hurting people. Sensible adults avoid people who frighten them. But milieu therapists need to become closer to frightening patients in order to continue to work with them. This is complicated and profound work that touches the inner life of the milieu therapist, as it touches the inner life of the child. *The milieu therapist's com-*

mitment to self-reflection and increasing self-knowledge parallels the child's struggle to heal and develop.

Energy. This work requires unusual amounts of physical and emotional energy—the kind of energy that flows from a relatively satisfying and healthy personal life. This is very hard work to do if one's own sense of self is under major attack, if one's personal life is in serious disarray, or if one's physical well-being is compromised by poor health. Physical energy is always needed to keep up with children, but milieu work also requires the kind of energy that can redirect depressed or troublemaking children into constructive play.

Our patients borrow our energy and attitude toward an activity or project until they can feel their own initiative and enthusiasm grow from within. Milieu therapists join in the activities they plan.

I remember a trip to a farm, when the guide told the kids to line up for their turn to milk the cow. The staff joined the line. At the end of the tour, the guide took me aside and criticized me and my staff because we wanted to milk the cow. She felt that we were taking the experience away from the children. In her mind, the proper role of the adult was to observe children at play.

I pointed out to her that our patients were able to value the activity and know how to do it through our participation. If we had held back, they may have also held back out of anxiety, fear, or reluctance to expose themselves. The adults modeled interest, skill, playfulness, and the willingness to try something new. It was hard for her to appreciate that school-age children would still need adults in this way.

Resiliency. *To be resilient, we will need to be open to observing and learning, to be actively resourceful in solving problems and finding creative new ways to reach children, and to be flexible in our approaches to patient care and program development.* We need to be open to approval and criticism of our approach from patients, their families, and our colleagues. Since units usually function at high speed, with constantly changing casts of patients and staff, they require staff initiatives to move at "therapeutic" paces and in "therapeutic" directions.

Resourceful therapists anticipate and plan management, rather than relying on reactive management. Therapeutic management requires constant rethinking about the interplay of group and individual needs: what structures should stay for all children and when the individual needs of a patient require modifications in the structure. Open, active, and flexible coping strategies that we require in staff are exactly what we are trying to develop in our patients as well.

Cooperation. Unlike the individual therapies, therapeutic management is not done in isolation; milieu therapists need to work together. This requires staff who:

- Are able to listen and talk about their work with each other (communication)
- Use collaborative problem-solving skills to develop a consensus in management approaches
- Enjoy and accomplish cooperation
- Use mature conflict resolution procedures to handle differences of opinion
- Maintain mutual respect and confidence in each other

Staff need to be able to debate and negotiate therapeutic management decisions with the best interests of the patients in mind. Just as mothers and fathers need to parent as a team, milieu therapists and the interdisciplinary team need to "treat" as a team. Milieu therapists need to develop the skills of good teamwork.

Intellectual Curiosity. Intellectual curiosity underlies the professional bond to our patients as much as respect and empathy. Milieu therapists need to remain curious about patients' pathology, existing abilities (even if they are relatively scarce or fragile), and potential for change, in the face of the patients' intense rejection of our efforts.

Curiosity counters our defensive efforts to simplify children into diagnostic categories or predictable life scenarios. Instead, we seek the complexity of possibilities for change in the midst of enduring pathology. Curiosity maintains our interest in a child or family even when we are emotionally upset or repulsed by their way of treating us. I have certainly known children I could not love or even like, but I have never met a patient that I could not take some interest in. Intellectual curiosity and psychological curiosity keep us open to new learning and the individuality of our patients.

Playfulness. Healthy people have fun. They delight in life. *Milieu counselors bring their own playfulness, sense of fun, and laughter to children and families who are in great need of some enjoyment.* This quality also includes a sense of humor. Many times we can head off major incidents by helping children see the humor in their behavior or our own.

Psychological pathology actually kills humor, makes it hard to laugh at oneself, and dampens enjoyment. We have to counter children's affinity for the negative feelings that preclude enjoyment and fun, such as shame, helplessness, frustration, and hopelessness. Staff members who can laugh at themselves can provide models for children or family members of how to manage frustration or failure by laughing at oneself. Playful therapists can guide children to the joyful in life, even in the midst of profoundly upsetting events.

Training

Milieu therapists may be selected because they have many of these qualities. But our staff training and supervision programs are also essential to develop the knowledge base of child development and child psychopathology as well as the professional orientation that is required to deliver therapeutic management. We alternate individual and group supervision and plan didactic inservice training sessions. Individual supervision allows for the private discussion of personal issues in the treatment of particular patients or help in handling conflicts with colleagues or unit administrators. Group supervision encourages peer support and learning. Didactic inservice training sessions teach child development, child psychopathology, and selected milieu treatments and management interventions. Continuing education experiences outside of the hospital bring in new ideas and treatment techniques.

Staff are asked to do a great deal and are expected to do it very well. They are not asked to do it without training or support. Many milieu therapists provide their service believing that this is one of the most gratifying experiences of their lives. They value their personal and professional growth. Milieu therapists develop collegial relationships and friendships that buffer the frustration and often deeply sad relationships that they form with patients and their families, who are constantly coming and going.

Milieu therapists usually stay in these jobs for one to three years. Nursing staff stay for several years and may stay longer if they assume the unit nursing administrative positions. Counseling staff stay for one or two years. We expect this turnover, because the counseling position is often a transitional position between college and professional training or other job choices. In some cases, counselors remain for several years and assume the senior counseling positions on the unit. Child-care career tracks can also be developed to encourage counseling staff to stay longer in these positions.

Organizational Structure

Therapeutic management requires an organizational structure that anticipates and plans for conflict and complexity through the delegation of clinical and administrative tasks according to experience, education, and training with clearly described lines of responsibility and accountability. Formal organizational structures should exist that provide behavioral job descriptions and designated lines of authority to foster constructive conflict negotiation. Without such structures, conflicts around clinical decision making can lead to counterproductive intrastaff relationships and antitherapeutic clinical interventions. Competition between different professional disciplines can become a fertile ground in which patients and family members can reenact maladaptive family interactional patterns.

Our unit organizational structure departs from traditional medical hierarchical organizational structures. The traditional hierarchical model fosters unilateral clinical decisions made from the top. It discourages clinical dialogue among staff from all levels of the organization. It parcels out clinical work in pieces, with no mechanism for synthesis. Lack of clinical dialogue about patient care underutilizes the initiative and creative thinking of milieu therapists.

Since milieu therapy is primarily done by nurses or unlicensed counselors holding the lowest-status jobs in a medical institution, their clinical observations and insights may not be heard or integrated in traditional central treatment formulations.

The Interdisciplinary Team. We have adopted the use of the interdisciplinary team in order to join the clinical visions of all staff at all levels of care. *The purpose of the interdisciplinary team is to harness and synthesize the clinical perspectives of staff with different training, expertise, experience, and daily exposure to the children and their families.* The team structure sanctions the existence of differences of opinion and formalizes the importance of synthesis in treatment plans.

The interdisciplinary team consists of the children's core treatment team (doctor, family worker, primary nurse or counselor), the specialists involved in assessment and treatment, and all staff who interact with the patients and their families during twenty-four-hour shifts and in special treatment groups. The formal structuring of these working relationships is designed to foster collaboration in clinical formulation and decision making and to create a conflict resolution path.

Organizational charts have been developed to establish clear lines of responsibility and authority, suggest channels of staff communication, and define clinical, administrative, and supervisory working relationships. Physicians, psychologists, nurses, social workers, art and occupational therapists, and teachers have unique but overlapping roles in assessment and treatment.

While recognizing different roles and functions, however, we emphasize active participation of all members of the treatment team. Despite differences in experience, professional credentials, salary, and responsibilities, the treatment of disturbed children requires an egalitarian spirit among all of the people involved in their care. The recognition and use of all staff members' contributions, commensurate with their training and experience, fosters a spirit of professionalism among the entire staff. This means decisions about therapeutic management will be informed by anyone who has relevant observations, insights, strategies, and understanding of the patient and family, regardless of professional status.

The core team works collaboratively to develop feasible and clinically relevant treatment plans. The patient's doctor is designated as the core team leader, with the responsibility for coordinating the comprehensive evaluation and treatment process. The doctor meets with the patient individually or with the family, according to the treatment goals. The family worker is responsible for coordinating the assessment and treatment of the family and social systems that support and treat the patient outside of the hospital. The milieu therapist is responsible for coordinating the daily assessment and treatment of the child in the milieu. All core team members communicate their observations and work to the full staff in regularly scheduled meetings.

Conflict Resolution in the Interdisciplinary Team. The interdisciplinary team works according to a written conflict resolution protocol that respects established organizational lines of administrative and clinical responsibility and accountability, as well as focusing on the best interests of the patient. Work is delegated according to the collaborative philosophy of the interdisciplinary team and the policies of licensing and accrediting agencies that oversee the unit's treatment. These agencies define and limit the administrative and clinical responsibilities and tasks assigned in job descriptions and delegated in organizational charts according to discipline-specific qualifications and credentials.

When conflict develops in the setting of treatment goals or choice of milieu treatment interventions, the core team leader has the responsibility for resolving the conflict through discussion and development of consensus among staff on an effective and common treatment approach. If the core team cannot come to an agreement, they seek consultation with the unit leaders (director and medical director), who oversee the overall clini-

cal and administrative functioning on the unit. The unit directors review the clinical options and seek feedback from other
key clinical staff—for example, the chief of psychiatry, nurse
manager, chief social worker, or activities specialists (the therapeutic recreational specialist or the occupational therapist, who
work almost half time in the milieu across all week and weekend
shifts). The directors then return to the core team with recommendations. If the core team remains unable to reach an agreement, they request that the administrative staff of the unit (director, medical director, nurse manager, chief social worker) discuss
the issues and make a decision.

This means that the most clinically senior staff members
who also represent the administrative leadership of the unit will
come to a decision reflecting the depth of their experience and
professional expertise. Their decision will also represent the basic
values and standards of the unit and, in some cases, may call
for a change in unit standards or procedures to accommodate
a unique clinical situation. Any conflict among the administrative staff is resolved through the organizational structure of the
unit—that is, "the buck stops" at the director's door.

This system will also monitor itself. For example, if the
cases of particular core teams are always in consultation, we
will analyze the reasons why conflict seems so unresolvable in
these situations. If too many cases are in consultation with the
administrative staff, we will analyze the working assumptions
and relationships between the primary team supervisors and the
administrative staff. In this system, the tools of the clinical
decision-making process are role flexibility, established forums
of discussion, supervision at all levels of the team, a well-defined
organizational structure with clear lines of responsibility and
authority (with one leader who all staff members ultimately
report to), and a clearly described culture of treatment that staff
are recruited with, oriented to, and held to.

We use cross-discipline supervision and performance evaluations. Choosing clinical options is considered the shared responsibility of all staff members. This collaborative responsibility
stimulates creative approaches from the combined efforts, observations, and expertise of all. Here is an example of how it works:

Kathy (a milieu counselor) lobbied to revoke Raoul's (age six) weekend passes because he returned from his home visit last weekend with questionable bruises and guarded stories about what actually happened.

Jill (a social worker) stressed Raoul's mother's attachment to and need for her son and ambivalence about keeping him in the hospital at all. She recommended a pass. We all knew about the mother's live-in alcoholic boyfriend who the mother needs as much as she needs her son. No one on the staff had met him yet.

During the discussion, we realized that we needed to involve the boyfriend in the parent-child activity program. Consequently, we decided to invite the mother and her boyfriend to spend time on the unit learning nonphysical ways of setting limits with Raoul. Rather than choosing one action or another (pass or no pass), we integrated perspectives from several staff members to inform our new treatment plan.

We shortened the pass for the upcoming weekend. At the same time, Jill discussed our concerns with Raoul's mother and her boyfriend and tried to find out what was happening on the weekend passes. Raoul's mother told us that he was getting into fights with neighborhood children and she needed to hold him back physically. Jill shared with them our appreciation of how difficult it is to manage Raoul's hyperactivity, temper tantrums, and generally disorganized responses under stress.

Kathy worked with the family to construct star charts and contracts to help shore up Raoul's behavior while on pass. They practiced some of these behaviors at parent visiting later in the week. We also ordered body checks to be completed following the home visit.

Time

Therapeutic management depends on a structured daily program that meets the clinical and developmental needs of the children and their families, helping them to increase their mastery over their bodies and their environment. Recreational and school activities are the natural arena in which school-age children master skills and develop competence, learn to relate to peers and adults, and acquire a sense of competence and self-worth (Erikson, 1950, 1980). Our milieu program incorporates these natural childhood settings, with the necessary modifications to fit our time-limited contact with our patients and their unique needs.

Our milieu program is modeled after the therapeutic activity programs designed in most hospital and treatment centers (Berlin, 1978; Erikson, 1976; Hoffman, 1982; Redl, 1966a; Redl and Wineman, 1951, 1952; Schulman and Irwin, 1982; Szurek, Berlin, and Boatman, 1971; Trieschman, Whittaker, and Brendtro, 1969). The program schedule, like all aspects of therapeutic management, is designed to contain, engage, and teach.

Our patients' problems have usually compromised their functioning in group situations. The hospital and treatment setting provides an opportunity for structured and professionally supervised interpersonal interactions and group participation, in selected activities, which are designed to bring a patient some measure of success and mastery of new skills, situations, or challenges.

For example, athletic activities—such as new games—are used that initially downplay competition and highlight the development of skills and team membership. Trieschman and his colleagues (1969, pp. 100–119) have presented Vinter's model of how to select activities according to dimensions of the activity: complexity and number of rules, who or what controls the activity, amount of physical movement, skill level for participation or winning, amount of interpersonal interaction, and the activity's reward structure. They also discuss the assessment of factors in the child (skill, motivation, and capacity for control in a particular activity) and in the group (cohesion, composition, and mood) as important dimensions of managing the milieu program (pp. 102–107).

Activity Group Program

The day is systematically programmed with mealtime, chore, bedtime, and personal hygiene routines and structured and unstructured therapeutic activities. Rules and routines stress conformity, just as therapeutic activities provide opportunities for expression of individuality and expression and rechanneling of strong emotions and impulses.

Most activities are organized around a group structure. Each group uses a particular activity or media to increase the patients' competence and self-esteem. A sample of possible goals for these groups are:

- Increase positive sense of self (self-esteem)
- Improve attention span and task completion strategies
- Develop a cognitive skill: ability to follow directions, organizational strategies
- Develop a coping skill: conflict resolution, problem solving, asking questions, listening to answers, waiting for turns, tolerating frustration, modulating intense emotions and impulses
- Develop a motor skill: skipping, running, hopping, swinging, or throwing and catching a ball
- Develop a social skill for adult-child interactions: working independently, listening, complying with rules, communicating, negotiating to get what you want, conversational skills
- Develop a social skill for peer interactions: communicating, negotiating, sharing, solving problems, helping, team work, becoming friends
- Learn to rechannel feelings and impulses in a structured activity

A child's participation in groups and unit routines is observed and assessed. These observations are written in the patient chart each shift. Milieu therapists pay special attention to the child's:

- Participation and quality of participation in the different groups
- Tolerance of frustration
- Ability to cooperate with adults or peers
- Reaction to physical, cognitive, or psychological challenges
- Interpersonal style with adults and peers
- Leadership style and potential

The milieu therapist for each child completes a milieu summary, which becomes a part of the patient chart and discharge summary. This summary describes the course of the child's treatment in the milieu and highlights the therapeutic management interventions that have been successful for that child.

The activity program is our major arena to help patients improve their relationships to peers (Selman, 1980, 1981; Selman, Jacquette, and Lavin, 1977). Small groups of active children, in which children learn interpersonal skills, simulate the real world. Most of our patients have had unsuccessful peer and group experiences and trouble making friends. We are particularly concerned about this, because negative peer relationships have been found to be a critical precursor to adult psychopathology (Kendall and Braswell, 1985; Robbins, 1966), adolescent delinquency and school dropout (Roff, 1961), and continued emotional and behavioral difficulties (Roff, Sells, and Golden, 1972).

Positive peer relationships are an essential part of normal child development (Hartup, 1976, 1983) and clearly buffer the impact of having a major mental illness or a troubled past and present family life.

We have incorporated various strategies to structure children's interactions in ways that can improve their peer relating skills:

1. Creating a positive peer culture (Vorrath and Brendtro, 1985); utilizing peers as "tutors" (Strayhorn, 1988)
2. Using peers as coaches for increasing social openness (Fantuzzo, 1988)
3. Establishing peer monitoring (Barth, 1986)
4. Using pair therapy (Selman and Demorest, 1984)
5. Relying on structured small-group treatment (Rose and Edleson, 1987)

In the structured small-group format, the leaders can control the group norms (for example, by rewarding prosocial actions and prohibitions against name calling), modify group cohesiveness (such as by assigning all children roles in the activity), and improve communication patterns (for instance, by teaching constructive ways of giving positive and negative feedback). They can also change status patterns—such as by assigning high-status tasks to low-status peers—and teach leadership skills.

The therapeutic activity schedule represents a balance of activities from the following four areas:

Motor groups develop motor skills and include:
   Movement group
   New games group (noncompetitive games)
   Gym group (skill practice and competitive games)
   Swimming
   Camping and outdoor activity skills
   "Work-It-Out" group or exercise groups
Affective and expressive groups help children develop adaptive ways to handle, express, and regulate affective material:
   Creative art
   Psychodrama (role playing typical problem situations)
   Storytelling (reading, writing, and dramatizing stories)
   Photography
   Music (listening, dancing, or drawing to music)
   Craft workshop (occupational therapy)
   Creative dance and movement
   "Anything Group" or drama (use of puppets, stories, structured board games to identify and express feelings)
Cognitive groups complement more formal school learning and incorporate grade-appropriate academic material:
   Reading (staff, parents, or tapes read stories and children read to each other)
   Outdoor education
   "All of Me" group (health education, including self-protection skills)
   Newspaper group

Cooking, unit community supper, family cooking
"Cars, Cards, and Comic Books" group (hobbies
and collections are started and shared)
World group (current events)
School discovery (preschool children learn letters,
colors, numbers)
Nutrition education
"Get Smart" group (drug and alcohol education)
Social skill development is embedded in all group experiences,
but specific groups are programmed to teach specific
social skills or handling of selected social settings, such
as:
A problem-solving group (emphasis on peer con-
flicts)
A small group (peer therapy between two children)
Outings
An eleven- and twelve-year-old group
A younger kids' club
Separate girls' and boys' groups

Exhibit 2 is a sample milieu schedule representing the rich-
ness and complexity of program planning.

Groups are named and planned to appeal to young children and stimulate learning and expression of feelings and experiences in age-appropriate ways. The "therapeutic" intent is
often embedded in a neutral activity, which allows for displaced
exploration of an issue or problem. We tried to avoid obvious
"hospital-sounding" names such as "feelings group" or "sexual
abuse victims' group."

Group size varies from large groups for all twelve children, to groups of six children, to groups of three or four children, down to the smallest groups for only two children. Since
most of our patients lack peer-relating skills, it is quite stressful
to be among other children all day. We try to minimize the demands of group living by offering children a daily schedule that
mixes various group sizes based on the goals of the activity and
the clinical and developmental level of functioning of the children. For example, a small group (peer therapy) involves two

children and a staff leader; groups of three or four children and two staff attend "Get Smart" (alcohol and drug education); six children and two or three staff go to the gym, outdoor group, and outings; eight to twelve children attend community meetings, watch movies, and participate in noncompetitive physical activities.

We also create groups around the development of a particular skill or management of a situation or issue. Skill groups teach constructive ways of handling a situation and provide outlets to express strong feelings and affirm the legitimacy of those feelings. We have created groups called:

- Complaint Group
- Apology Group
- Dropout Group (kids who refuse to go to tutoring)
- Tough Kids' Group (for boys who have been abused)
- Problem-Solving Group

Other groups deal with a difficult or challenging situation:

- Goodbye Group
- Transition Group
- Getting What You Want Group
- Being a Good Friend Group

We try to name groups using the words of children and avoiding hospital jargon:

- Get Smart Group (drug and alcohol education)
- Craft Workshop (occupational therapy)
- Anything Group (expressive arts)
- Cars, Cards, and Comic Books (school-age hobbies)
- School Discovery (school-readiness skills)
- All of Me (health education, including self-protection skills)
- Stepping Out (preadolescent outings)
- Work It Out (physical and relaxation exercises)
- Older Kids (preadolescents plan and carry out the activities with staff observer)

Exhibit 2. Sample Milieu Schedule.

TIME	MONDAY	TUESDAY	WEDNESDAY	THURSDAY	FRIDAY
7:00-7:30	RISE-N-SHINE	RISE-N-SHINE	RISE-N-SHINE	RISE-N-SHINE	RISE-N-SHINE
7:30-8:00	INSPECTION	INSPECTION	INSPECTION	INSPECTION	INSPECTION
8:00-8:30	BREAKFAST	BREAKFAST	BREAKFAST	BREAKFAST	BREAKFAST
8:30-8:45	MORNING MEETING	MORNING MEETING	TEETH, CHORES 8:30 MORNING MTG 8:50-9:00 FREE TIME 9:00-9:30	A group 8:30-10:15 B Group	MORNING MEETING
8:45-9:30	FREE TIME	FREE TIME		SW—m NG	FREE TIME
9:30-10:30	WORKSHOP ● OUTDOOR GRP FREE TIME	A Group B Group ALL OF Garden ME Group	PLAY GROUP WORKSHOP ● OUTDOOR GRP	small groups or OT STUDENT GROUP	A GRP B GRP NEWS-PAPER CREATIVE ARTS
10:30-10:45	SNACK	SNACK	SNACK	A-GRP SNACK 10:15 to 11:45 B Group	SNACK 10:30-10:45
10:45-11:45	CARS CARD COMICS B GRP FREE GET TIME SMART	GYM FREE GROUP TIME	FREE TIME IN ROOMS	A GROUP CREATIVE ARTS 10:45-11:15 SW—m NG	10:45-11:45 B GRP SPORTS ALL OF GROUP ME
11:45-12:30	INSPECTION	INSPECTION	INSPECTION — SMALL GROUP	INSPECTION	INSPECTION
12:30-1:15	LUNCH TEETH CHORE	LUNCH TEETH CHORE	LUNCH TEETH CHORE	LUNCH TEETH CHORE	LUNCH TEETH CHORE
1:15-2:15	School Discovery NEW GAMES NEW GAMES	NUTRITION GROUP SELF DEV GRP DEVELOP MENT GRP	STORY/DRAMA PSYCHO DRAMA STORY DRAMA	1:15-1:30 GET READY FOR GROUPS 1:30-2:30 GOAL GRP A Group WATERWORKS B-Group	GET SMART A-Group B-GROUP
2:15-2:30	GET READY FOR COMMUNITY MTG		GET READY FOR COMMUNITY MTG		GET READY FOR COMMUNITY MTG

Schedule chart (handwritten). Rotated table; days run left→right, times top→bottom.

Time	Day 1	Day 2	Day 3	Day 4	Day 5
2:30–3:00	Community meeting	Community meeting	Community meeting	Community meeting	Community meeting
3:00–4:00	Personal Time	Personal Time	Personal Time	Personal Time	Personal Time
4:00–4:15	EVENING MTG	EVENING MTG	EVENING MTG	EVENING MTG	EVENING MTG
4:15–5:15	SMALL GROUP — WORK IT OUT — WORKSHOP●	FREE TIME — FREE TIME — WORKSHOP●	FREE TIME 4:15–4:30 / 4:30–5:15 COMMUNITY SUPPER ANYTHING GROUP	FREE TIME — WORKSHOP● CARDS, OARS AND COMICS	FREE TIME 4:15–4:30 / WORKSHOP● 11 & 18 y/o group or FREE TIME
5:15–5:30	FREE TIME	FREE TIME	5:15–6:00 COMMUNITY SUPPER ANYTHING GROUP	SHOWER AND INSPECTION	FREE TIME
5:30–6:00	SUPPER & CHORE	SUPPER & CHORE	SUPPER AND CHORES	SHOWER AND INSPECTION	SUPPER & CHORE
6:00–7:00	SHOWER AND INSPECTION	6:00–6:30 SHOWER & INSPECTION / 6:30–7:30 PARENT-CHILD ACTIVITY	SUPPER AND CHORES	PARENT-CHILD ACTIVITY	SHOWER AND INSPECTION
7:00–8:00	OUTING	7:30–8:00 SHOWER AND INSPECTION	7:00–7:30 SHOWER AND INSPECTION / 7:30–8:30	7:00–7:30 SNACK	7:00–9:00 ___
8:00–9:00	HOMEWORK	7:30–8:00 SNACK / 8:00–8:30 TV-TIME	HOMEWORK TIME	7:30–8:30 T.V. TIME	MOVIES
9:00	OUTING	8:30–9:00 QUIET TIME	8:30–9:00 QUIET TIME	8:30–9:00 QUIET TIME	—

LIGHTS OUT

● CHILDREN CANNOT BE SCHEDULED FOR APPOINTMENTS DURING GROUP TIMES THAT HAVE A BLACK DOT ●

Education

An on-unit tutorial program meets the children's educational needs. Formal tutoring takes place Monday through Friday and is integrated into the daily milieu schedule. A homework period is built into the evening schedule. Milieu staff assist certified special education teachers during tutoring time with the educational assessment and school assignments.

Since our unit is a short-term program, we do not have a separate school. We emphasize reintegration into existing school programs as soon as possible. The tutors coordinate each child's schoolwork with the child's previous school setting, using the same books, when possible. Some children transition to their community schools while still coming back to the unit after school hours. Cognitive learning also takes place in the activity groups — for example, math skills in cooking groups and science in outdoor education groups.

Teachers coordinate the child's educational services, which include evaluation and assessment of academic needs and learning style, remedial teaching in academic problem areas while in the hospital, and development in posthospital educational recommendations, in collaboration with the child's school teacher. Teachers make weekly reports on the patient's study habits, learning style, and academic performance. These reports become a part of the child's chart and are sent to the child's posthospital school setting as part of the discharge package.

Family Participation Program

Family members are active members of the interdisciplinary team. Our overall treatment approach is based on the central importance of children's family context (current, past, missing, or substitute) to their healthy development and treatment.

Our goal is to help parents regain control of their families, through understanding of their children's developmental needs, feelings, and behavior. We try to help them learn how to communicate and discipline their children more effectively. We start with helping family members (emphasizing the parents) to express and understand their feelings about hospitalization, including feelings of shame, guilt, anger, anxiety, helplessness, and relief. By creating a climate of mutual respect, we are more likely to help families overcome resistance to change and develop confidence in their own capacities for healing and growth.

Parents, patients, and their siblings work and play together with focused treatment goals in multiple treatment structures. The family treatment program includes the following components, which are individualized for each child and family in a treatment plan:

1. *Family and parent meetings.* Each family is assessed in terms of family history, dynamics, and interactional patterns that are buffering the impact of mental illness and that are contributing to the patient's problems. We try to determine what changes are necessary and possible to allow the family to be a part of the solution to their children's problems. A family worker is assigned to each family and meets regularly with the parents and other subgroupings of the family, as indicated in the child's treatment plan. Family or parent meetings may be co-led by the patient's doctor and milieu worker. Helping the family members feel comfortable and understood is a primary goal of individual family or parent meetings.

2. *Parents' group.* Parents meet with other parents of hospitalized children for support of each other, validation of the difficulties in hospitalizing a child, information sharing, and education. Group leaders encourage parents to share their feelings about hospitalization, seeking help for their children and their families, problems with finding community resources, and adjustment to this crisis time in the life of their family. Parents share their questions and concerns about unit practices and issues throughout the hospitalization (Mirkin and Koman, 1985).

3. *Parent-child activity group.* Parents and children form small evening groups to improve the quality of the parent-child relationship through learning new behavioral and communication interactional patterns. The curriculum includes

units on practical parenting skills, communication, limit setting and discipline, reward systems, self-esteem, and play. Activities and role playing are used to increase interactive learning. Each parent-child set adapts the didactic material to their own focused goals (DeSalvatore and Rosenman, 1986; Simon, 1982).

4. *Parent participation on the unit.* Parents spend several hours per week on the unit as co-therapists with milieu workers. This allows for alliance building between parents and staff, parent modeling of staff-child interactions, opportunity for parents and children to practice new communication and discipline strategies, and opportunities for milieu staff to get to know and appreciate parents. Parents and children have specified goals, such as a parent learning to praise the child or the child learning to take time out without arguing (Critchley and Berlin, 1981; DeSalvatore, 1989).

5. *On-unit visiting.* Visiting on the unit is unstructured time between family members and the children. We inform parents that they are in charge of their children during visiting. We will only intervene if unit safety or routine is disrupted and we will help them, whenever they request help. This is their opportunity to enjoy each other. Staff observe family styles of interaction and communication (Adessa and Laatsch, 1972).

6. *Therapeutic home visiting.* Home visiting allows children to stay connected to their family, neighborhood, and community. Children and parents bring home behavioral contracts in which they practice new ways of dealing with troublesome behavior or situations. This is the children's chance to keep up their friendships and group connections (for example, some children continue participation on sports teams or in clubs). Home visiting counteracts the potential for children and families to become further alienated from each other during the hospitalization (Parmelee, 1982).

7. *Sibling group.* The sibling group provides support and information to all siblings of hospitalized children. It meets at the same time as the parents' group. Siblings have the opportunity to share feelings and ask questions about their

brother or sister's emotional problems and psychiatric hospitalization.

Children have often not had the opportunity to hear other siblings share similar feelings of fear (can you catch it?), anger (over broken possessions or scary incidents), guilt (over being the "good" one), shame (at having a "bad" brother or sister), self-blame (I caused this, because I told on him), and relief (the house is peaceful, I get more attention), or lonely (I miss my brother or sister). Some children are envious of their sibling who is receiving so much attention and can take part in "fun" activities and trips while in the hospital.

Leaders also assess siblings, try to identify problem areas, and refer children for evaluation when indicated. We try to create a younger sibling group (ages ranging from five to eight years) and an older sibling group (ages ranging from nine to sixteen years).

8. *Parent-child milieu groups.* We try to create some groups that are natural settings for children and parents to play together. Family cooking or the community supper are opportunities for parents to nurture their children, teach their own favorite recipes, and share their own family or cultural styles. On athletic night, children and their parents can pick a game and play it together. Story telling in the evening involves the staff reading stories to the parents and children. Parents are encouraged to select or bring books from home. Staff modeling of nighttime routines with books is emphasized at this group. We often tape a parent reading a story and let the child listen to it while in the hospital and then bring it home later. Parents love to hear themselves on tape. This practice also emphasizes the unique role parents have in their children's lives.

The programming of the time that children and their families spend on the unit is designed to provide generally comforting and growth-promoting experiences. The general program schedule is altered for patients and their families to allow them to have the greatest degree of success in the milieu.

Conclusion

Therapeutic management starts with the environmental context of treatment, which sets the stage for the interpersonal interactions between patients, families, and staff members. Culture, space, people, and time are designed to protect, engage, and teach patients and their families.

The institution's culture is defined by explicitly stated values and the atmosphere or spirit created by the people and space. Physical space is designed to support the therapeutic and developmental needs of the children and their families. Staff are recruited for specific qualities that reflect and match the unit treatment values of hope, respect, and understanding. The unit program provides a rich and structured schedule of routines and special activities to enhance skill development and treatment goals through systematic design of the motor, affective and expressive, cognitive, and social areas of development. The child's educational needs are programmed into the activity program, and specific remedial work is accomplished in tutoring sessions. Families are integral members of the treatment team, and so the milieu program includes a variety of specially designed groups to include parent and sibling participation in treatment.

This framework of treatment creates the holding environment in which therapeutic management can shape the interpersonal interactions between children and staff. The interpersonal holding environment is based on the triad of empathy, communication, and discipline.

Sal Lion

CHAPTER 2

The Interpersonal Context of Therapeutic Management: Empathy

The environmental framework of treatment sets the stage for the creation of the interpersonal context of treatment during Phase I of our model of therapeutic management. Just as normal childrearing relies on daily adult-child interactions around the mundane and profound happenings of childhood, therapeutic management pays special attention to the potential of daily interactions to protect, engage, and teach patients.

The interdependent processes of empathy, communication, and discipline form the basis of socialization in healthy childrearing. *The interpersonal foundation of a therapeutic management program is also made up of the critical triad of empathy, communication, and discipline.*

Empathy consists of our efforts to feel and understand the children's point of view—what they are feeling and thinking and why they are doing what they are doing. We use the children's perspective to decipher what their words and behavior are trying to say and do. Communication consists of listening to the children's messages (words and behavior) and responding verbally and nonverbally with empathy. The discipline process con-

69

sists of steps by which adults teach children society's standards and rules and how to follow them.

In this chapter, we discuss the interpersonal holding environment, focusing on the practical skills needed to create empathic connections. In Chapter Three, genuine communication is described, and in Chapter Four, growth-promoting discipline is outlined. Chapter Five describes the corrective modifications required for emotionally disturbed children who are unable to make use of the normal socialization process.

We begin this chapter with a discussion of the triad and conclude with a description of the empathic formulation: our translation of what the child's behavior is trying to say and do for the child.

The Triad

The triad of empathy, communication, and discipline are the ingredients of the normal socialization process that all children need to develop into loving, trusting, competent persons with integrity. Socialization takes place in the children's relationships with the parenting adults in their lives. Adults use these relationships to help children develop:

- Self-control
- Acceptable ways of getting needs met and wishes granted without violating the needs and rights of others
- Adaptive ways of coping with stress
- Acceptable ways of expressing feelings
- Mutually satisfying relationships with adults and peers

Any hospital or residential treatment setting will have to provide the ingredients of the socialization process needed by all developing children. Empathy creates the fertile ground in which communication and effective discipline can develop between children and adults. Discipline *not* based on empathic connections and true communication may bring about behavioral compliance. But it will not develop the child's capacity to love and trust adults in authority and to develop in time internal standards and controls for commitment and adherence to society's standards and codes of behavior.

Our model of therapeutic management incorporates the complex mix of ingredients from the full socialization process outlined in Table 2. The triad of empathy (step 2), communication (step 3), and discipline (step 4) are at the heart of this process. The ingredients of socialization have been culled from the childrearing literature, integrating principles and practices from humanistic, cognitive, and behavioral approaches (for example, Clark, 1985; Dangel and Polster, 1984; Dinkmeyer and

Table 2. The Normal Socialization Process.

---

1. *Love.* Love with warmth, support, and affection.
2. *Empathize.* Respect, understand, and affirm feelings.
3. *Listen and talk.* Communicate effectively.
4. *Utilize the discipline (teaching) process.*
   a. *Have expectations, values, rules, and limits.* Set developmentally attainable standards and rules.
   b. *Be clear and give reasons.* Clearly explain standards, rules, and limits.
   c. *Say what's acceptable and unacceptable.* Respectfully evaluate the child's attitudes, words, and actions.
      1. Endorse: approve, praise, and encourage.
      2. Discourage: disapprove and criticize.
   d. *Be a good model.* Model acceptable and adaptive behaviors: practical problem solving, conflict resolution, adaptive coping, honesty, prosocial behaviors, and constructive interpersonal skills.
   e. *Invite participation and collaboration.* Encourage developmentally feasible parent-child dialogue and child initiative in relationship building, value setting, rule making, and problem solving.
   f. *Teach consequences of behavior.*
      1. *Acknowledge good behavior (good consequences).* Notice and celebrate when the child obeys rules, copes well, and lives up to standards.
      2. *Give penalties (negative consequences).* Give reasonable, effective, and developmentally fitting penalties when the child breaks the rules.
         (a) Ignoring a child.
         (b) Reprimands.
         (c) Natural consequences.
         (d) Logical consequences.
         (e) Behavior penalties.
   g. *Provide opportunities for reparation.* Provide opportunities for reparative actions and words (apologies).
   h. *Forgive the child.* Accept the child's apologies, forgive the child, and communicate this to the child.

McKay, 1976, 1983; Faber and Mazlish, 1980, 1987; Forehand and McMahon, 1981; Ginott, 1965, 1969; Glenn and Nelsen, 1989; Gordon, 1970; Nelsen, 1987; Patterson, 1975, 1976; Patterson, Reid, Jones, and Conger, 1975).

The table presents steps in a process that starts with a loving adult-child relationship and leads to socialization through empathy, communication, and effective discipline. The cycle goes like this: If children feel loved and understood, they are more likely to listen to adults and talk to adults about their concerns and wishes. Also, if they feel loved and understood and can communicate with adults, they are more likely to cooperate with the discipline process and use the discipline process to learn how to cooperate. Finally, children who have internalized positive values, have self-control, and can trust and love others are children who are more able to participate constructively in their own socialization.

A word about love. Our therapeutic triad does not start there. We do not start off loving our patients, and we may or may not ever love them. We certainly never will love them as a family member can love them. We do not replace or substitute for parental love and constancy. In fact, we need to assist in "parenting functions" without this basis in love and trust. This is one reason that the socialization process will look so different in an inpatient or residential setting. The basis of our relationships with our patients is the respect and commitment we extend to them, regardless of their capacity to evoke affection or love and without the biological or family bonds that exist between our patients and their biological, adoptive, or foster families.

Empathy

Empathy is the process we use to enter the inner world of the children. Through the empathic stance, we are able to stand in the children's shoes, listen with their ears, look out through their eyes, think with their brain, feel with their heart, speak with their words, and believe with their soul. We need to actively search children's behavior, symptoms, words, feelings, and silences to find their inner selves. As Havens (1986, p. 25) explains, "The first order of clinical business is to find the other . . . not in the sense that the patient feels found out or criticized, but so that the patient feels found."

When we see Lisa hurting herself, when Andrew greets us with insults and taunts, when Ralph "streaks" down the hall, when Paul is found trying to sneak off the unit, we try to find out what he or she is needing, saying, or hoping to resolve with these actions and words. With the empathic stance, we accept the child's perspective and work within it. We do not need to agree with it or approve of it. Empathy does not mean giving children everything they long for or everything they want. Empathy has to do with searching, understanding, and affirming.

Therapeutic management starts with empathy, and in this way it works from the inside, not the outside, of children. We are interested in the subjective meaning of an action, rather than the overt effect of that behavior on us. When we describe children's actions as "manipulative," we may be describing how they make us feel, not what the children intend to accomplish with the behavior.

Paul (age nine) finished his time-out for teasing during story time. He was sulking in his chair and visibly trying not to listen as Suzanne (an occupational therapist) read the story. Mel (a counselor) noticed and asked Paul to come into the hall with him. Mel knew that Paul's sulks soon moved on to troublemaking of one kind or another. Mel asked Paul what was bothering him.

Paul answered with a tirade against Suzanne, emphasizing how unfair she was only to him, how she never gave a time-out to Maria, how she never listened to his side of the story, and how he was not going to take this from her anymore. He also compared her to his foster mother, who always took the side of her own children and never listened to his side.

"I'm sorry you feel so bad," Mel said. "I feel bad when I feel things are unfair, too . . . "

"Yeah, sure," Paul interrupts. "You always take Suzanne's side."

"I don't know what Suzanne did, but I can see you're pretty mad," Mel said. "No wonder you can't stand listening to her. Now that I know how you feel, I can appreciate how much control you're

showing in that group. Do you want to sit with me for a while out
here, until you cool down?"
Paul didn't answer, but he sat down next to Mel.
"Do you want me to help you write Suzanne a note, telling
her your side of the story?"
"Nah, I can write it myself. Just get me the paper."

Mel listened to Paul. He affirmed how Paul felt and helped
him stay in control and out of trouble. Mel did not try to question the reality of Paul's account of the situation. He did not
try to defend Suzanne or interpret Paul's experience of Suzanne.
He did not attempt to clarify Paul's contribution to these incidents. There are times when interpretation, clarification of reality, advice giving, and confronting children with their responsibility for trouble should take place in therapeutic management.
But there are many more times when the first order of business
is to try to understand and appreciate what the children are feeling and thinking and to let them know that we understand their
perspective on a situation. With our empathy, children can learn
to adapt to what they perceive to be "unfair" reality and post-
pone their need to fight adult limits.

This is what we mean by an empathic response. This is
the basis of all the other communications and interventions we
will try with children. Responding empathically has nothing to
do with detective searches for "the truth." We want to work within
the children's "truth" and create a bridge to other truths. This
sequence is particularly necessary when children are feeling
strong emotions.

As Ginott (1965, p. 22) points out, "When a child is in
the midst of strong emotions, he cannot listen to anyone. He
cannot accept advice or consolation or constructive criticism.
He wants us to understand him. He wants us to understand
what is going on inside himself at that particular moment."

The empathic stance is easier the more similar the child's
perspective is to our own perspective, and harder the more unlike a child's thoughts and feelings are. Since we are no longer
children, understanding children is always more challenging,
because children have their own developmentally determined

ways of thinking and feeling. Working with disturbed children, we need to be prepared to stretch and distort our perceptions and expand our tolerance for painfully raw negative affects. Psychotic children or children with idiosyncratic views of reality require us to enter new inner worlds of distortions and misconceptions.

Heather (age seven) lived in a private world of fearful and powerful internal figures who personified good (Jesus) and evil (the pointy-headed monster). These forces controlled her actions and tortured her with vindictive judgments about her unworthiness. Heather worried whether they would ever accept her efforts to be good and let her be happy and free.

Her nurse, Joy, spoke to her one day following a difficult weekend in which Heather had been very withdrawn and seemed to be talking to herself.

"I want to talk to you about your weekend. Your parents noticed that you were very worried. I wondered whether you were battling with Jesus and the pointy-headed monster again."

"No," said Heather. "Go away."

"You know, Heather, I think your struggle is very important. The struggle for good over evil and happiness over sadness is very important."

"You don't know," whispered Heather.

"I fight the same battle," Joy continued, "but I talk about my battle with different words. You are all alone with your battle. So you feel these things in very private ways and have named them with your own personal words."

Heather put her head down, clasped her ears with her hands, and hummed softly. Joy knew that the inner voices were trying to drum out her words. But Heather was listening intently to Joy.

"I know you're worried that your words sound 'crazy.' The words may sound crazy to some people, but I don't think your worries are crazy. Your feelings are very real. You deserve the chance to feel them with others. I want to help you express them in less private ways, so that others can understand you."

Heather looked up and stared at Joy. "I can't tell Mommy."

"Maybe we can draw some pictures for your mommy and invite her to join us sometime."

"Okay."
"The pointy-headed monster is not the only force to help
little girls be good and triumph over evil. We can help Jesus and
the monster be kinder with their powers. I believe that you may
find life less painful and confusing if you can learn to share more
with others."

These are the moments we study and train for. We want
to be able to understand what children are feeling and needing
at these times. The more we understand who children are and
the unique ways they may have of trying to do something and
how they are feeling, the more effective our efforts will be to
communicate with them.

Dramatic and mundane empathic moments construct the
profound context in which treatment takes place. Working with
children, we need to appreciate how frustrating it is for them
when they want to wear the red socks but they are in the laundry or how infuriating it is when the menu promised pizza and
the kitchen sends up fish sticks. The following is an example
of the empathic stance during mundane moments:

Dr. D (a psychologist) entered the bathroom just as Andrew (age
seven) was yelling at Kathy (a counselor). His pig-shaped sponge,
"Oinky," was missing. He was refusing to take a bath. Dr. D looked
very concerned.

"Can I help? I heard that Oinky was missing. You may not
know it, Kathy, but Andrew really depends on Oinky. I feel terrible
that Oinky is missing. I hope we can find him soon."

"I've got an idea," Dr. D said. "Until we find him, we could
make a new pig and pretend it's Oinky's cousin. I could cut a piece
of an old towel into a pig shape and Andrew could bring it into the
bath with him."

"What do you think of that, Andrew?" asked Kathy.

Dr. D's empathy stemmed from his understanding of the
importance of bathtime rituals to a seven-year-old. He did not
know whether the pig had a special emotional significance for
Andrew the way some objects can for some children (transitional
objects; Winnicott, 1965). Maybe it was the interruption in the

bath routine or maybe the pig was given to him by his mother. We often will never know. The point is, children can have intense feelings about what adults may consider minor events.

Children in residential treatments can attach special importance to things, people, places, or rituals that help them stay connected to their nonhospital lives. We need to accept and respect these reactions even when we may not know much about what they represent. Empathy with the child's experience can start with our acceptance and acknowledgment of the experience. We do not need to find the unconscious intrapsychic roots of anxiety or anger to respect these feelings.

Michael (age eight) was pestering Ruth (a counselor) again. He kept touching her hair, pulling at her clothes, and insisting on sitting on her lap. Ruth was feeling smothered and irritated with his clinging.

When she walked into team meeting, she heard Michael's social worker telling the staff that Michael's mother had been admitted to a psychiatric hospital the previous evening following her visit to Michael. She was suicidal again. Ruth knew immediately that Michael was reacting to his own predictions about his mother's fragility. He had often been the one in the family to know about her deepening depressions before they were detected by her therapist or before she was able to verbalize them herself.

Ruth returned to the unit with a renewed commitment to Michael. She was able to offer her lap, tolerate the clinging, and set limits on the poking with a different attitude and spirit. She rejoined Michael and gave him a big hug. He looked surprised and then smiled.

They talked later about his worries about his mother. Ruth helped him call his mother at the hospital. That night, he slept with her picture under his pillow.

Empathic understanding must precede our individual responses to the children. Our empathy with them helps us try to imagine how they will hear what we are trying to say or understand what we are trying to do. The empathic stance positions us to search for the proper words, gestures, and body language to convey what we need to.

Empathic understanding can help us soothe and bring out the best in children, rather than miss the point or intrude and bring out the worst. Our understanding can also help increase our patience and tolerance and stimulate our creative responses to children. In this way, the empathic response brings out the best in ourselves.

Healthy children are likely to respond positively to our empathy, but our patients have more complex reactions to being understood. Some children receive our understanding with relief, and the process of communication begins. Other children may distrust, misunderstand, or simply be deaf to our meanings when they are really upset. These are the "relationship-resistant children" described by Trieschman and his colleagues (1969) in their chapter titled "Establishing Relationship Beachheads." They point out that the invasion metaphor aptly describes the initial resistance that our best efforts may encounter when we try to connect with emotionally disturbed children.

Many children cannot digest kindness without feeling hungrier than before. The emotional connection threatens their need for isolation and independence from adults who have been too consistently irresponsible, indifferent, mean, or sarcastic. These children will need time and resourcefulness to be able to take in our understanding and respect for who they are and what they have been through. Children with low self-esteem feel unworthy of our understanding. We will need to regulate dosages of our understanding and kindness, just as we regulate the dosages of our other "medicines." Other children cannot value words as useful ways of getting their point across. They cannot hear our words as useful to them. Many do not believe our words. We will need to be thoughtful about how and when we share our empathy with sensitive and vulnerable hearts.

The empathic stance requires adults to observe, listen, and talk within each child's personally and developmentally determined point of view. The empathic stance shapes and tunes our responses to what each child can accept, understand, and integrate.

The Empathic Formulation

The empathic stance leads to the empathic formulation, which is the initial step and the guiding framework in the behavioral treatment of emotional problems (Harper, 1991). *The empathic formulation is our best guess about what children's behavior means to them, says for them, and does for them.* The empathic formulation ties our developmental and dynamic understanding of children to the problem behaviors that we observe and the behavioral treatments that we design to change those behaviors. The dynamic aspects of a formulation focus on the conscious and unconscious meaning of the behavior to the children, how the behavior is tied to their sense of self and other, and how the behavior fits in their characteristic ways of defending and coping.

The empathic formulation explains a child's problem behaviors and answers the following questions: How does the unacceptable behavior serve the child? How does it resolve inner conflict, communicate strong feelings, solve problems, or cope with stressful situations?

In the empathic formulation, we decipher the child's words and actions and translate them in terms of the child's past and the subjective meanings for the child. Our understanding of children can be based on extensive observations and formal evaluations. Other times, we will need to formulate our understanding of children quickly and with few details. Our intuitive grasp of the details of children's lives may be our best clinical tool. In the following vignette, Johnny had only been on the unit a short time.

"Get the fuck out of here," screamed Johnny (age eight). "I don't have to listen to you. I didn't ask to come here. I don't have to talk to you. Leave me alone."

I stood outside the locked seclusion door. The mess around me told the story of how six staff had got Johnny in the quiet room. Furniture was lying where it had been kicked, and torn art work was hanging from the walls. The staff were meeting in the staff room, and the main argument was about whether or not to transfer this eight-year-old boy who had been on the unit for less than twenty-four hours. The school had referred him for an evaluation because he was fighting with peers and wouldn't obey his teachers. He could not read and seemed completely unmotivated to learn.

"Johnny, you're right," I responded. "You don't have to listen to us or talk to us if you think it'll hurt you. You only have to cooperate if you stay here. I need to unlock the door and talk to you about staying here. Please sit in the far end of the room and I'll sit at the doorway. I don't want to get hurt.

"I know you're very strong and I know you hit and throw things when you get mad. You may get mad when we're talking so I want to protect myself. I also don't want you to run away when I open the door. You may leave this unit if we can't help you but I want us to think about this first. If you leave, I want you to leave safely."

When I unlocked the door, I saw Johnny crumpled up on the punching bag in the far corner. Sweat was dripping from his mostly hidden face, which was buried in his arms.

"I told you to get the fuck out of here. I can't hear a word you're saying. I . . . "

"You've had such a tough day," I interrupted. "But I guess you're used to it. You've had such a tough life. It's amazing you're still alive."

"Don't talk about my life. You don't know me. Leave me alone. You . . . "

"No. That wouldn't be fair. You've been left alone too much. You've done a lot for yourself, but I think you deserve some help now. I . . . "

"You can't make me do anything. I don't have to tell you anything."

"I need to help you. For your mother, because she's not here to do it herself. She didn't have you so you could grow up angry and unhappy. She wanted you to grow strong and competent. She wanted you to have fun and play with friends. She wanted you to love her, and she wanted you to feel her love."

Johnny had grown perfectly still. His face was completely buried in his arms. He was beginning to breathe more smoothly.

I continued, "I wish I'd also known your father when he was a little boy. I wish I could've helped him learn to manage his anger in safe ways. He deserved the kind of help from adults all kids need. He still deserves help, but it's too late to save your mother. I bet he'd be glad if I could help you not end up in jail like he is."

This was the unbelievable reality that Johnny lived with. His father had killed his mother when he was six months old, during one of their frequent fights. He was in a local prison, where he was appealing his life sentence. Johnny lived with his maternal grandmother and some aunts and uncles. He had been a behavior problem since he was three, and the family said he was just like his father. He had only seen his father a few times when he was much younger. He followed his whereabouts in the local paper, which reported on the happenings of this highly publicized murder.

I felt that Johnny had enough talk for now. I did not want to overwhelm him with the connection we were feeling as I read what could be the secret longings of his heart.

"I can't promise that we can make a difference or that we can help the way your parents could—if they were here. But I can promise to try. Trying hard is worth a lot even if it doesn't work at first. We give credit around here for trying. It would work better if we tried together, but I want to give you a chance to think about that. You have another half hour of time to take. Do you want me to leave the door unlocked?"

"Yes."

Our formulation of Johnny's dramatic life story informed the empathic connections that this dialogue illustrates. Johnny was convinced that he would be nothing if he was not just like his father. His father had not learned to read, and Johnny was loyally following in his footsteps. Since he had not known his father long enough to ask him, Johnny had to guess at what his father would want him to be like. Johnny was going to be tough like his father. He was even suspended from school for concealing homemade weapons in his school locker.

There was a deeper, invisible (some call it unconscious) reason for his fighting and destruction of property. Johnny feared that if he was not like his father, if he was more like his mother, he would be murdered, too. These were powerful forces to shape his character and behavior. Add to this a violence-prone family life in an inner-city housing project, an overwhelmed grandmother who was tragically reminded of her dead daughter every time she looked at Johnny, and the family's vivid fear that he would be just like his father, whom they despised openly. After all, he looked just like him.

This was our formulation, and it helped us retrace our steps with him. Our efforts to get him to conform to our rules and trust and befriend us were premature. We were expecting a relationship that Johnny had steeled himself against. Fear and past failures had taught this proud child that he was better off alone. He was not about to depend on people who were so foreign to him. One thing was clear. Johnny was going to be the most obnoxious and talented tough guy on the unit. He preferred showing off what he did well rather than trying to learn new ways. Why be an awkward, "good" boy when he had the potential to win the fear and admiration of every other kid on the unit? As for adult approval and love, it was out of his reach. The mere sight of an adult caused rage to bubble up inside. What a mess adults made of their lives. What right did they have to tell him what to do?

Our empathic formulation was the "code" to decipher Johnny's symptoms or troublemaking behaviors.

The Code

We need a code because the meaning of symptoms is often obscure to us and unconsciously known by the patient. We assume that there is meaning in symptoms and that the symptoms serve the child:

- They communicate what cannot be put into words.
- They try to solve problems.
- They manage the child's psychological distance from other people.
- They both conceal and reveal the child's inner self.
- They help control the environment by eliciting predictable responses.
- They tell us how the child has learned to cope.

They are the connection between the events of the moment and the child's history.

The empathic formulation derives from the psychodynamic formulation, which summarizes and organizes into central themes all that we know about a child (Coppolillo, 1987; Kalogjera, Bedi, Watson, and Meyer, 1989; Perry, Cooper, and Michels, 1987; Rossman and Knesper, 1976; Shapiro, 1989). With the empathic formulation, we see the world from the child's perspective. With the psychodynamic formulation, we understand how and why the child needs to act this way.

We also include biological factors in the code. The biological contributing factors in a child's behavior can often explain why the child's symptomatology has taken one form rather than another. We will also not search for psychological meaning in symptoms that are clearly caused by physical or neurological diseases (temporal lobe epilepsy) or medication side effects (toxic levels of a medicine) or cognitive deficits (low IQ or language processing deficits).

Many of our patients are unable to make connections between their actions and their pasts. We need to translate for them. These translations can relabel behavior for the child and parents in ways that help motivation and self-acceptance.

> Lisa (age eleven) was more frequently disliked than liked or understood. She maintained a safe distance from people with her aggressive behavior and clever verbal insults and putdowns.
>
> She was annoyed and then amused when Fran (a counselor) started to call her a "porcupine."
>
> "Lisa, you remind me of a porcupine," he explained. "Every time we start having a good time, you do something to spoil it. Like yesterday when you started kidding me about my big nose after we had had a nice walk. I'm pretty sensitive about my nose. I was hurt. Then I thought about it on my way home last night. I guess it was too soon for us to become good friends. You might need to keep your distance. I hope we can plan for this better in the future. But you should know, I like porcupines! They are independent and intelligent and lovable. You just have to figure out how they want to get close. Okay?"

Fran's metaphor and explanation were empathic. They allowed Lisa her defenses but avoided the usual discussions of why she was so obnoxious. He communicated his understanding to her without asking her to change the behavior. He also recognized that even a casual friendship was a big expectation for Lisa.

Often we don't have the code, and our best response will be a question. When we ask children what happened to make them so angry or unfriendly, we are letting them know that we are interested in their history and their point of view, even if we are clearly limiting their behavioral expression of it. Our translations of the meaning of behaviors also need to guide our words without making interpretations to children who need the "cover" of their symptoms.

> Maria (age twelve) wouldn't go on the movie outing with the group. She wanted to remain on the unit with Ralph and Heather, two patients who were not permitted to go on the outing. Paul (a counselor) and she were making hot chocolate and watching TV.
>
> "I noticed something, Maria," started Paul. "You can't enjoy something, when someone else is missing out, can you? Do you feel guilty when you're so lucky and they aren't?" Maria looked at the floor and didn't answer, but she seemed to be listening closely.
>
> Paul continued, "I can see how you try to even things out. But I don't think giving up things for yourself really helps people. Enjoying yourself is kind of separate. You know, having fun fills us up, Maria. It renews our energy and interest in helping others."
>
> Paul knew that Maria was struggling with her sense of disloyalty and guilt as she compared herself to her psychotic mother and limited father. Her suicidality was an extreme example of her attempts to even the score with her tragic mother, who was now a homeless bag lady wandering the streets of Maria's neighborhood.
>
> Maria stared at Paul and smiled, "Is that how you do it for us?"
>
> Paul smiled back. "Yes. When I've had a real bad day here, I go for a ride on my bike or I listen to a tape. My bike and music make me feel good and I get filled up inside."
>
> Maria spent the rest of the evening helping Paul and playing games with Ralph and Heather. Before she went to sleep that night, she told Paul that she wanted to go on the movie outing next week.

The code also helps us sort out the problem behavior and help the patients save the *good in the bad*. We need to know what in the maladaptive behavior has to be saved and how to save it, and what needs to be jettisoned and how to make the children do that. For example, aggression contaminates assertion in psychopathology (Stechler and Halton, 1987). This contamination makes it hard for children to assert their identity and their needs or wishes without also causing trouble. The good gets buried in the bad.

> Michael (age eight) was whining and clinging to Judy (a nurse). She asked Michael to take a time-out for whining.
> When he returned, she said, "Good job, Michael. I know you want more attention from me. You deserve my attention. I didn't like the way you reminded me and asked for my time, but I'm glad that you didn't let me forget about you and what you want. Let's try to find another way for you to tell me next time."

Here's another example:

> Donna (ten years old) started swearing at Ralph. She was furious that he had teased her about her new haircut and tried to poke her in the butt. Peg (a chief social worker) asked her to take a time-out. When she had finished her time, Peg suggested that they take a walk. Donna complained that Peg didn't understand her feelings.
> "I heard what Ralph said. It must have hurt your feelings."
> "He's a fucking asshole. He had no right to touch me on the butt . . . in front of everyone."
> "I didn't see that. I'm sorry. But you're right to put up a fuss if someone violates your privacy like that. It's really good to see a girl stand up for herself. I hope we can work out a way for you to do the right thing without getting into trouble yourself."

Conclusion

We start our interpersonal interactions with children by assuming that they need our commitment, empathy, and willingness to listen and talk with our actions and our words. The empathic stance keeps our attention on the inner world of the children and focuses our thinking on the search for their meaning in the symptoms and troublemaking behaviors that confront us. The empathic formulation is our best guess at what the children's behavior means, says, and does for them.

Equipped with this understanding, we can attempt to listen, talk, and act. Communication with children is the product of empathy and the foundation of effective discipline.

Surprised Lion

CHAPTER 3

The Interpersonal Context of Therapeutic Management: Communication

Effective communication is one of our most powerful therapeutic tools. Therapeutic management and therapy in all its other forms depend on our capacity to communicate with children. We can do all sorts of "right" things, but they will not lead to healing and development unless we can communicate our understanding of children and what we are trying to do with them. It is the sense of being understood and helped that children seek, even more than the experience of getting what they want or being agreed with. This understanding, in the service of helping children, is the water that primes the pump when we are looking for motivation for treatment or even some degree of cooperation in treatment. Everything that we do and provide for children must convey our efforts to connect with them.

Communication consists of the two complementary processes of listening and talking. *Good talking starts with good listening,* as suggested in Faber and Mazlish's wonderful book, *How to Talk So Kids Will Listen and Listen So Kids Will Talk* (1980). This title makes the point that all communication is a two-way street, with messages from one person being received by another person. Effective communication consists of practical skills of good listening and helpful talking that grow out of the empathic stance and set the stage for effective discipline (Dinkmeyer and McKay, 1976, 1983; Faber and Mazlish, 1980, 1987; Ginott, 1965, 1969; Gordon, 1970; Grisanti, Smith, and Flatter, 1990; Dumas, 1992).

Good listening and helpful talking are the tools to teach children about their emotions and the emotions of others. Emotional education begins when children learn what they are feeling, why they are feeling such emotions, and how and when to express them. We must respond to children in such a way that they can accept the legitimacy of all feelings — the positive, the negative, and the ambivalent — and so that they can distinguish between feelings, fantasies, and actions. Constructive discipline "permits" all feelings and wishes and "restricts" some actions and ways of expressing feelings and wishes.

Although basic communication skills are the same for healthy and disturbed children, we need to modify them to design therapeutic communication.

Therapeutic Communication

Emotionally disturbed children cannot be expected to respond positively to the communication skills described in the typical parent training literature. These children challenge our skills and resourcefulness. We need to refine our timing and sensitivity in order to communicate with emotionally wounded or developmentally delayed children.

Thus, our communication efforts make "end runs" around emotional, cognitive, interpersonal, and biological pathology. *More than any individual message we will ever convey, it is the communication of our wish to hear the children and to have them hear us that they will feel and remember.*

Therapeutic communication begins with the caring and respectful attitude with which we listen, talk, and carry out our procedures or chat about everyday occurrences. It is used when we ask children to do something, when we set a limit, when we criticize or correct, when we restrain or seclude, and when we say goodbye to children. It extends to the kind of therapeutic conversations we have with children about their past lives, their views of themselves, and their intense feelings. Redl (1966a) calls these *life-space interviews*. They take place when the milieu counselor makes use of an incident at the moment it occurs to soothe, teach, or clarify a psychological issue for a child.

Therapeutic communication occurs in every phase of therapeutic management. Even when we are managing behavioral crises with physical restraint or seclusion, we use constructive talk, listening, or silence to convey our continued caring and support to the children causing the trouble. Therapeutic communication consists of good listening, helpful talking and nonverbal reactions, and helpful physical contact between adults and children.

Good Listening and Helpful Talking

Listening starts with empathy and leads to good talking. People's verbal and nonverbal reactions convey their listening. Good listening helps us to pick helpful words or gestures that shape our reactions to children. This kind of talking brings out the best in children. It comforts, invites intimacy, and heals (Faber and Mazlish, 1980, p. 36). Helpful talk nourishes children's self-respect, sense of competence, optimism, and hope. It smooths out their daily life, as well as the greater worries of their whole lives.

Helpful talk is committed to honesty, information giving, respect, and kindness. Helpful talk is aimed at what is useful for children. It motivates them to find more adaptive ways of coping and relating to others. To nourish an emotionally wounded child's spirit, we need to believe in what we cannot yet see, to forgive, and to enthusiastically acknowledge all effort and accomplishment (even if it is really little!). We will be able to recognize helpful talking using one simple guideline: this is the way we want children to talk to us!

Helpful talking consists of choosing the right words that can assist children to adjust to demands or procedures that they cannot cope with on their own. In an eight-hour shift, a milieu staff has hundreds of opportunities and challenges of this kind:

Jimmy (age ten) arrived on the unit with three large green garbage bags containing all his possessions. Unit policy required a search and labeling of all possessions when a child was admitted to the unit. Jimmy was very upset about a "stranger" going through his stuff.

Ruth (a counselor) said the following: "I'm sorry we need to do this. I understand how embarrassing and upsetting it can be to have a stranger looking through your stuff. It's a real invasion of privacy."

"You bet," said Jimmy. "That's why you're not gonna do it."

"I'm sorry, Jimmy, we need to do this for every child because sometimes kids bring things that are unsafe or against the rules of the unit."

"I don't got any unsafe stuff."

"I have a suggestion. We can keep your stuff in the staff room until later. Then you can do the search with a counselor in your room with the door closed."

"I won't have no fucking girl going through my stuff," stated Jimmy.

"Why don't I see whether one of the men counselors can do it with you?" replied Ruth. "Brent and Steve are on tonight. They are really nice and they will undersand what you mean. They can help you label your stuff, so if one of the other kids says your stuff is theirs, we will know it is really yours. You can mark your name or initials wherever you want, so they won't spoil anything. Some things aren't allowed in the bedrooms."

"I'm keeping my stuff with me," retorted Jimmy.

"We have storage space in the staff room. No one is allowed to touch it without your permission," patiently continued Ruth.

Ruth was trying hard to respect Jimmy's right to privacy and his fierce attachment to all that was left of his life before he came to the hospital. Her explanations, special provisions about when and where the search could take place, and her firm insistence on adherence to the rules combined with acknowledgment of Jimmy's feelings facilitated Jimmy's adjustment to the unit.

Interpersonal interactions can be a problem during the initial stages of treatment: when adults require children's respect and cooperation before the children are able or willing to give them, or when adults demand respect from patients and give none in return. Children like Jimmy may swear and accuse staff before they are able to believe staff and cooperate with them. Some children cannot tolerate too much caring and try to repel staff efforts to "help them."

We can try to meet them on more neutral ground. Although we will eventually try to create mutually respectful interactions, at the beginning we give respect even if it is not returned. In this way, we are modeling to the children how we hope they will respond to us. We are modeling the ways that we would like the children to speak to us.

Helpful talking during ordinary moments builds an atmosphere of understanding. Ordinary moments occur when we assist children to cope positively with daily demands such as getting out of bed in the morning, dressing, brushing teeth, going to school, doing chores, or playing alone or with others. This consists of much talking about the obvious: what we are doing, why we are doing it, and explicit offers to help out. Repetition of the obvious is necessary because to our children we are strangers in a strange place and we may be taken for other adults they have known who have not behaved kindly or responsibly. Our rules, routines, food, talking, and demands may be quite alien to some children. Our earnest efforts to clarify can reassure children about what we are trying to do, even if they hate our actions or are perplexed by our rules.

Michael (age eight) was whining about the fish for dinner. Dr. P (a psychiatrist) said, "I know you hate fish. Will it be too hard to eat some of it? Then you can have dessert. You can always substitute with a peanut butter and jelly sandwich. I'm sorry dinner is such a drag tonight."

Paul (age nine) was complaining that he had to stay in the living room. He wanted to play alone in his room. Pam (a nurse) said, "Paul, I know you like to be alone. There isn't much time for that around here, is there? It's hard to be with the kids all the time, isn't it? What do you hate most about it?"

Heather (age seven) hated to take showers or baths. She was screaming and trying to hide under her bed the first night on the

unit. Diane (a counselor) said, "Heather, I know taking a bath up-
sets you. I know it's scary because you just came and you don't
even know us. I know you had bad things happen in bathtubs. That
won't happen here. I'm sorry you're so upset. I want to help."

Ralph (age twelve) got the news that his father wasn't coming to
visiting night. He started yelling, swearing, and punching the door.
        Dr. E (a psychiatrist) said, "Ralph, I can see you're upset.
It must feel like such a dirty trick when you look forward to seeing
someone and then they let you down. I can't let you yell and punch
like this. It disturbs the other kids. Your punches may damage the
door. With all the disappointment around here, the place would
look like a mess if we allowed punching.
        Said Ralph, "Shut the fuck up."
        Dr. E replied, "Let me get you a punching bag. I don't want
you to hurt your hand. You have some powerful punches."
        "Leave the bag right there!" screamed Ralph.
        "No, I'm going to put it in the quiet room. You could close
the door and yell and punch to get it out of your system. Later we
could try to get some time in the gym together. I really am sorry
about your dad; you've been working so hard all day; I don't want
you to lose it now. You have a right to feel really upset. Let's figure
out what to do with it, so you won't get into trouble."

While all of the above are examples of helpful talking,
let's take a closer look at the last one. Dr. E's words could not
change Ralph's disappointment but they could help him through
it. Our efforts can serve as life preservers for a child who is about
to drown in overwhelming feelings. They do for Ralph what
he is unable to do for himself.

The adult's empathy and skillful talking begin the process
of guiding Ralph through the difficult emotions that usually un-
hinge him and lead to major troublemaking. Dr. E fully intends
to set limits on Ralph's "swearing and vandalism," but she starts
out by setting a tone of understanding by acknowledging Ralph's
feelings. She clearly distinguishes Ralph's legitimate feelings from
his "illegitimate" actions that break unit rules. If Ralph can accept the emotional support that Dr. E had given him before he
becomes overwhelmed by his intense feelings, Ralph can head
off the need for a greater means of containment.

Consider the following example:

The excited children were waiting to go to the swimming pool. Swimming is one of the children's favorite activities of the week. Helen (a therapeutic recreationalist) was trying to locate the hospital van.

She finally joined the group with a long face. "I hate to tell you this, kids, the van is broken, we won't be able to go swimming this week. I'm sorry. We'll try to think of something else to do."

Johnny (age eight) loved to swim, and this was the first week that he was not restricted to the unit and was able to go to the pool. He began to swear and yell.

"Unfair—you did this on purpose. Why didn't you tell us before?"

What response could Helen give to Johnny that would convey good listening and understanding (empathy)?

Helen responded to Johnny as follows (he was swearing throughout): "Johnny, you're right to feel angry with us for letting you down. You did your part and we disappointed you. Please take a time-out for swearing in the quiet room, and I'll be in to talk to you after you finish your time-out."

Helen's response paid attention to both Johnny's feelings and his behavior. She accepted and validated his feelings but also rejected and put limits on his behavior. This is therapeutic communication. The discipline phase of her response helped to decrease the group's increasingly volatile expression of rage and frustration. Using the time-out routine depersonalized her disciplinary response to Johnny. The time-out invoked the unit structure and reminded the children about the rules they needed to follow. In affirming Johnny's legitimate feelings, she was validating what the entire group of children were feeling and saying. The time-out gave Johnny a cooling off period. This was clearly helpful talking.

Not Good Listening

There are also ways of talking to someone in distress that involve "not good" listening, which then leads to "not helpful" talk (Faber and Mazlish, 1980). In not helpful talk, the adult does not listen or pay attention to the child's experience of a situation. Helen could have responded to Johnny in any of the following ways:

Minimizing feelings. "There's no reason to get so upset. We can go next week." Or "It's foolish to feel that way, we're going to find something else fun to do." Or "You're probably just tired and blowing the whole thing out of proportion." Or "It can't be as bad as you make it out to be."

Avoiding and distracting. "Come on smile, you look so cute when you smile." Or "Your tutor says that you're able to control your temper better in school and that helps you do better in reading." Or "What did you watch on TV last night?" Or "Let's talk about what we'll do now."

Philosophizing. "Johnny, you have to learn to roll with the punches." Or "Life is like this. Things don't always turn out the way you want." Or "In this world, nothing is perfect."

Advising. "You know what you should do? You love to play baseball. Why don't you get the group to go outside and play ball. You could suggest that we bring snacks and stay out as long as if we went to the pool." Or "You should stop yelling and swearing because you're getting yourself into more trouble."

Questioning (implying fault). "Didn't you know the van breaks down a lot?" Or "Why didn't you ask whether we could go?"

Defending the other person or situation. "You can't blame the morning staff, they didn't know." Or "Just think of the poor hospital staff, who need to depend on such an unreliable van." Or "The hospital is nice enough to have a van and to arrange swimming for you at all."

Pitying. "Oh, you poor thing. This is terrible! I feel so bad for you." Or "Poor Johnny, you were counting on this trip." Or "Nothing ever goes right for you, does it?"

Psychologizing. "I bet the real reason you're so upset is that your mother didn't come last night." Or "Are you really upset because your roommate is leaving tomorrow?"

These are typical responses of people trying to help someone. They are usually not intended to be mean responses. Some
are accurate. But being a good listener is not about being "right"
or "wrong." It is about being helpful. The responses are unhelpful
because they do not address Johnny's immediate feelings. Many
of these responses may even be useful to Johnny later on during a dialogue about this incident. But adults can block communication by preaching, prophesying, criticizing, and going
on and on in endless monologues that stifle dialogue. In unhelpful talking, advice and instruction precede efforts to understand the child's experience and convey this understanding to
the child.

Practical Skills of Good Listening and Helpful Talking

Certain adults intuitively know how to listen and talk to children. Others can learn communication skills. There are iden-
tifiable characteristics of warm and effective ways of relating to
children that we all use when we are at our best. Thus, we can
dissect the constructive adult-child interchanges that foster positive connections between children and adults and find the principles of helpful listening and talking. This section reviews the
following means of communicating:

- Paying attention to children's experience
- Reflective listening
- I-feeling statements
- I-information statements
- Paying attention to children's interests
- Encouraging questioning and exploration
- Answering questions
- Helping children be individuals
- Using childhood fantasy
- Using humor and whimsy
- Note writing

We discuss each way of communicating with children to help
develop the kinds of adult-child interactions that can facilitate
development and create change.

Paying Attention to Children's Experience

Giving our full attention and interest to children's experience conveys our acceptance and valuing of their feelings, whether we find them to be appealing or ugly, true or false, moral or immoral.

Ginott (1965, p. 58) warns us that "if we want to teach honesty, then we must be prepared to listen to bitter truths as well as to pleasant truths. It is from our reactions to his expressed feelings that the child learns whether or not honesty is the best policy." The "concentrated attention" which is the basis of all our later verbal exchanges can be as healing as the words themselves (Grisanti, Smith, and Flatter, 1990, p. 77).

We can convey concentrated attention by using nonverbal cues such as facial expressions, eye contact, moving closer, gentle touches, and stopping what we are doing. We can adjust these movements to what seems to help a particular child open up, rather than act out or shut down.

> Donna (age ten) wandered over and sat next to Dr. R (a psychiatrist). Dr. R was writing notes and covering the floor while milieu staff were at lunch. Most of the children were out, but Donna had been restricted to the unit.
>
> Donna complained, "I'm so bored." She seemed irritable and withdrawn.
>
> Dr. R listened and continued her writing. She was trying to be careful because Donna had never approached her in this way. Usually Donna joked with her from afar or they got into battles over things like putting boots on to go out in the snow or refusing to go for her therapy appointments. She showed interest through some sympathetic nods and sounds.
>
> "I hate to be bored. I always do something stupid. I remember how bored I was before I played with those stupid matches."
>
> Dr. R put down the chart and gave her full attention to Donna's description of boredom and playing with matches. Donna had burned down her apartment building. Dr. R had never heard about this sequence of feelings and behaviors before the fire. Now she was able to understand Donna's vulnerability to impulsive acts like fire setting when she was feeling alone and abandoned.

Dr. R listened quietly and intently. She only asked brief questions to help Donna continue telling her story. Donna seemed calmed
and distracted by the opportunity to tell this story. She returned to her
lunch and began to talk about what she wanted to cook for community
supper that evening.

Dr. R was able to select the kind of attention that could
help Donna open up and share. At first, Donna needed her
casual manner, and later on, she benefited from her exclusive
attention. Good listening means careful observation. We need
to notice whether our words or actions are helping children feel
more open and comfortable. Listening with sensitivity requires
our interest and flexibility. Sensitive listening leads to *reflective
listening*.

Reflective Listening

We must convey our understanding of the children to the children themselves. Our responses should convey what we know
about their feelings from their tone, words, and actions. Like
a mirror, we attempt to reflect the children's emotions without
adding our own corrections, judgments, or opinions. The function of an "emotional mirror" is to reflect feelings as they are,
without the distortions of our analyses, interpretations, and clar-
ifications (Ginott, 1965).

Reflective listening translates the emotional messages in
children's actions and tone. This helps them feel understood,
learn what they are feeling, and learn how to put these feelings
into words. Then they can move on to why they have these feelings (insight) and make choices (when, where, what, and to
whom) about how to express their feelings (behavior and words).

Young children and emotionally wounded children often
cannot figure out complex feelings, especially when they are contradictory or painful. They cannot understand the relationships
between events and their feelings. Our capacity to put the complexity and agony of their experience into words is the beginning
of our work with many children. We are putting the troublemaking into words, giving children "a vocabulary for their inner

reality" (Faber and Mazlish, 1980, p. 18). We pay particular attention to acknowledging our patients' feelings behind the troublemaking and their feelings about our limit setting.

> Jimmy (age ten) threw a chair as he stomped his way to the quiet room. He had "messed up" again and would be missing the rest of the group. When Keith (a counselor) approached the quiet room, Jimmy yelled out, "Get out of here, you fucking asshole. This place sucks. You don't know what it's like to be in a fucking prison."
>
> Keith sat on the bench outside of the quiet room and looked sadly at his folded hands. "You're right, Jimmy. I haven't been in hospitals and institutions like you have. It seems too unfair to be true, that you have been in so many institutions. You must feel pretty alone with those feelings sometimes. It must be pretty hard to take, being kicked out of a group again."
>
> Jimmy, "You don't know what the hell you're talking about."
>
> Keith, "I'm trying. But you're the expert."

I-Feeling Statements

Staff members have strong negative feelings, too. When we talk about our anger, frustration, fatigue, and disgust, we try to say what we are feeling without attacking or blaming. I-statements convey our disapproval, fears, anger, and disappointment. They focus on a particular behavior, not the person who did it. This preserves the children's self-esteem, while we try to contain, stop, and change their troublemaking.

The therapeutic use of I-statements requires more careful consideration with emotionally disturbed children. These children are too sensitive (and in some cases too numb) to disapproval to use adult feelings constructively. Conveying negative feelings therapeutically requires the careful choice of words that avoid sarcasm, ridicule, blame, and humiliation.

> Donna (age ten) had started to swear obscenely to Ralph when he threw sand and smashed her castle at the beach.
>
> Vivian (a counselor) heard the swearing and escorted her to the van to take a time-out, saying that "I don't like the swearing, but I can listen to you if you can find some other words."

Maria (age twelve) would not let Barbara (a nurse) come into the quiet room after she had finished taking her time-out.

"You hate me!" Maria exclaimed.

Maria had attacked Barbara in the van that afternoon. Barbara responded, "No, I don't hate you, Maria, but I did hate your kicks, spits, and bites in the van this afternoon."

I-Information Statements

We can choose to leave out our feelings when we convey our disapproval and focus on the consequences of a behavior. This is more neutral and perhaps more "traversable" ground for the disturbed child. These statements also focus on the behavior, not the person. By focusing on the consequences of an action, we can further depersonalize the situation. We can explain and clarify a rule or the reason for a procedure.

I-Information statements happen frequently in a therapeutic milieu, because we do not assume that children cooperate easily or well with authority.

Andrew (age seven) pushed open the door that led from our unit onto the neighboring pediatric unit. This was considered "running away," and the standard response for running away was a twenty-four-hour restriction to the unit. Julie (a nurse) explained to Andrew, "When you stepped outside the unit, I was so worried because I didn't know whether you had the control to come back yourself. I remembered that you once ran away from your foster home for two weeks."

"I was just fooling around."

"I'm sorry, Andrew, but the rule is the same for everyone who goes through those doors. It is the beginning of walking off the unit. When the consequence is so serious, we use strong rules that don't change for anyone."

"Well, that's unfair and stupid. I'm not going to take no twenty-hour-restriction for pushing open the doors and putting one foot outside."

"I'm afraid you're going to have to stay on the unit for twenty-four hours," Julie quietly insisted.

We explain a lot about what we do and why we do it, because our children come from different family styles, cultures, and socioeconomic settings. Our rules may be very different and in some cases contrary to what the children are expected to do at home.

> David (a counselor) was trying to get Paul (age nine) to take his daily bath.
> "I only have to take a bath once a week at home," Paul complained.
> "We want kids to take baths so that they can feel good about themselves," tried David.
> "I don't care about that. It's not fair to make everyone be the same."
> "We need to find a rule that is good for everyone. Sometimes the rule isn't fair to an individual kid. I'm sorry. My job is to help you follow the rules, so you'll need to follow this one. Is there any way that I can make it any easier for you?"

Paying Attention to Children's Interests

Communicating our interest in the children's experience should extend beyond their psychopathology and feelings to their games, books, pictures, TV shows, stuffed animals, clothes, hobbies, and opinions on any subject. Our interest can revive a child's waning attention, distract a child who is becoming emotionally overwhelmed, or encourage a child who is becoming discouraged.

Our interest is in the children's likes and dislikes and opinions. We can communicate this interest when we show our attention, ask questions, return to subjects in future conversations, take pictures of an activity, watch a child do something, tell others about what a child has done in front of the child, save something a child has made, or ask to join a child in an activity.

When an adult joins a child's activity, it gives that activity a new status in the eyes of a child who may not value an activity only played by children. We can steer the child who is about to make trouble on to a new course by our attention and participation (Redl and Wineman, 1952).

> Maria (age twelve) was trying to use the new needlepoint stitches that Dorothy (a counselor) had taught her the previous evening. She was waiting for a visit from her social worker, who had recently talked to her father.

Bill (a counselor) noticed that Maria was getting frustrated and looking upset. He went over and sat next to her. "Hey, how do you do this stuff?" he asked. "It looks so hard. Could you show me a stitch?"

Maria laughed shyly, "I'm no good at this. Look at the mess I'm making."

"You're better than me. Can you show me how to do the stitch? I'll watch you untangle it first."

Interest in children involves the frequently forgotten technique of "chatting" with a child. We can ask children questions about their experiences, which builds ego capacities. Our chatting with children helps them describe and reflect on their experiences, define their feelings, delineate their needs, value their experiences, refine their perspectives, and remember, question, and compare their experiences.

Encouraging Questioning and Exploration

We try to help children question and explore the assumptions they carry around about themselves, their past, other people, and the future. Some of these assumptions close their minds and hearts to new experiences. We talk in such a way that children will question maladaptive assumptions about themselves and others.

Simply reassuring children will not lead them to different conclusions about themselves. Children who tell us that they are unlovable will not feel more lovable when we tell them that we love them. They are much more likely to believe that we can hold this opinion because we do not really know them. In this way, reassurance alone can alienate children who need to hide themselves for fear that we will discover the "truth."

We can "undermine" false and negative self-opinions by pointing children to specific information that counteracts their conclusions.

Jimmy (age ten) showed his bookends in community meeting, "Wanna see my ugly bookends? I put the ends on backward. I'm stupid."

Leslie (a counselor) answered: "I know you think you're stupid, Jimmy, but I like those bookends. I like the way you de-

signed the pictures on the end. I like the colors you chose. You
didn't drip the paint."
     Jimmy: "I'm gonna throw them in the trash."
     "If you don't want them," Leslie queried, "can I have them
for my desk at home? But first, can you tell me anything you like
about them?"

Avoiding reassurance and promoting questions becomes crucial
in the process of helping children change their notions about
some profound aspects of their self-concepts, such as feeling they
are competent, lovable, or worthwhile. Pathological self-concepts
underlie a lot of the maladaptive things children do. We can
help children begin to question and explore their automatic negative responses to themselves, other people, or situations.

     As with each communication skill, we try to encourage
questioning and exploration in more mundane or trivial areas
in order to build these skills for use in emotionally packed areas.
In the school setting, we use the curriculum to encourage and
develop children's curiosity. Helping children share openly about
seemingly minor matters will build a greater sharing ability.

Answering Questions

Children ask a lot of questions. Emotionally disturbed children
ask fewer questions. Their confidence in dialogue and their curiosity have been blunted by their problems. There is often too
much they do not want to know or fear knowing about themselves, their families, or their lives. Knowing has hurt them.
Therefore, it is particularly important to answer questions when
they are asked, even if they may seem trivial or personal. It
is the questioning process that we want the child to value. A
child's questions and an adult's willingness to answer and explore the topics introduced by the child help convey the value
of talking with adults.

     We keep reference books readily available in the public
living spaces of the unit to encourage "researching" a child's questions about weather, geography, different cultures, religions,
famous people, records for achievement, historical events, and

Table 3. Resources for Answering Children's Questions.

---

1. Dictionaries
   Macmillan Picture Wordbook. New York: Macmillan, 1990.
   The Lincoln Writing Dictionary for Children. Orlando, Fla.: Harcourt Brace Jovanovich, 1988.
   Macmillan Very First Dictionary: A Magic World of Words. New York: Macmillan, 1983.
   Macmillan Dictionary for Children. New York: Macmillan, 1989.
   The American Heritage Student's Dictionary. Boston: Houghton Mifflin, 1986.
   Thorndike-Barnhart Children's Dictionary. New York: HarperCollins, 1988.
2. Encyclopedias
   The Kingfisher Children's Encyclopedia. New York: Kingfisher Books, 1989.
   The Young Children's Encyclopedia. Chicago: Encyclopaedia Britannica, 1988.
   Random House Children's Encyclopedia. New York: Random House, 1991.
3. Atlases
   The Times Family Atlas of the World. Topsfield, Mass.: Salem House, 1988.
4. Almanacs
   The Information Please Kids Almanac. Boston: Houghton Mifflin, 1993.
5. Books about facts
   Bragonier, Reginald, and Fisher, David. *What's What: A Visual Glossary of the Physical World.* Maplewood, N.J.: Hammond, 1990.
   Guinness Book of World Records. New York: Bantam Books, 1989.
   Leokum, Arkady. *The Big Book of Tell Me Why: Answers to Hundreds of Questions Children Ask.* New York: Purlieu Press, 1989.
   Macaulay, D. *The Way Things Work.* Boston: Houghton Mifflin, 1988.
   The Do It Yourself Genius Kit. New York: Viking Penguin, 1988. (Step 1: Facts; Step 2: Amazing Facts; Step 3: Incredibly Amazing Facts; Step 4: Stupendously Incredibly Amazing Facts.)
   Goldman, Amy. *Where Fish Go in Winter and Answers to Other Great Mysteries.* Los Angeles: Price, Stern, and Sloan, 1987.

---

animals. Table 3 lists a basic reference library for school-age children who may have delayed learning or may come from less bookish environments.

Children also ask us personal questions. We always need to respond to their interest and concern, but we do not always need to answer their specific questions with facts from our personal lives. They can use personal information against us the next time they are mad at us.

Mrs. B (a nurse) and Maggie were talking about families. Maggie (age six) was asking Mrs. B a lot of questions about her family.

Mrs. B's father had died in a car crash the year before she began working on the unit. She told Maggie about this one evening when Maggie was asking her about her family.

A week later, Mrs. B sent Maggie to bed early for disrupting the unit. Maggie was furious with her for being so unfair. She brought two cars to bed with her. Whenever Mrs. B walked by her room, she made car zooming sounds and then crashing sounds. Mrs. B stared at her in disbelief when she got the point.

Maggie smiled sweetly and said, "The daddy died in the crash and I'm glad."

When questions are personal, we need to respond with a clarification about what is private and what we feel comfortable sharing. Mrs. B was answering Maggie's questions about whether anyone she loved had ever died. She could have answered her questions without saying who had died in her life. Maggie was looking for comfort because she feared that her mother would die. She was undergoing minor surgery that week.

Clarifying private and public information comes up when children ask us about sex. This is often awkward.

Steve (a counselor) was putting Andrew (age seven) to bed. Andrew asked Steve if he ever had wet dreams. Steve was startled. He asked Andrew to explain what he meant by a wet dream. Andrew did have the accurate meaning, which he had learned from Ralph that afternoon.

Steve answered, "Most boys have them when they become teenagers."

"But do you have them?" persisted Andrew.

"I don't want to answer that question about myself, because that is personal and private. But I want to answer your questions about what happens to boys' bodies when they grow up."

Andrew responded, "When will I have wet dreams like Ralph? Is there a lot of water? Can you drown?" He asked many more questions and was content to leave Steve's personal experience out of it.

Other times, questions cannot be answered because we are busy with more pressing matters. At these times, we acknowledge the questions and explain our dilemma and promise to return to the questions when things calm down or time permits. One possibility is to ask the child to write down the question and have a secretary put it in our mailbox. The important point is to find some way of letting children know that questioning is good and that we are glad they approached us. We are setting the groundwork for treatment relationships.

Helping Children Be Individuals

Our responses can help children begin to notice the differences between themselves and other children. This starts the process of the more serious differentiations required for healthy psychological development, such as Maria differentiating herself from her psychotic mother. Our responses can clarify differences in people and situations, modeling for children the helpfulness of observing and figuring out the uniqueness of self, others, and situations.

> Betsy (a nurse) and Maria (age twelve) were cooking dinner one evening.
> Maria commented to Betsy, "This is like our kitchen knife that my mother used when she cut herself the last time she was at home. You know, I thought of using it when I wanted to hurt myself last time. I couldn't find it. My father must have thrown it out."
> Betsy gulped and kept chopping the vegetables for the spaghetti sauce. "Did you really want to hurt yourself?"
> "I wanted to die."
> "Like your mother?"
> Maria stopped to think. "I don't think so. I was mad. My mother gets really sad. I don't think that my mother ever wanted to live."
> "What about you? Do you ever have times when you feel like living?
> "Yeah, I guess I'm not like my mother. But I wonder sometimes."
> Betsy was quiet and then went up and gave Maria a hug. "You know, you can be like your mother in some ways and not in others. I bet you'll notice some similarities as you grow up. And

people who knew her may see some likenesses. Maybe you can
be like she would have been if she had had a different chance like
you have now."

Using Childhood Fantasy

We can help children cope with an overwhelming or merely unpleasant reality by invoking our own fantasies for them or encouraging their own fantasies to ease the present. Our words can
convey our *desire* to fulfill children's wishes even if we can't or even
while we set limits on their maladaptive attempts to get something.

Although we cannot grant children's every wish or sanction all their behavior, we can communicate our approval of
the wish and our belief that children deserve to get what they
want. This is reassuring on many levels to children. Providing
in fantasy what is unavailable in reality also models a substitute form of gratification for children.

> Everyone was grumpy at supper tonight. The children were com-
> plaining that the hospital was trying to starve them to death with
> this awful food. Kathy (a counselor) passed out extra crackers to
> help the fried fish go down better. She then started a game.
> "I'm sorry you guys hate this stuff tonight. I'll talk to the hospi-
> tal nutritionist and see if we can scratch fish from our menu. Let's
> play a game tonight. I want to give each kid their favorite meal. Let's
> start with you, Ralph. What do you want to have for dinner tonight?"
> "Pizza, fries, and a Coke," said Ralph.
> "Here you go. What about you, Raoul?"
> "Cheeseburger, fries, and a large Coke."

Fantasy helps with minor annoyances and frustrations,
and it serves children in profound ways. Fantasy gives painful
yearnings and memories a place to go. Fantasies that are shared
can help childen connect with others, and this can be comforting.

> During free time Raoul (age six), Michael (age eight), and Paul (age
> nine) created a tent city out of sheets, boxes, and pillows. They
> were intensely interested in creating this private world, where
> adults were not allowed. Julie (a nurse) helped them make signs to
> attach to the house: "KEEP OUT," "PRIVT," and "NO CONSLRS
> AND DOCTRS ALOWED."

The boys were playing out one of the scariest parts of their lives. They did not know where they would go after the hospital. In real life, they had no control over this decision. In their play, they were in control of where they would live and who would live there with them. They didn't want adults to make the decisions. Julie was especially glad to see Raoul playing. She knew he had been talking about running away. He missed his mother.

Some of the most poignant moments occur on an inpatient milieu, when children's play reveals how much they are missing an absent or dead parent or when children's play reenacts past trauma. We can comfort and heal by helping children use their imaginations.

Maria (age twelve) was withdrawn and silent. Clare (a nurse manager) knew that she was thinking about her mother. Maria had been working on her book about schizophrenia that afternoon. She was asking questions about her own schizophrenic mother and was trying to write a book for other kids who may have the same questions.

Clare asked Maria if she wanted some hot chocolate. They made the chocolate and sat down in the back of the living room while the other kids watched a TV special. "I guess you have been thinking of your mother tonight?" Clare asked.

"Yup," Maria responded curtly.

"I read your book about schizophrenia. Schizophrenia is a terrible disease. I felt so bad for your mother, who could not be the mother she wanted to be. I also felt bad for you. You deserved a healthy mother. If your mother was not so sick, and you were living at home with her tonight, what would you like to be doing with her?"

"I don't know," said Maria quietly as she thought about Clare's question. "I guess we would be watching the TV and she'd be telling me to do my homework."

Using Humor and Whimsy

Spontaneous humor or whimsical reactions to situations can diffuse negative feelings and tension. They can restore perspective to a child, groups of children, and adults, and they can help children save face in certain situations. As Faber and Mazlish (1980, p. 78) put it, "If you can reach your child's head through his funny bone, more power to you." Redl and Wineman (1952, pp. 172–175) talk about the "tension-decontamination" effect of genuine humor when the point is to laugh with, *not* at a child.

We have to be more careful with humor when we work with emotionally wounded children. Problems with reality often make plays on reality confusing and incomprehensible. Our children often do not have what it takes to laugh at themselves. Low self-esteem and self-doubt render children more sensitive to remarks about themselves and more likely to experience what we consider a good-natured joke as an insult or offense. It is always better to err in the direction of being too earnest with a child than too glib.

When we choose to use humor, it must be entirely free of sarcasm and ridicule if it is to help children. The following is an example of a child who is refusing to sign a contract. (See Chapter Seven for full discussion of contracts.) We use this procedure to engage children and formalize an agreement that we need to make with them in order to accomplish something. Children often refuse to sign their contracts when they are ambivalent about participating in our rules. This is a vulnerable time, because we can easily incite troubled children.

Ellen (a counselor) knew that Paul (age nine) was beginning to put up a fuss about signing his contract. Paul had broken the rule about staying within ten steps of the group when he had been outside the hospital with the day staff. Ellen was concerned that without a contract for staying with the group, Paul might run away when they went outside for the next outdoor group. The contract routine required that he write the promise to stay with the group on a contract form and sign his name to the contract.

Knowing Paul's tenacious capacity to insist on his own slightly "illegal" variation of a routine, Ellen tried to "lighten up" the procedure before Paul had dug in too deep: "Hey Paul, if you don't want to sign your contract with your hands, why not sign with your toes? As long as at least one counselor can recognize your name, it will pass."

Ellen then helped Paul remove his socks and place the pencil between his toes. When they knocked on my door, they were both giggling. Paul covered the top of the contract and asked me to read the names at the bottom. After recognizing the names, Paul proudly told me that he had written his name with his toes.

Ellen explained to me, "Paul had a problem. His hands didn't want to write his name."

"Paul, you have such a smart body. When one part doesn't want to follow the rules, you let another part take over and this keeps all of you out of trouble. I'll have to remember that one!" I exclaimed with admiration.

Note Writing

Children love to get mail. When we write something down, it takes on great importance. There are therapeutic reasons for reviving the "old-fashioned" practice of writing notes or letters to each other. We can write notes and draw pictures to say things that kids may not be able to hear when we are face to face with them. Notes also help in institutions when children are ready to hear after you have gone home or when you have several days off. They are another means of conveying our wish, our need, our hope, and our willingness to connect with a child, regardless of the internal and external obstacles to communication.

Children are usually impressed when an adult goes to the trouble of writing them a letter. Notes can also underline the importance of what we have already said by repeating our points. And notes can be reread and kept. Pictures are useful, too, since they can be hung on the wall. Both pictures and notes are ways of talking to a child even when we are not there. We use notes and drawings routinely in goodbye books to tell children what we like about them, what we'll remember, and what we'll miss. We write notes when we want to congratulate a child who is less likely to accept our praise verbally or in public.

Heather (age seven) had been to court. She had been withdrawn and preoccupied since she returned. She refused staff bids to play or talk with her. Then Lisa (a counselor) yelled out, "Heather, you have a letter in the office."

Heather walked slowly to the office and picked up a big

envelope. She sat down on a nearby bench and started to read the letter. As she read it, she began to smile. This is what Lisa had written:

Dear Heather,
WE THINK THAT YOU ARE VERY BRAVE AND GOOD!!!!!!!!
WE MADE YOU THIS MEDAL. WE ARE GLAD TO BE YOUR FRIEND!!!!!!
                        Your friends, the staff (we all signed it)

Enclosed in the letter was a picture of Heather sitting in court. Pinned to her shirt was a big medal that said, "Brave Heather." The medal was removable. She took it off and stuck it to her hand. She returned to her group with a smile on her face.

Evening staff members developed the "good-night note," which children find taped to the foot of the bed when they wake up in the morning. Being reminded of a success from the evening before helps them begin a new day with the memory of a recent success. Brent (a counselor) wrote this note to Maggie (age six), on Garfield stationery:

Dear Maggie,
        Congratulations on your GREAT bedtime! Thanks for staying in bed and playing quietly with your Garfield, while we were trying to help Ralph get back in control. YOU were a real help! Have a good day! See you tonight.
                                          Your friend,
                                          Brent

Other times, good-morning notes reassure children who have been unruly that they can start again the next day and that the evening staff will not retaliate the following evening. Here is one written to Johnny (age eight):

Dear Johnny,
        We hope your day goes well. Try not to let your difficult night ruin a new day. We can talk tonight. Even though you have an early bedtime, there will be plenty of time for us to have a good time before you need to go to bed. We know you are going to have some bad times, but it will not stop us from liking you at the other times.

We remember how helpful you were on Monday night. (You remember it too!) We don't expect you to be perfect. Let's see if we can figure out what will help you next time. Have a good day! See you tonight!

> Your friends, Steve, Pat, Stacy, Keith, Kathy, Brent, Pam, and Lisa (evening staff)

Parents also write good-night notes when they are on the unit to visit their children.

Dear Paul,
> We were so proud of you tonight. I hope we can all try like this when we get home together. We're learning how to be better parents, and you are learning how to listen better. Thank you. We love you.
>
> Mom and Dad

A note can also help bridge the times we are not on the unit. Or sometimes it's better for a child to listen to a note and not a person. When there is an incident on one shift that cannot be resolved on that shift, the involved staff often write a note to be shared with the child later.

Jimmy (age ten) was in seclusion when Barbara (a nurse manager) was leaving for the day. She had worked with him for most of what had been a horrendous afternoon. It had started with her discovery that Jimmy had plugged up the toilets. He was quite delighted with the stench and chaos that ensued. When asked to help clean the bathroom, he refused and needed to be physically restrained and brought to the quiet room. He remained in the quiet room and sang obscene limericks about Barbara, as she and the day staff cleaned up the overflow from the toilets. Later, he also threw a pail of soapy water at Barbara while washing the walls of the quiet room.

When Barbara tried to talk to Jimmy at the end of the day, he started shouting obscenities. Eventually she helped him write a contract that stated a series of alternative chores he needed to complete before he resumed his participation in the activity program. She wrote him the following note when she was leaving for the day:

Dear Jimmy,
> I'm going for the day. I'm honestly glad to be going. It has been a really awful day. I hope you can rest tonight, as I plan to. I hope things go better tonight for you and for me. I'll see you tomorrow and we can talk about today, if you want. I just wanted to let you know that I still like you, even though you know how frustrated I was today. I didn't like some of the things you did today, but I still remember the other things I like about you (the way you read to Raoul yesterday). I think we'll have to expect some hard days like this until you learn new ways of telling us about your disappointments and frustration. As I drive home, I'm going to remind myself of the good times we've had together (remember baking cookies last week?). I hope you can too.
>> Good luck, your friend,
>> Barbara

Not Helpful and Destructive Talk

Both not helpful talk and destructive talk are of course the opposite of helpful talk. We have to include this section, because *everyone who does therapeutic management will not talk constructively at least some of the time.* We cannot completely avoid this problem, but we can try our best to be positive and helpful. Not helpful talk and destructive talk bring out the worst in children. They irritate, create distance, and wound the spirit (Faber and Mazlish, 1980, p. 36). These kinds of interactions undermine children's best ability to cope and master challenges. Not helpful and destructive speech can incite feelings of anger, revenge, discouragement, or dangerous levels of rage or despair. Inadequate or negative responses to children can also urge them on to become disobedient, rebellious, stubborn, aggressive, self-injurious, or passive.

Both not helpful talk and destructive talk can be used by adults who intentionally want to hurt children or by adults who are unaware of the impact of their words on the children. Sometimes we are sadistic, and at other times we are just ignorant or inept.

Not helpful talk is subtly injurious; it occurs when our words are not useful or are insensitive to children. This kind of talking does not seriously harm them but fails to facilitate their efforts to cope.

Destructive talk is obviously harmful. Most people would not endorse it once it has been pointed out. When we use words destructively, we insult, threaten, blame, ridicule, accuse, shame, bully, or respond cynically and sarcastically. All of these reactions are occupational hazards for those of us who work with emotionally disturbed children, since these children are frequently talented at getting us angry and frustrated. Have you ever said any of the following:

Insult. You are just like your lazy, freeloading mother.

Threat. Stop struggling. Someone is going to get hurt and it isn't going to be me.

Blame. Thanks a lot, Paul. We can't go out because you made us late.

Ridicule. It has now taken you more time to tie your shoes than it took the Egyptians to build the pyramids.

Accusation. Stop trying to con me. I know you put the jam on Cindy's seat.

Shame. Michael, stop crying like a baby. Act your age!

Bullying. Get going or I'll get you going.

Sarcasm. You will be finished with time-out in ten minutes if by some miracle you can keep your mouth shut that long.

When you say words like this or when you hear others say them, you know it's not right. But similar interchanges can occur in even the best treatment program (or normal family). We are not saints or robots. We work with children who can be very difficult. We get tired, frustrated, angry, resentful, disgusted, discouraged, and revengeful. These are the feelings that prompt such responses. This is when the harmful responses pop up, no matter how well intentioned we have started out. Respect for what children are feeling, saying, or trying to do is not easy to maintain throughout some very difficult situations.

Some clinicians may try to rationalize destructive talking as "part of the real world" or "what the child was asking for anyway" or "what the child deserved anyway." Insulting, blaming,

ridiculing, shaming, or threatening should never be rationalized
or defended in any way. They are mistakes. Our patients and
their families are rarely in need of more of the "real world." Thus,
like not helpful talk, destructive talk is inevitable but unacceptable.

What to Do When We Use Not Helpful or Destructive Talk

The ratio of good to bad talking is part of what defines the culture of caring that adults offer children in a setting. It is never
determined by only one person or one interaction. It is created
and recreated daily by a group of adults who intervene with a
group of children. Not helpful talk occurs in all institutions, but
it should never be the predominant mode of communication.
Unhelpful interactions should be considered mistakes to be
avoided and regretted when they occur.

We need to acknowledge making mistakes, just as the children we are trying to treat must acknowledge and deal with their
mistakes.

Not helpful and destructive talking needs to be followed
by "helpful" apologies.

> I was on the telephone in my office when I heard Ralph (age twelve)
> racially taunting Maria.
>
> I stormed out and yelled, "Get in the quiet room. I won't have
> this kind of teasing on the unit! You have a lot of nerve being so
> mean."
>
> I'm ashamed to this day of my furor and the contempt on
> my face, which my words alone can't convey.
>
> Ralph looked shocked and then hurt. But he regrouped
> quickly and yelled "You fucking whore" at me and "You greasy
> spic!" at Maria, as he ran into the quiet room, dumping a chair as
> he ran.

I was right and I was wrong. Ralph was wrong and Ralph was
right. My excessive anger and contemptuous tone were so wrong
that they made the limit I set unfair. I had been as insulting to
Ralph as he had been to Maria. We all "lose it" every once in
a while, but we need to acknowledge and respond to our mistakes. In this case, I wrote Ralph an apology.

Dear Ralph,
    I am sorry for getting so mad at you this afternoon. It was unfair to talk to you like I did. I am glad the other staff were there to help you when I was not very helpful.
                                                        Your friend,
                                                        Dr. Cotton

Wally (a nurse manager) joined Ralph in the quiet room and talked to him about the incident. He agreed with him that I was unfair to talk to him like I did. Wally helped him take his time-out and informed him that I had written him an apology. Wally offered to read it with him when he was ready.

    No one can do this work if they are unprepared to make mistakes, apologize for them when they happen, and learn how to not make them in future interactions. Milieu therapists are constantly offering and seeking collegial support and feedback when they hear and use not helpful or destructive talk. Other times, individualized clinical supervision and teaching are necessary. Administrative actions (job probations and terminations) are called for when supervision and teaching are not sufficient to bring about more effective communication skills.

Nonverbal Communication

Children listen to more than our words. "It's not *what* you say but *how* you say it that counts" is verified by research that found that what we say accounts for only 7 percent of what people (adults) actually hear (Mehrabian, 1972). Children are probably even more susceptible to nonverbal cues than adults (Trieschman, Whittaker, and Brendtro, 1969).

    Our nonverbal messages are particularly salient when children are emotionally overwhelmed and irrational. At these times, they can focus intently on what we are doing while we are speaking words. Emotionally disturbed children may have a greater need to use nonverbal channels of communication if they have language deficits or if words have proved meaningless in families who speak with violence, broken promises, or distorted images of reality. Children from violent families have learned to read nonverbal cues as a way of surviving life-threatening situations. Nonverbal channels may also be culturally or socioeconomically more consonant with the child's dominant style of communicating. Nonverbal messages are conveyed through voice, facial expression, postural messages, or silence (Silberman and Wheelan, 1980).

Voice

Our voices convey different nonverbal messages depending on our choice of volume (loud or soft), speech pattern (flow of words), inflection (emphasis), and emotional tone. We can tell Lisa to take time out for swearing, and the same words can lead to compliance or more trouble, depending on our voice. We can say to Lisa, "Lisa, please take five minutes for swearing" with a moderately loud, evenly paced declarative sentence (assertive nonverbal behavior), or we can scream it with fast, jack hammer–type speech in an exclamatory sentence (aggressive nonverbal behavior). We can also ask Lisa to take her time-out with a soft voice, using frequent pauses and questions (nonassertive nonverbal behavior). Assertive voices help to convey firm, clear messages, which cut down on confusion and encourage compliance by conveying that we mean what we say.

The voice contributes to the emotional tone of the message. Emotional tone is particularly important when talking to emotionally disturbed children who may be more attuned to this dimension than any other. The tone needs to match the words. When emotional tone contradicts our actions and our words, it breeds distrust and confusion and blocks communication. If we are exuding anger and our words are saying that we are not upset or if we are saying words of affection and our voices convey boredom, children will "hear" the anger and boredom. The words get buried by the emotional tone. Emotional tone can amplify the significance of words when it affirms their meaning. Just as assertive voices help set a limit, soothing voices help convey comfort and support.

Facial Expression

Our faces and eyes also convey important nonverbal clues to children. The emotional message expressed in our eyes and on our faces is the primary factor in determining people's responses to our communications (Mehrabian, 1972).

Fran (a counselor) noticed that Michael (age eight) winced when he told him to go to his room. He felt uncomfortable about his relationship with Michael. He asked Paul (a counselor) about it.

"I noticed that, too. Did you know that you scowl a lot at Michael when you are telling him to do something? You radiate anger when you're around that kid," Paul responded honestly.

Paul's words hit home. Fran began to notice that he was exceptionally aggravated by Michael's meek, passive resistance. He realized that he had been unaware of how angry he felt when Michael started to whine. His voice was harsh and his words were clipped short as he "barked" orders to Michael. When he tried to refrain from yelling at him, he glared and his face was tense with anger. It became clear that Michael was wincing and defending himself from Fran's rage.

Eyes can open wide, narrow, glare, look away, pay attention, or shed tears. Children know a lot from watching how we look at them and what kind of eye contact we try to give them.

Ralph (age twelve) was in locked-door seclusion. He was yelling sexual insults at Lisa, who was sitting in the adjoining living room. He started accusing her of seducing her uncle, who had sexually abused her. Keith (a counselor) heard this and ran down the hall, furious that Lisa had to listen to this.

Heather saw him coming and ran up and grasped his arm. She pleaded, "Keith, take the fire out of your eyes. It's burning me up."

Keith was shocked by her words. In her psychosis, Heather was seeing the pure emotion. She talked with the metaphors that described her direct experience of his anger.

Keith called for Becky (a counselor) and asked her to deal with Ralph. "I'm too angry to deal with this now. I'm scaring the kids." Before he went into the office to cool off, he approached Heather and sat down next to her. "I took the fire out of my eyes, Heather. I hope you won't be afraid of me now."

Our facial expressions can help to get our point across or they can cancel out our messages.

Postural Messages

Postural messages are conveyed by hand gestures, body stance, and physical position or proximity to a child (Silberman and Wheelan, 1980). Our hands can convey different messages as they choose to point, make fists, fidget, beckon, or clap. Hands can make V's for victory, circles for congratulations, and peace signs for a truce when children are fighting. Our body stance can be challenging or supportive as we try to calm troubled children. If adults stand face to face and shoulder to shoulder to children during an argument, the children may perceive the adults as "challenging" rather than helpful (Wyka, 1988). In a "supportive stance," staff members can stand at an angle to children, at least one leg length away, with hands visible at their sides. Kneeling or sitting next to children can often defuse a power struggle.

Our distance from children during interactions should respect their personal space. Personal space is that area surrounding our body that we consider an extension of our physical self (Wyka, 1988). When we intrude on that space, we may threaten children. Other times, we can sense that we need to be in that space to comfort and connect with children. Children's personal space will vary depending on their mood, the situation, their personalities, and their relationships with us. Different cultures also have unique and implicit expectations about acceptable nonverbal cues that regulate body language. We need to be in tune with children in context, because the impact of our presence can change according to the particular situation and the shifting boundaries of the children's personal spaces.

Maggie (age six) was launching another miserable bedtime. She had already been given extensive time-outs, had been removed from her room twice, and was challenging the conditions set for her to remain in her room. Emmy (a nurse) knew that Maggie was going to push through every limit established by the evening staff.

Emmy entered the quiet room and sat quietly on the end of the bench. Maggie was lying down and hiding her face in her arms. Emmy started humming and gave Maggie a pat on the shoulder. Maggie tensed up and pulled back at first. Emmy kept patting and began to give her a gentle back rub. Maggie's whole body relaxed and soon she was breathing smoothly.

"Do you need some more time in here to calm down and relax?" Emmy asked softly. "Or are you ready to return to your room now?"

Maggie nodded that she was ready to go back. Emmy suggested that she give her five more minutes of a nighttime back rub once she was in bed. Maggie nodded and smiled.

Emmy was astonished, because Maggie usually repelled staff's affectionate gestures. She had thought that maybe Maggie missed some affectionate, physical contact at bedtime, which was usual for six-year-olds. It was Maggie's body signals that tipped Emmy off to Maggie's readiness to accept this comfort from her.

Emmy was equally good at picking up Maggie's signals that she was losing control.

Maggie was furious that her parents were not visiting that night. Her parents were attending her older sister's piano recital. Maggie had clobbered Michael that morning, because he had teased her about her big lips. Maggie had just stolen his seat during TV time.

Emmy approached her carefully, telling her what she already knew—that she had to take a time-out in the corridor for hitting Michael. Maggie sat stubbornly in Michael's chair and clenched her fists and glared as Emmy approached.

Emmy stayed back and casually said, "Maggie, I hope you can take your time-out quickly so that you won't miss too much of the movie. I'll save your first seat until you come back. Why don't I give a count of ten? One . . . two . . . three . . . "

Emmy didn't even look at her. Maggie growled and made her way to the corridor on the count of seven.

Silence

There are times when we have to talk with silence. This means that we sometimes need to admit the inevitable defeat of words before we begin. Our words and the children's words.

We use our understanding of a child to make the decision not to talk. Timing of what we say is as important as what and how we say it. Saying the "right thing" at the wrong time can be as disruptive as saying the "wrong thing." It doesn't work to keep talking to children who are unable to listen or use the words. Even more serious are the times that our words incite children to greater distress and more troublemaking.

Therapeutic silence is different from punitive, indifferent, or hostile silences. Silences can be misinterpreted; children will not know why we remain silent unless we tell them. When we decide not to talk, we should provide a simple and clear description of what we are doing and why. Otherwise, children will come up with their own reasons for why we have abandoned words or why we are leaving them alone in a room.

> Paul (age nine) was furious that Heather had smashed his Lego jail. He had spent hours carefully constructing the windows and doors. He had made three floors and was working on the roof when Heather ran down the hall and wildly lashed out at his project, while laughing hysterically and taunting him.
>
> Paul threatened to run away and started to run off the unit. The staff needed to bring him to the quiet room. When they tried to comfort him and supported his right to be angry, Paul started to swear and punch the walls. Leslie (a counselor) said, "Paul, I'm sorry this happened. I won't talk anymore about this now. I don't want to get you into any more trouble. My words seem to be making things worse. You don't deserve this. When we can, we'll talk."
>
> Leslie sat outside the quiet room and waited until he was able to listen and talk.

Here's another example:

> Ralph (age twelve) was packing his stuff for an overnight visit to a potential residential placement. He was leaving in the morning.

> Dr. G (a psychiatrist) walked by the room. "Can I join you, Ralph?"
>
> Ralph looked up with sad eyes, which quickly turned to an angry glare. "Get out of here. Leave me alone."
>
> "I can get some juice for each of us," said Dr. G neutrally. "I promise to keep quiet and just sit here with you. You're doing a good job with a difficult time."
>
> "Okay, but you promised to shut up."

Silences like these require the art of conveying comfort, understanding, and respect without uttering a word. Silence is needed when words are too powerful and painful or when words are too limp and trite for the children's experience.

Communicating with Touch

Physical contact is a powerful form of nonverbal communication. Physical contact is developmentally a part of most children's close relationships. Although there are significant clinical and legal complications to touching other people's children, especially if those children have been victims of sexual abuse, we sometimes need to touch them if we want to create a more normal, nurturing setting. Children with language processing deficits, which are common in inpatient and residential populations, are particularly dependent on nonverbal communication.

Physical contact is especially important with children. As Silberman and Wheelan (1980, p. 79) point out, "How we express physical affection should vary with the age of the child, but the need for affectionate physical contact does not diminish with age." Young children are in particular need of physical contact, because they are just learning how to use words and how others use words. Infants and toddlers spend large amounts of time being touched and held by caring adults. School-age children determine their own personal balance of touching with adults and have strong opinions about where and when it should occur. Touching is a part of most children's intimate relationships. In addition, touching is of primary importance in certain cultures.

Affectionate touching expresses love and support in positive situations, just as firm, gentle holding restricts and protects in negative situations. In our setting, we rely on physical holding to restrain children who are upset or unable to safely control themselves when they are overwhelmed with anger, frustration, or sadness. (Chapter Five discusses physical holding and presents guidelines for physical contact in negative situations.)

Helpful Touching

Helpful touching expresses our affection, support, empathy, and protection. Physical contact can help us communicate what words cannot express. At other times, children can "listen to" and "accept" our touch, when our words can only aggravate or alienate.

Specific guidelines for therapeutic and developmentally necessary touching are difficult to establish because individual and cultural interactional styles are so different. The general guidelines for determining when staff should use physical contact in positive situations are outlined in Table 4.

We should always ask the question "Who is the touching for?" Children's needs should always determine whether we use touch and physical proximity to comfort them (Redl and Wineman, 1952; Trieschman, Whittaker, and Brendtro, 1969). Children's response to our physical closeness or touch is our gauge of whether the touching was helpful or not.

Heather (age seven) was running wildly through the unit. It was visiting night, and her parents were unable to come because of car problems. She refused various staff offers to play a game or go off the unit for a snack with the "Lean on Me" group. Heather zoomed through the halls beeping and screeched to a halt when she came on a family playing a game on the floor or eating a snack.

The noise and potential danger of running down one of our toddler visitors required Jill (a social worker) to ask Heather to stop running and find a quiet activity.

When Jill put her arm on her shoulder, Heather shuddered

Table 4. Guidelines for Helpful Touching in Positive Situations.

---

1. Touching should only be used when it comforts, supports, guides, and expresses approval and affection.
2. Touching should meet the needs of the child, not the needs of the adult.
3. The form of physical contact should respect the child's cultural and family style of adult-child interactions, history of positive and traumatic adult-child physical interactions, developmental level of functioning, and special needs due to biological and psychological vulnerabilities.
4. Sexual and punitive touching should never be used.

---

and winced. She flung herself against the wall and yelled, "Help, help! Jill is hitting me. She wants to kill me."

Jill asked for help from Pat (a nurse). She thought that her touch had been experienced by Heather as an assault.

In the following example, Ralph (age twelve) was able to share his disappointment, following a counselor's kind interest and comforting hug:

Ralph slammed down the phone. He walked into the sun room and picked a fight with Paul. Soon Paul was in tears, and Ralph was jeering over his success. Brent (a counselor) gave him a time-out for teasing. He swore and stormed into the quiet room.

After giving him a few minutes to calm down, Brent knocked on the door and walked in. Ralph was curled up on the bench with his back to the door. "Get the fuck out of here! Leave me alone!"

Brent hesitated until he noticed Ralph's heaving shoulders. He sat next to him and hugged him. "I'm sorry things aren't working out for you tonight."

Ralph moved to embrace him and hid his teary face in his shoulder. "They don't want me home this weekend."

Physical proximity and friendly touching can control rising levels of excitement, anxiety, restlessness, or anger. We can walk into a bedroom to speak, rather than staying at the doorway. We can sit next to a child during a meal or hold a hand or put a friendly arm on a shoulder. We can stand up to speak to a standing child or sit and kneel while talking to a sitting child. We can walk down a long corridor to ask a child to obey, rather than yelling from the other side of the unit. Supportive and friendly touch can be a quiet way to comfort, remind, and redirect attention.

Physical touch needs to be curtailed or modulated when emotional disturbance and histories of physical and sexual maltreatment lead to tactile defensiveness or distortions in a child's experience of an adult's intentions and actual touch. Traumatized children will also need the support and caring of our touch to help heal and develop the normal capacity to give and receive physical contact. However, children with histories of traumatic touching need to be approached with exquisite appreciation and respect for their individual needs.

Lisa (age eleven) had been sexually molested by her maternal uncle since she was six years old. Robert (a counselor) felt extremely uncomfortable about her habit of clinging and rubbing up against him when they were waiting in line or sitting watching TV. He also was uncomfortable with his response: he would freeze when she touched him or try to move away. Robert and Lisa did not acknowledge these interactions. He shared this discomfort with his supervisor, Joan (a social worker).

Robert was an extremely nurturing person who always had a child on his lap, holding hands, or hanging off his shoulders in the warm and physical ways that children have of playing with adults. Robert knew that Lisa's touch was different; she knew how to stroke, caress, and position her body in ways that were subtle but explicitly sexual.

Joan commended Robert for his clinical insight about the quality of Lisa's touching. She also pointed out that she was impressed that he had so accurately figured out that his response was clinically inadequate. It was a proper and safe response that protected Lisa from further sexual maltreatment, met his needs, and fulfilled the unit protocol for physical contact between staff and children. But it fell short of therapeutic management of the situation.

Joan suggested that he talk to Lisa about the situation and that they include Dr. B, Lisa's psychiatrist. This allowed Lisa to have someone else present who could later help her with her feelings about what Robert said and help her follow the plan they developed for this problem.

Robert, Lisa, and Dr. B met the following day. Robert started their meeting off in the following way: "Lisa, I wanted to talk to you so I wrote you a letter to help me say what I want to say. May I read it to you?"

Lisa, "Sure. But why do ya need to write it down?"

"Because it helps me to think and say it better. Anyway, I want to give an extra copy of this to Dr. B because you may want to talk to him about this when we're finished. Okay?"

Dear Lisa,

I like being your counselor, and I think you are working very hard preparing for the move to your new residential center. We also have fun in outdoor group and I appreciate all that you contribute to the psychodrama group.

I wanted to talk to you about a problem I see with the touching that goes on between us. I know you have worked hard on protecting your body and learning how to act with adult men. I want to be very careful so I will be a different adult man for you than your uncle was. I know he liked you, too, but he was very unfair to bring you into a sexual touching relationship. He should have picked an adult for a sexual relationship and kept being an uncle for you.

I want you to know that you can have a relationship with an older man without sexual touching. You and I can have the kind of touching that kids like to give and get from adults and that most adults like to give and get from kids. But I think your experiences have confused you about what an adult wants and likes from you.

I have moved away when you have touched me because I do not feel comfortable. You must have noticed. You also notice that I let the other kids sit on my lap, hold my hand, and rub up against me. I don't let you do this with me. That is not because I like them better than you. It's just that our relationship will need to have less touching, until you can learn again how to touch like a child and I can learn to not worry that my touching will be okay for you.

I want to be a good counselor and friend. I think we should make a plan that lets us both agree what is okay touching for you and for me. Maybe Dr. B can help us with the plan.

Your friend and counselor,
Robert

The meeting went well, even though Lisa was hurt and angry at times. Her doctor met with her after the meeting and helped emphasize Robert's intentions to be a good friend, but a responsible and safe male friend. There were many complications, but certainly one of the most searing was Lisa's belief that she was only likable and desirable as a sexually pleasing woman, not as a cute, lively, cuddly kid. Long-term sexual abuse had taught her the adult skills of sexual engagement, and she was unable to distinguish them from her normal childhood wishes for physical closeness and playfulness with adults. Robert and Dr. B were able to help her begin to disentangle her touching and needs for touching, hopefully to free the way for her to be able to experience the healthy adult touching that all children enjoy and need.

Not Helpful and Destructive Touching

Just like talking, touch can be not helpful or destructive. Not helpful touching misses the opportunity to facilitate children's best efforts at coping or learning. It may not be explicitly destructive, sexual, or illegal, but it is still extremely hurtful. Adults sometimes resort to poking, jabbing, pushing, grabbing, pulling, and yanking. Usually these behaviors occur when annoyed or frustrated adults are trying to get a child to do something. They tend to produce similar feelings of anger and frustration in children. Children are also embarrassed and sometimes fearful when treated this way. These behaviors often trigger more intense feelings in our patients, because previously abused children believe this could be the prelude to greater violence. Since adults are almost always physically stronger than young children (not the case when you are working with adolescents), these physical "reminders" are misuses of adult strength. Although we may not intentionally use them this way, they are clearly forms of intimidation. We are also modeling mildly aggressive behaviors to children who are all too likely to use mild or serious aggressive behaviors to get their way or express their point of view. Therefore, we need to avoid these interactions.

Destructive touching occurs when adults physically punish or interact sexually with a child. *Adult physical or corporal punishment and sexual interactions with children are never helpful or therapeutic to children in treatment centers. They are always abusive.* Adult sexual molestation of children is always illegal. The situation is less clear about corporal punishment. Cross-cultural differences in childrearing methods do exist, and some cultures support the use of physical punishment. As of 1988, only nine American states explicitly bar corporal punishment in their school systems (American Academy of Child and Adolescent Psychiatry, 1988).

Physical punishment continues in some treatment settings. This may seem justifiable because the occasional use of spanking is sanctioned in some cultures and in some childrearing and clinical manuals (Lickona, 1983; Barkley, 1987). However, most childrearing manuals oppose spanking as a counterproductive disciplinary action. It does not foster mutual respect between parent and child because children usually resent their parent's use of greater strength.

Spanking provides an example of an aggressive solution to a conflict. It doesn't model the use of words instead of force to deal with conflict. Furthermore, it does not teach kids why what they did was wrong or what they should do instead (Lickona, 1983). We explicitly prohibit the use of physical punishment as a disciplinary action in our setting because we think it is never justified with emotionally disturbed children and it is rarely the only or the best disciplinary action for any child.

Although our patients may be physically assaultive to us and may stimulate the wish to return physical hurt, our therapeutic relationship will never recover from such interactions. Our long-term developmental and treatment goals are seriously compromised when we resort to physical punishment. It fails to contribute to a child's development of self-control and coping skills.

Children cannot be expected to trust or positively identify with physically mean or out-of-control adults. In addition, children who have been physically punished usually feel sorry for themselves, instead of feeling sorry for what they did or learning to take the point of view of the people they have offended. A properly designed therapeutic management program will never need to use physical punishment.

Institutional policy and procedure manuals should explicitly forbid the use of physical punishment and punitive interventions. These regulations should also clearly state the reasons for prohibiting physical punishment: (1) the children are not our children; (2) we will use alternatives to assert adult authority; (3) we are professionals who have developed other "safety valves" for relieving our personal tension and frustration; (4) we have developed alternative penalties to teach consequences for misbehavior; (5) we do not want to jeopardize the development of mutual respect between staff and children; and (6) many of our patients have had a lifetime of aggressive models — they don't need more.

The media frequently report incidents of sexual abuse of patients in institutions or by individual therapists. These tragic reports attest to the continual dangerous potential for sexual molestation of children in therapeutic relationships and treatment centers. Some adults may argue that children can be comforted by sexual contact, or that their self-esteem can be enhanced by their choice as a sexual partner, or that to repel their sexual overtures will hurt their feelings. These are the rationalizations of sexual offenders. No matter how lonely or unreachable a child may be, we are never justified in offering sexual interaction as a therapeutic solution.

Prevention of Not Helpful Adult-Child Interactions and Institutional Abuse

The likelihood of not helpful talking and touching increases in institutions where staff are untrained, unsupervised, and unmonitored by clinically more experienced and professionally trained staff. Milieu treatment is most commonly carried out by milieu counselors who have had no professional training and may receive no supervision. In some cases, they may have had no previous experience with seriously emotionally disturbed children. In hospitals, milieu work is enhanced by nursing personnel who have received professional training. However, it is essential that milieu treatment personnel receive the training, ongoing supervision, and support of professionally trained clinicians. This will give them the necessary skills of therapeutic communication with children to supplement their own family histories and personal styles of interacting with children.

The likelihood of sexual and physical abuse of children also increases in settings when staff (1) live loveless and isolated personal lives and depend heavily on their patients for emotional gratification; (2) have problems controlling their sexual urges and regulating their anger, frustration, and sadism; and (3) are untrained and poorly monitored in the therapeutic management of vulnerable children with traumatic histories and significant psychiatric illnesses. Staff training, supervision, and monitoring ensure that staff follow the philosophy and procedures of an institution and that the values of the institution will be carried out in professionally designed adult-child interactions.

Children in treatment centers will always be vulnerable and provocative. However, we can protect them by hiring competent adults with psychological and moral integrity and then training and supervising these adults in professional techniques of therapeutic communication. We can also give them the psychological and emotional support they need in the demanding and complicated work of therapeutic management.

Conclusion

Therapeutic management starts with skillful communication between adults and children. Helpful listening and talking bring out the best in children and pave the way for further development and healing. Training and supervision of milieu therapists focus on teaching the art and practical skills of empathic listening, helpful talking, positive touching, and creative outreaches to the inner world of the child. These connections with our patients form the foundation of our discipline system.

A mad Lion

CHAPTER 4

The Interpersonal Context of Therapeutic Management: Discipline

The purpose of discipline is to teach the child. This is the real meaning of discipline, where discipline is the educational process "that develops self-control, character, or orderliness and efficiency" (Fraiberg, 1959, p. 244). The foundation of an effective discipline system is an emotionally secure adult-child relationship built on empathy and effective communication.

Self-control and adaptive coping develop out of constructive adult-child interactions. Children cooperate with adult disciplinary actions through compliance or negotiated compromises balancing their wishes with adult expectations in order to maintain positive adult-child relationships. *Most discipline situations require a two-part adult response to children: adults respond to feelings with understanding and to behavior with approval or limits.*

Discipline is only one step in the total process of socialization introduced in Chapter Two (see Table 2). The socialization process is actually a product of adult-child reciprocal interactions. The adult role is to love, empathize, listen and talk, and utilize a discipline process with children. Children contribute to the socialization process in terms of their capacity to make use of adult love, empathy, communication, and discipline.

130

Adults use their controls for children, until children can develop internal controls. The adult role in the discipline process is one of a nurturing teacher in which adults:

- Set reasonable expectations
- Model acceptable behavior
- Support the children's best efforts
- Encourage any improvement
- Enforce reasonable penalties
- Invite child participation in the process
- Forgive following penalties and reparation
- Communicate this forgiveness to the children

For their part, healthy children learn from the discipline step if they are able to:

- Understand what they did wrong
- Feel sad or angry about their misdeed
- Differentiate between the adult giving them a penalty and the misdeed
- Acknowledge responsibility for their actions
- Feel angry with themselves and regret for what they did
- Make amends
- Transform anger and regret into resolves for the future
- Accept the adult's forgiveness
- Use the image of this process to mobilize self-control in the future

This is the normal sequence of constructive adult-child interactions during the discipline process that all children require to develop internal control.

Hospitals and residential treatment settings provide the components of this process to children in their care, adding the corrective steps needed for emotionally disturbed children with psychiatric pathology. The corrective steps consist of modifications to the normal process to allow our patients to complete the discipline process. The child's parents and staff members share the responsibility for the discipline process in treatment centers.

The steps of the discipline process are outlined in Table 5.

Table 5. The Discipline Process.

Step 1. *Establish expectations and values.* Translate expectations and values into clear, developmentally attainable rules and facilitating routines.

Step 2. *Explain.* Give reasons for standards and rules.

Step 3. *Endorse some behaviors and discourage others.* Encourage acceptable behavior and discourage unacceptable behavior through approval or disapproval and constructive criticism.

Step 4. *Model acceptable and adaptive behavior.* Model compliance with standards, adaptive coping, and resourceful compromise.

Step 5. *Encourage participation.* Allow dialogue and negotiation about values, standards, and some of the rules and penalties (within children's developmental and clinical capacities).

Step 6. *Teach consequences of behavior.*
   a. *Acknowledge good behavior (good consequences).* Notice and celebrate when the children live up to the standards.
   b. *Deliver penalties (negative consequences).* Use ignoring, reprimands, natural and logical consequences, and behavior penalties.

Step 7. *Let them make amends.* Give children the chance to express regret and make reparation.

Step 8. *Forgive them.* Accept the children's apologies and reparations, forgive them, and communicate this to them.
   a. *Let them know that you forgive them.* Communicate your forgiveness to the children.
   b. *Foster their capacity to forgive and learn.* Help the children forgive themselves, learn from their mistakes, and learn alternative ways of behaving.

In this chapter, we will discuss steps 1 through 6. In Chapter Seven, we will complete our discussion of the discipline process by describing the reactive contract, which is our routine response to behavioral crises and rule violations. The reactive contract incorporates the final steps in the discipline process: penalties (step 6), the child's reparative words and acts (step 7), and the adult's forgiveness (step 8).

Step 1: Establish Expectations and Values

Adults are the source of standards and values in children's development. During step 1 of the discipline process, adult standards, values, and expectations are translated into rules and routines. These rules and routines become guideposts for children as they balance external expectations with internal wishes and goals. Adult expectations prescribe certain behavior, such as kindness and honesty, and prohibit or limit other behaviors, such as violence and disrespect. In this way, adults create boundaries of acceptable action for children.

Rules and routines form the impersonal structure used to translate adult expectations into unit culture. Unit rules are a set of consistent expectations that preserve order and stability in the treatment community. They need to be useful, fair, and feasible. Routines describe the sequence we expect of how, when, and where to do something; examples include mealtime, bedtime, or bathing routines. Rules and routines bypass individual styles of setting or complying with rules, differences in family styles and values, and the vicissitudes of personal relationships. Some children will be able to adhere to this impersonal structure before they are able to incorporate values from individual adults (Redl, 1966b, p. 78).

Every group of people, such as families or communities, needs rules to help regulate their lives together so that people can get what they want when possible, give what they need to when necessary, and accomplish something for themselves in work, relationships, play, and personal development.

Under the umbrella of the idea of a rule, we talk to children about how we expect them to relate to each other and adults; how to be honest and truthful; how to act on the unit, in the hospital, and in public places; and how to cope with frustration and strong emotions. *Rules allow us to be proactive about behavior, rather than reactive.* Rules are a format for child-adult discussions about expectations and limits. Rules represent our "long-term decisions" about how children in our settings should behave (Silberman and Wheelan, 1980).

Rules and routines are a part of the developmental territory of childhood. School-age children are naturally drawn to the information and comfort communicated in rules. Emotionally disturbed children have an even greater need for consistency and predictability in order to feel comfortable, secure, and protected. Codifying our values and expectations into clearly stated, reasonable, developmentally feasible rules and routines enhances children's adjustment to a treatment setting. Consistency and predictability are forever challenged in treatment settings by staff rotations through three daily shifts, staff leavings, changes in clinical philosophy and administrative leadership, patients in crisis, and frequent changes in the patient group when the length of stay can be as little as a couple of days.

Goal and Purpose of Rules

The goal for rules is to achieve conformity in behavior, just as the goal for the empathic formulation, therapeutic contracts and activities, and psychotherapy is to work with the child's individuality.
The key to a rule's efficacy is consistency. The purpose of a rule is to create a dependable, safe, and comfortable environment. Consistency creates sameness and reliability, which convey safety and dependability to children. If children know that counselors will always say yes to their attempts to avoid aggression and no to entering the hallway during crises in managing other patients, the children can feel comfortable in moving on to other concerns. The consistency of a rule is like the consistency of a mother's appearance and behavior in the life of a baby or toddler. The absolute length of time present or absent is not as important as the regularity of the schedule. A rule becomes an "easily tested handle on the world for the child" (Smith and Smith, 1976, p. 128). It is the same rule with the same automatic, predetermined consequences for all times of day, for all staff whatever their discipline or relationship to the children, and for all children regardless of changing circumstances.
Rules should not exist for situations where consistency is not clinically indicated or feasible. Rules can be written with qualifying statements, or they can be written for general situations. For example, we can state that there should be no toys in the quiet room when children are taking time-outs, unless their individual treatment plans state that they may have toys with them. We can then include a provision like the following in the individual treatment plan: "Maggie is learning how to take time well with the help of her teddy bear friend." Therapeutic flexibility is implemented at the level of the individual treatment plan, which accommodates the individual clinical and developmental needs

of our patients. Therapeutic flexibility is not inconsistency in the application of the rules. Flexibility in rules should be a planned clinical strategy, not the product of inattention, ignorance, or an individual staff member's personal decision.

Program development centers around the sometimes conflicting values of consistency versus clinical flexibility. An effective program is characterized by the ongoing dialogue about the need to be both consistent and flexible between day and evening shifts, nurses and doctors, parents and staff members. We should always be assessing whether the rules fit our values, the patient population, the setting, and the treatment goals. For example, the rules can be "too loose" when there are younger or more disturbed children on the unit and "too controlling" when there is a more preteen group of kids, who will need opportunities to exercise their initiative and self-control.

Cultural and familial differences between staff members often lead to intense disagreements about the rules for mealtimes, standards of room cleanliness, frequency of bathing, use of TV, and always the use and restrictions around food. The important process is the clarification and continual revisions of rules to gain staff consensus and flexible accommodation to family values and style.

Orientation of new and part-time staff is also necessary for staff adherence to the developmental-clinical rationale for the use of rules in general and for consensus and consistency with regard to the use of particular rules. Failures in consistency are inevitable (as every parent knows). When inconsistency is too prevalent or flexibility is absent, therapeutic management is disrupted and milieu treatment is jeopardized.

Kinds of Rules

The basic unit rules apply to all children, and they have the same automatic consequences for all children. Basic unit rules are divided into Big Rules and Smaller Rules, according to issues of physical safety and danger. Violating a rule is making a mistake. Discipline involves learning from mistakes.

All rules are important, but the Big Rules jeopardize the

physical safety of children and staff (and property), and the Smaller Rules jeopardize the emotional, ethical, and psychological well-being of the children and staff and treatment community. Since all rules are necessary and important, we want to help children distinguish what is dangerously unacceptable and what is unacceptable and serious but not as dangerous. For example, we do not condone teasing, but we would prefer that children yell insults at their peers rather than physically attacking them. Ultimately, we would prefer that they express their frustration or disappointment without violence, taunts, or teasing.

When children break a Big Rule, they make a Big Mistake. When children break a Smaller Rule, they make a Smaller Mistake. Our program emphasizes that we think all people make mistakes. Some people learn from their mistakes, and the mistakes make them smarter. Other people never learn from their mistakes, and this keeps them in trouble all the time. This framework appeals to the concrete nature of a young child's thought.

Table 6 lists Big Rules and the typical behaviors that violate these rules (Big Mistakes).

Table 6. Big Rules and Big Mistakes.

Rule 1. *Keep myself safe.*
Big Mistakes: violence, physical fighting, sexual activity with someone else, touching another person's private parts, possession and use of drugs and alcohol on the unit, leaving the unit without staff permission, possession of sharp or dangerous objects, keeping money in a bedroom, hiding, leaving the group while off the unit, self-injurious behaviour, suicidal ideation and behavior, fire setting, running away, bulimia, failure to eat.

Rule 2. *Keep others safe.*
Big Mistakes: violence; physical fighting; sexual activity with someone else; touching another person's private parts; rape; flashing; possession of drugs or alcohol on the unit; giving drugs to another patient; possession of matches or sharp or dangerous objects on the unit; inciting unitwide disturbances; verbal and physical threatening; fire setting; cruelty to animals.

Rule 3. *Keep the things around me safe.*
Big Mistakes: vandalism, punching or kicking walls, breaking windows, graffiti, fire setting, smearing feces.

The Big Rules deal with safety, the unit's foremost job. Protecting children from their troublemaking behavior and the troublemaking behavior of their peers is not easy when aggressive, self-injurious, and sexual behavior is quite common. For example, the majority of our patients have histories of sexual abuse. We needed to create a special set of "Privacy Rules" that take into consideration the great probability of reenactment in these traumatized children. We excuse only one child at a time to go to the bathroom, and only one child at a time is allowed to change clothes in a room. We also installed windows in bedrooms and instituted frequent night checks to ensure that children remain in their own bed.

In this example, Maggie breaks a Big Rule:

Maggie's (age six) bedtimes were the worst. She was unable to settle down and usually ended up in a verbal and physical battle with a staff member. Melissa (a counselor) was trying to talk to her through her screaming when she kicked her in the shins. She was walked to the quiet room by two staff, and Melissa remained outside.

When Maggie had calmed down, Melissa went in and talked to her. Melissa told her that she would need to start her bedtime in the quiet room the following night. Maggie cried and insisted that it was unfair.

"Maggie, I want to help you follow the rules and I want to protect people from your kicks, punches, and spits. Hurting people is a Big Rule on the unit, and breaking that rule is a Big Mistake. This means that we have to make big changes in your bedtime routine until we can be sure that you won't hurt anyone again."

Table 7 lists important Smaller Rules and the Smaller Mistakes that violate these rules.

It may be surprising to see consideration and honesty on a list of "smaller" rules. We emphasize in our words and eventually in our penalties for rule violations that this is a question of relative seriousness and importance. The Smaller Rules are very important, but infractions are not dangerous. These rules deal with actions that jeopardize the quality of life on the unit, and they encourage more responsible and constructive ways of

Table 7. Important Smaller Rules and Smaller Mistakes.

Smaller Rules
  1. Be considerate to kids and staff.
  2. Listen to and cooperate with staff.
  3. Tell the truth.
  4. Respect other people's things.
  5. Follow the routines, rules, and program.
  6. Talk without swearing.

Smaller Mistakes
  1. Teasing
  2. Name calling
  3. Interfering
  4. Ignoring staff
  5. Lying
  6. Borrowing without permission
  7. Stealing
  8. Breaking a rule
  9. Not following the routine
  10. Not participating in a program
  11. Swearing

---

dealing with people and situations. In other words, they convey our standards for kind and respectful dealings with each other.

In this example, Maggie breaks a Smaller Rule:

Maggie (age six) kept building blocks after Dr. B (a psychologist) had told her it was time to clean up for lunch and put the toys away.

"Maggie, please clean up and put the blocks away. I'll give you a count of five. One . . . two . . . three . . . four . . . five . . . "

Maggie didn't look up and started building a new fortress.

"Okay, Maggie, you need to take a time-out for not listening," said Dr. B.

Maggie pouted and crawled to a time-out chair. When her time was up, Dr. B said, "Good job! You made a mistake and didn't listen, but you did a good job taking your time well. I can give you a star on your star chart for taking your time well."

Kinds of Routines

Routines are sequences of rules for specific contexts that help structure a specific time of day or activity. These rules build routines by specifying a sequence of expectations for particular times of the day or for dressing, toileting, bathing, eating, and sleeping. Exhibit 3 is a page from the unit rule and routine book, written jointly by the staff and children. It illustrates how we write the rules that make up a routine. Notice step 3, written by the children, which clearly relates to a common problem among the children.

Rules and Routines for Special Times and Places

We also have rules and routines for particular places, such as staff-only spaces, the hospital lobby, or the van. We structure activities with specific rules designed to help children do the work of that activity, such as personal time in bedrooms, school tutoring, TV time, visiting, and home passes.

We also use rules and routines for groups of children doing special activities or going on an outing. In these rules, consequences are the same for all children involved in the activity or trip—for example, rules for a trip to the beach or rules for starting a club.

And then there are individualized rules that apply to only one child and have either automatic, predetermined consequences or negotiated consequences. Individualized rules for individual children are written up as treatment plans and change according to their developmental and clinical needs. For example, a frequently assaultive child may have a transition program that anticipates the aggression and provides for a unique sequence of events when it occurs. We may also want to help a child learn about how rules work by allowing the child to develop a contract about the consequences of loud talking during TV time.

Steps 2 and 3: Explain, Endorse, and Discourage

This phase of the discipline process focuses on explaining the reasons for the rules in clear and developmentally fitting ways and specifying the limits of acceptable behavior. We set the boundaries of the limits by specifying the behaviors that we endorse at one end of the limit and specifying the behaviors that we discourage or criticize at the other end of the limit.

Exhibit 3. Sample Description of a Unit Routine.

What to do at Mealtimes

1. Kids sit in living room. Quiet kids are called to the table first.
2. Kids pick a seat and stick with it. Once you lift the tray cover from a meal, you need to keep that meal.
3. No switching trays without staff permission. If you have a special tray, you may switch.
4. No playing with food.
5. Talk to the kids at your own table. You may talk to staff by raising your hand.
6. You may have dessert, if you eat half of your meal. Please ask staff for permission to start eating dessert. Kids lose their dessert if they start to eat it without permission.
7. Kids can leave their seats with staff permission. Raise your hand to get it.
8. To clear, raise your hand. Quiet kids are called to clear.
9. Clearing rules:
   a. Throw all paper in garbage.
   b. Empty all liquids into the sink.
   c. Save all unused food and utensils for collection and trade-ins.
10. THANK YOU AND ENJOY YOUR MEAL!

We explain the reasons for our expectations and rules by talking to children about why we have general rules and particular rules. Although taking the "because I said so" approach may initially seem easier, it does not do the long-term work of educating children about the reasons and value for order and structure. Thus, whenever possible, we need to include reasons with our requests.

"Andrew, please finish your chore (sweeping the dining room floor). If everyone does their chore, we can start afternoon cartoons and the unit looks really neat!"

"Ralph, you'll need to take a time-out for swearing. We really need to help you break that habit before you go back to school."

"Lisa, you'll need to take a time-out for touching Ralph in his private parts. We need the privacy rules, because it's important to respect the other kids' bodies. You each deserve respect and protection.

"Too many kids have problems with touching. They have not been respected themselves by adults and other kids, so they don't know how to respect other people's privacy."

Explaining rules starts when a child comes to the unit. We ask other children to help us "orient" the new child to how things work in this new place.

Andrew (age seven) and his parents arrived on the unit. Joy (a nurse) greeted them. After showing Andrew his room, she asked Michael (age eight) to show him and his parents around. Joy stayed with them, adding missing information and correcting any inaccurate or personalized renditions that Michael might come up with.

Children are good tour guides. They introduce the unit and its culture from a child's point of view. They explain what interests, confuses, or worries them (they spend a lot of time on the bathroom and kitchen). Adults tend to orient children from an adult perspective, missing details that would be more important to a child. Children spontaneously bring up rules when they are explaining the unit. Their explanations are usually clear and firm.

When children give distorted views of the unit or do not take the job of orientation seriously, staff will "remove them" from the job.

Michael (age eight) was giving Andrew (age seven) and his parents a tour of the unit. He pointed to the quiet room. "This is where they torture you."

"Michael, please tell Andrew what we really use the quiet room for," interrupted Joy, who was following along behind.

"I'm right. I hate the quiet room. Especially when they lock the door and don't open it."

"It's okay to tell Andrew what you like or don't like about the unit. You can tell him that you don't like the quiet room when we lock the door. But he also needs to know that kids often use the quiet room and we do not lock it. He needs to know why we lock the door, when, and for how long and stuff like that. I bet his parents really want to know these things too."

We have a large, multicolored, laminated rule and routine book that hangs in a prominent place listing general unit rules and specific rules for unit routines for mealtimes, bedtime, community meeting, van trips, or going outside. This book was made by the children. The children have printed and drawn pictures on large pieces of colored paper. It is revised frequently by kids and staff. Kids are asked to refer to it when they have questions.

Staff use the rule book when they want to evoke the impersonal structure of the unit.

Paul (age nine) was teasing Maggie about her red hair. "Watch out the rabbits don't eat you. Bunny rabbits love carrots!"

Maggie clenched her fists and started moving toward Paul.

Dr. G (a psychiatrist) intervened. "Paul, please look in the rule book. I think the rules say you can't tease. Come on, I'll look with you."

Paul and Dr. G spent some time sitting on the sofa reading the rule book. Paul critiqued the rules and Dr. G tried to defend them. Maggie sat down and also became interested in this "game." She and Paul found common ground in their dislike of the bed-time rules.

Dr. G kept encouraging them to discuss the rules and their opinions. "Hey, this is interesting. You both have some good ideas. Although I need to help you follow the rules, I don't expect you to like them."

"You never listen to us when we try to tell you something," said Paul.

"We can't argue about them in the situation, like just then when Paul was teasing, but we can argue about them now, when we are just talking. Why don't you two design your own family? Write out the rules that you think would be good for kids (and parents, too)."

Invoking institutional rules has other benefits when we see (or feel) a power struggle coming on with a particular child. Both Paul and Maggie have strong oppositional streaks. They were very good at getting into power struggles with staff over minor requests. Dr. G was successful in the previous vignette because he sidestepped a direct confrontation with Paul by redirecting his battle to the rule book and the impersonal structure of the unit. He managed to set a limit (which Paul followed) and allowed Paul his favorite activity of arguing. He then helped both Paul and Maggie find an outlet in fantasy for their wish to control and be in charge.

Respecting children's separate power and decision-making capacities is an essential part of asking them to engage in treatment. Requests to follow rules or carry out procedures should always be preceded by "pleases" and concluded with "thank you's." When we say "please" to a child, we are acknowledging that we are requesting something from the child and the child has the power to comply or not to comply. When we ask Ralph to "please take his time-out," we are altering the authority message to include our "lack of power" confronted by his "power" to obey or disobey. When we say "thank you," we are acknowledging that the child made the decision to cooperate with us. A "please and thank you culture" models for children how we would like them to talk with us.

We have devised several helpful principles for the creation of useful, fair, and feasible rules, drawing both on our own experience and on the child management literature (Becker, 1971; Silberman and Wheelan, 1980; Smith and Smith, 1976; Trieschman, Whittaker, and Brendtro, 1969). Table 8 summarizes principles for the design and use of rules during the discipline process.

Step 4: Model Acceptable and Adaptive Behavior

Actions speak louder than words, and adult actions teach "louder" than words in the discipline process. In fact, children will imitate our actions, whether we intended them to do so or not. If we show them the "right way," we are more likely to see them act that way.

In treatment settings, there are many opportunities to show children how we follow our own rules, show self-control, adaptively regulate and express feelings, negotiate compromises with our colleagues, obey the dictates of our bosses, and cope with stress. When we are driving, we need to pay special attention to speeding limits, parking regulations, and road signs. On

Table 8. Principles for Making and Using Rules.

1. Make them clear, concrete, and specific. They should be clear to the children and the staff. Specific details tell children what, how, and when to do it.
2. State them positively: "When you finish your morning routine, you can watch cartoons"—not "If you do not do your morning routine, you cannot watch cartoons."
3. Make the rule suitable to the children's age, developmental status, and abilities. Make it reasonable in terms of the setting.
4. Make the rule enforceable. How will we (and the children) know if the rule has been broken or followed?
5. Teach children what the rules are and post copies of the rules in their space. Can they remember the rules?
6. Discuss the rules with the children. Take the time to explain the reasons for the rules and how the community of children and staff will benefit from the rules.
7. Prepare and explain consequences for breaking a rule in advance.
8. Notice and comment on adherence to the rules. "Catch kids being good."
9. Let kids help make up and write the rules.
10. Don't expect the kids to like the rules. Let the kids know this.

the unit, we have the chance to be nonaggressive and effective models while we carry out the discipline process. Talking about why and how we come to our values and goals helps children learn how to be thoughtful and concerned.

We can model praising and encouraging children, and we can model the way we disapprove of and criticize children. These are social skills that children need to have for participation in groups. Children also learn from and model our disciplinary style. We can offer rational, mature models or impulsive, excessive models who scream, threaten, and blame.

When staff make mistakes, children are interested and impressed when they can make their own reparations and apologies. This models the steps in the discipline process that we are trying to help a child complete. Staff model how to follow rules when they comply with the rules designed for them. They can model compromise and negotiation of rules when they discuss their differences of opinion and try to come to compromises with each other. There are also opportunities for staff to discuss personal reasons and styles for disagreeing with a rule while still complying with it. When staff disagree among themselves, they can model adaptive arguing.

Ruth (a counselor) and Joy (a nurse) were sitting in the living room while the kids watched TV and planning the cooking group that they co-led. Although they were jointly in charge of this activity, they both dreaded these planning sessions because they had such conflicting ideas about the group.

"I think the last group was totally out of control," said Joy.

"I don't think so," said Ruth. "The kids and their parents were really enjoying the group. If we had tried to quiet them down, it would've made everyone feel uncomfortable and squelched the fun."

"Well, I don't want to lead another group like that one again," responded Joy with barely suppressed annoyance.

Ruth looked frustrated. "What do you suggest?"

"I'm wondering whether we better rethink this whole arrangement. I don't want to hurt your feelings, but maybe it's not possible for us to lead the group together. We have such different styles. I think our disagreements are interfering with the running of the group."

"You're not hurting my feelings, because I agree with you. Maybe we should think about it some more. I need to calm down about my feelings. Let's talk about it later this week?"

"Okay," said Joy, looking relieved.

At this point, they noticed Paul (age nine) intently looking at them with a worried expression on his face. Joy called him over and asked him what was wrong.

"You're fighting," he said in a whisper.

Ruth and Joy looked at each other and Ruth calmly responded, "You're right. We don't agree about something, so we're arguing. But don't worry. Joy and I can disagree and still be friends. We've decided to talk about it later. We're too emotional now."

"That's right, Paul, Ruth and I are friends and we usually work well together," Joy confirmed.

"Do you ever leave and never come back?" Paul asked.

"No. Not over anything like this," Joy responded quickly. "If we're going to leave, we would plan it and tell the kids. I wouldn't leave a job that I love, just because I had an argument. We have lots of arguments about ways to help you kids."

"Hey Joy, remember yesterday, when we were arguing about whether Johnny was ready to leave the quiet room?"

Paul smiled and got the point.

We also model basic values of trust, loyalty, honesty, and caring in our daily interactions with each other. Kids certainly notice when staff thank, comfort, encourage, teach, and assist each other. *The educational value of a helping and collaborative staff is frequently underestimated.* We can model these interactions in ordinary and remarkable moments.

Meg (a counselor) was holding her arm and crying in the hallway after she had helped to place Ralph (age twelve) in seclusion. Stacy (a counselor) quietly hugged her and walked her to the staff room.

"I'm sorry you got hurt, let me help you," said Stacy. "You did a good job. I saw him punch you. I know how strong Ralph can be. Let's go into the staff room for a minute."

The children were listening and watched as she led Meg into the staff room. Some counselors stayed behind and assured the kids that Meg was going to be all right and that Stacy would comfort her.

Step 5: Encourage Participation

Within children's developmental and clinical capacities, we can encourage their initiative and participation in the discipline process. *Children learn to use good judgment by practicing good judgment.* Although treatment settings for emotionally disturbed children have to establish greater structure around rules and routines, they also need to use every opportunity to include children in the formation and revision of rules and routines. If we do not allow children to use their initiative and good ideas around management of themselves and their community, we miss an opportunity to strengthen those skills and strengthen children's sense of themselves as positive members of a community.

When children question existing rules, we need to encourage dialogue and collaboration. We can convert angry and futile protests into constructive action, which may change a rule or lead to a better understanding of why the rule was designed in a particular way.

Michael (age eight) complained that he could not use the unit video games during TV time. They were reserved for specially supervised times during the week. He became sullen and started to swear under his breath. Dr. A (a psychiatrist) heard him in the TV room and knew that this was going to lead to bigger trouble. She asked Maria (another patient) to help Michael turn his complaints into suggestions for a new policy for the use of video games on the unit. Dr. A suggested that Michael bring this up at community meeting.

The next day, Michael and Maria presented a "formal proposal" at community meeting. Keith (a counselor) told them that the old policy was written that way because we didn't want the equipment damaged by inexperienced users. Maria suggested that kids could learn how to use the equipment and pass a test. This added a "credentialing" step to their policy that said that a child needed to go through a training session to use the equipment independently. They also suggested that misuse of the equipment would lead to loss of credentials.

The staff decided to change the routine and include Michael's and Maria's suggestion. Michael also received lots of praise for his contribution.

Arguments or dialogues about the rules were also redirected to the unit complaint and suggestion box.

The "older kids" were disgusted with the 9:00 bed hour. Ralph, Lisa, Maria, and Donna were asked to put their complaints in the complaint and suggestion box. Complaints were read at the daily community meeting.

When Clare (a nurse manager) read their complaints, she thanked them for their comments. "Thanks for complaining in such a mature way. It's easier to listen to your ideas this way than at night when kids start getting loud at bedtime."

"We think you make us go to bed too early. We're not babies," said Ralph (age twelve).

"The time to go to bed is unfair to some kids. It's hard to make a good rule for all the kids. It's hard to live in a group of younger and older kids. We need to make a bed hour that will be okay for the younger and older kids, for the kids who have trouble falling asleep, for those who can go to sleep easily, for the kids who are grouches if they don't get lots of sleep, and for those who need just a few hours of sleep a night," responded Clare.

"I don't need that much sleep. At home I go to bed when I want to," said Maria (age twelve).

"I know the rules are different here than at home for some of you."

"Yeah, stupid," said Lisa (age eleven).

"Well, I'm just going to try to explain another reason why we did it this way," continued Clare. "We want to be sure that we leave enough time for the evening staff to help the kids who need their attention, before they go off duty. The night staff is smaller, and they don't have the time to give individual attention to the kids."

"I don't want no story read to me," interrupted Donna.

"For some of these reasons, we need to keep an earlier bedtime. But maybe you can all form a committee to come up with suggestions to help the older kids be allowed to do something different once they're in bed. Like listen to music? Maybe you could ask an evening staff member to be the staff representative on the committee."

The kids looked distinctly disinterested in this process. They just wanted to get their way. However, Clare and Mel (an evening counselor) were able to get them involved in making some special arrangements for older kids who could earn later bedtimes.

Of course, children are not content to be sent to committees. They would rather have us change the rules, but we can often help with individual modifications within the rules (for example, radios with earphones, books and flashlights under the covers, Friday night "late-nighter" clubs) or redirect children to designing their own bedtime routines for use at home. We want to introduce the child to the process of constructive "complaining," which includes both complaining and making suggestions.

Step 6: Teach Consequences of Behavior

When children act, the consequences can be good or bad for themselves or others.

Step 6a: Acknowledge Good Behavior

Teaching consequences should start with positive consequences for positive behavior. Praise and encouragement are powerful teachers of acceptable behavior. We make a special effort to notice when a child does something right. We want the child to experience something good because of it. We can become so focused on what a child is doing wrong, especially when it is seriously or dangerously wrong, that we overlook the smaller increments of improvements. Rewarding good behavior is the best way to build positive skills (Clark, 1985; Wagonseller and McDowell, 1979).

When we praise and encourage children, we are teaching them how to acknowledge the good in themselves and their peers. The "contagion" effect of positive feelings and mutual support is as powerful in a milieu as the power of hate and aggression. *We should never take any degree of cooperation or compliance for granted when we are working with disturbed children.* We make a point of giving them credit for anything that they do right. This sounds easier than it actually is.

On an inpatient unit, there is such a necessary emphasis on controlling dangerous behavior and delivering negative consequences for noncompliance that it is easy to become blind to good behavior. It almost takes special training and vigilance to find the good in the midst of the chaos.

"Ralph, good work. First time you were at the meal without a time-out."

"Maria, thank you for reading to Raoul and Paul while we were busy helping Ralph (restraining him following an assault)."

"Raoul, you did an *excellent* job not interfering when we were helping Ralph."

"Kids, the staff and I want you to know how much we enjoyed community meeting today. We didn't have to give one time-out. Did you notice that we had a chance to give everyone their turn, and we didn't have to rush? Good work!"

Our praise and enthusiasm convey attention and encouragement for the hard work required to follow rules and learn from mistakes. *Encouragement "primes" the motivational pump in children who have failed too often.* Frequently our patients have given up trying to be good or trying to please adults. Our praise for even partial successes tells them that they can succeed. Praise and encouragement start to reroute patients back to the normal socialization process, in which children obey because it feels good, gets them adult affection and approval, and helps them do what they really want to do. Our job requires a lot of cheerleading. Praising what is acceptable in a child's behavior is the most powerful strategy for helping children develop adaptive coping skills and competence.

Praise and limit setting are not incompatible. Sometimes we can catch children doing something right as we give them penalties for breaking another rule.

"Heather (age seven), please take a time-out for spitting at Michael. You can come right back after it's finished. You've done a really good job following the rules during the rest of the group. I'll save your place for you."

"Thank you, Johnny (age eight), for helping set up for TV time. You'll need to take a time-out for changing the channels without staff permission, but welcome back after your time-out."

Johnny (age eight) was going to court on Wednesday. On Monday, Gino (a therapeutic recreationalist) noticed that Johnny had had no seclusion episodes in the last week and a half. He brought it up in team meeting. Dr. Z, his psychologist, predicted that he would probably resort to some old ways as the court appearance got closer. He thought we should do something special today to recognize this growth in self-control before there was a slip.

The staff cut a blue ribbon out of blue construction paper and all signed it. They glued Velcro on the back so that he could wear it if he chose to. Gino gave it to him in evening meeting at the beginning of a new shift. The ribbon said,

Johnny
Self-Control Award
10 Days Without Seclusion
Keep Growing Those Controls
From Ruble 2B Staff

That night, Johnny started yelling at Maggie (age six) for bugging him. He was sent to the quiet room to settle down. He asked Allyson (a nurse) if she could hold his ribbon. He carefully removed it, and Allyson agreed to hold it until he returned. He mentioned casually later that night that it was the first ribbon he had ever received.

Step 6b: Deliver Penalties

This is the penalty or punishment step of the discipline process. Behaviorists call this the *response cost* (Barth, 1986, p. 159). A penalty is a negative consequence for doing something wrong, just as a compliment or praise is a positive consequence for doing something right. Most children will make mistakes along the way to developing internal control and the capacity to live by adult standards and limits. An effective approach to discipline capitalizes on these mistakes to teach children. Positive consequences encourage children to continue a particular behavior, and negative consequences motivate children to change or stop another kind of behavior. Sometimes adults need to structure consequences; at other times, naturally occurring negative and positive consequences are the logical effect of acting in certain ways.

Not all punishments or penalties promote positive development. When penalties are kind and firm, they are valid components of the discipline process for normal and disturbed children alike. But when penalties are designed to retaliate for the child's misbehavior, they do not contribute to positive socialization. Parents, counselors, and teachers give penalties in order to teach, not retaliate. Retaliatory punishment has no place in a therapeutic treatment center, and most regulatory agencies specifically forbid "punishment" in this sense.

Our model of therapeutic management assumes that our patients will cause trouble and that our job is to stop the trouble and teach children to learn from their mistakes. Therefore, our question is *how* to therapeutically punish, not *whether* to punish. We need to choose from various kinds of penalties, matching the penalty to the child and the misdeed. The penalty step in therapeutic management builds on the methods of punishment used in normal childrearing (Clark, 1985), with the modifications necessary to make these practices therapeutic.

When a child breaks a rule or misbehaves and we decide there should be a negative consequence, we have five different kinds of penalties to choose from:

- Active ignoring
- Reprimands
- Natural consequences
- Logical consequences
- Behavior penalties

Active Ignoring. Withholding our attention is one way of penalizing a child. Childrearing manuals recommend "active ignoring" (1) to weaken unwanted, passive misbehavior such as whining, fussing, loud crying and complaining, insistent begging; (2) to discourage temper tantrums in toddlers; or (3) to avoid power struggles (Clark, 1985; Silberman and Wheelan, 1980; Wagonseller and McDowell, 1979).

Children learn that the behavior they are using will not get them what they want from adults, because the adults will

not do business with children who act that way. When we ignore, we also avoid inadvertently rewarding a behavior. Ignoring does not work when the consequences of the behavior will
be too destructive for the child or others, or when property
damage will be too great. Ignoring will also not work when loss
of parental attention does not offset the benefits for a child of
acting in a certain way. Ignoring works if parents have a positive relationship with a child (the child misses the attention) and
if they use it consistently with a particular behavior.

For our patients, ignoring has some complications. We
do not have long-lasting positive relationships on which to base
our responses. Children who have had relatively neglectful childrearing experiences interpret ignoring as indifference or hostility. We often have to pay attention to negative behavior in order
to teach that "attention getting" is a legitimate childhood wish
and that there are "good" ways of doing it and "unacceptable"
ways of doing it. We first need to communicate that our patients deserve our attention and our help by giving them more
initial attention than usual.

We often use ignoring for parts of behaviors. We can accept a child's request at face value and ignore the demanding
tone. We can accept a child's talking about frustration and pain
and ignore the descriptive use of swears, or we can accept an
attempt at an apology and ignore the tone of voice. We can talk
about a child's good shift and ignore the difficult night that preceded it (assuming that the night staff carried out their discipline
jobs at the time of the trouble.)

We need to assess individual incidents in terms of our best
guess about whether children are on their way to something bigger, whether allowing this behavior will lead to a negative group
contagion, and whether it is "tolerable." If tolerable, we can use
"planned ignoring" (Redl and Wineman, 1952, pp. 158–160).
Our patients frequently have brief show-off or back-talking behaviors that they need to perform to settle down. When these
actions are only defensive beginnings, we can avoid causing
something bigger by not challenging them. Other times, ignoring
these actions will inspire greater troublemaking. Constructive
ignoring is a difficult clinical intervention to use.

Heather (age seven) became anxious when other children were causing trouble on the unit. She usually stayed out of the immediate fray and soothed herself by touching her vagina. Helen (a therapeutic recreationalist) noticed that Heather's hand was in her crotch while the kids were watching television. Ralph (age twelve) had just blown up and was being physically held in the quiet room. Helen went over and sat next to Heather. She said nothing about the masturbation, and Heather started twirling her hair.

Johnny (age eight) shouted to Colleen (a nurse), "Get the fuck out of here or I'll punch you out!"
    Johnny had awakened while Colleen was completing her night checks. She thought he must have been disoriented and frightened when he found her looming over his bed. She ignored his swearing and his threats.
    "I'm Colleen, Johnny. I'm doing the night checks. Do you want me to put on the light for a minute? I'm sorry for waking you."
    As she talked quietly, Johnny calmed down and fell back to sleep.

Lisa (age eleven) and Donna (age ten) were giggling during the community meeting. Jim (a counselor) had noticed that they had been in high spirits outside. It was a beautiful spring day. As they got louder, Jim ignored them and asked the group if they wanted to do anything special outside in the time before dinner. Lisa stopped talking to Donna and raised her hand with a suggestion.

Reprimands. We can use words and gestures to convey our disapproval: "I don't want you to climb on those trees. I don't want you to tease Jimmy with your bigger bag of potato chips." This is usually a first step in trying to modify unacceptable behavior. When a child's better self is temporarily out of order, we can often convey a clear message of our disapproval with a friendly gesture or brief remark. Redl and Wineman (1952, p. 160) call this *signal interference.*
    Like every other normal intervention, it is trickier to do with our patients, because they may get upset or paralyzed by criticism. On the other hand, they may be immune to critical words so that they don't listen, or they may distort the intentions and messages of what we say due to faulty reasoning. We

need to be particularly aware of our nonverbal signals and our choice of words when we express disapproval or criticism.

When reprimands are used at the start of trouble, they often can help a child stay out of bigger trouble.

Leslie (a counselor) noticed that Raoul (age six) was playing happily with Michael's red racing car during personal time. Michael had invited him to play with him. She knew that Raoul had trouble with stealing other kids' things. He called it "borrowing."

When she was announcing cleanup time, she asked to speak to Raoul quietly in the hall. "I just wanted to remind you that we don't allow kids to borrow other kids' toys without permission."

Raoul looked at her intently and didn't say a word. He grasped the red racing car in his left hand more firmly.

"I know you like Michael's red car, but I hope you can remember to leave it in Michael's room at the end of personal time. Remember how much fun you've had. If you want Michael to ask you in again, you better keep his toys safe."

Donna (age ten) and Lisa (age eleven) were beginning to get very silly during Thursday supper.

"I'm worried about the increasing silliness between the two of you," said John (a counselor) as he moved over to be closer to them. "I just wanted to remind you that you need to be quieter at supper. I'm glad to see you having fun. But this isn't the same as outside conversation. Do you need to change the subject? You've done so well today that I don't want to see you spoil it now."

Becky (a nurse) asked to speak to Ralph (age twelve) in private. "I don't like the way you're starting to talk to me," she said. "Can you find another way of telling me you're angry, so that I can listen better?"

The following is a list of guidelines for expressing disapproval to children in helpful ways:

1. *Be brief and calm.* This does not mean that you do not express your feelings of disapproval. You can be more effective if you can limit emotional intensity during reprimands. Acting too angry distracts children from the lesson to be

learned: they may enjoy "the show," they may welcome the intense emotional attention they are receiving even if it is negative, they may feel they are being punished because you are angry (not because they are doing something wrong), or they may develop excessive guilt feelings or feelings of self-hatred.

2. *Criticize a behavior, not the person.* Don't say "You're bad." Say "You did a bad thing" or "I don't like it when you taunt Andrew." This distinction is a part of the bigger picture, which emphasizes that you can like children and not like what they do.

3. *Name the behavior.* Provide accurate and specific information about the undesirable behavior. Don't use hospital jargon. If a kid kicks, refer to kicking, not "assaultive behavior."

4. *Stick to the present.* Try not to pull in other areas of disapproval as well. The children will then discount your comments if they feel like they have "lost" anyway. They will need to ignore you if they feel ganged up on.

5. *Include ways to make amends with the reprimand.* For example, "I'm so angry that you marked up the walls. I expect you to clean it up now. Would you like me to get you the proper cleaning stuff?"

Reprimands do not work if the individual child or group is too unhinged to hear them. If the adult-child relationship is not in good shape, the adult does not have a positive influence on the child (Redl and Wineman, 1952). If the child's behavior is determined by attention deficits or language processing problems, the child will be less able to use words of warning.

Natural Consequences. These are consequences that occur automatically following certain choices and behaviors. When a child is considerate or generous with a friend, the result could be an invitation to a birthday party. A natural consequence of wearing sneakers on a snowy day is wet, cold feet; getting up late means missing morning cartoons; if you tease someone who strikes out in a baseball game, you get teased when you miss the catch in the outfield. Adults teach children by allowing them to experience these natural consequences. Children learn the connection between their decisions to act in certain ways and the consequences of those behaviors.

We need to protect children from the natural consequences of their behavior when (1) immediate danger to the children or another person or property exists, (2) long-term negative consequences are at stake, or (3) the children are too young to prevent the natural consequences (Glenn and Nelsen, 1989).

Our patients often lack the ego capacity to see cause-and-effect relationships clearly. When they argue that "I didn't do it," they often truly believe their version of the story. We also need to monitor the use of naturally occurring consequences in disturbed children who will bring about these punishments for their own irrational motives. For example, depressed children will use natural consequences to meet their distorted needs to be punished for excessive feelings of guilt. Aggressive or suicidal children or those who injure themselves will bring about excessive and dangerous natural consequences.

The concept of natural consequences is built into privilege systems that connect increasing freedom to use of safe and adaptive behaviors (see Chapter Five).

Logical Consequences. A good logical consequence follows the "three R's": *related* to the behavior, *respectful* to both child and adult, and *reasonable* to both child and adult.

Adults or peers set up logical consequences. Logical consequences can be both positive (for behaviors we want to see more of) and negative (for problem behaviors we want to discourage). When children complete their morning routine early, an adult can give them extra cartoon time or make a special breakfast. If children are discovered making obscene phone calls to the hospital operator, they are restricted from phone use for a period of time. If the group of children are too disruptive (not listening to counselors, arguing and teasing with each other, unable to physically settle down), then the staff can decide to cancel an off-grounds trip. When choosing the logical consequence, the adult attempts to make the penalty logically fit the nature of the misbehavior.

On the inpatient unit, we substitute behavior penalties even when the situation offers natural or logical consequences. We use short time-outs (a form of behavior penalties) when we believe that a natural or logical consequence would impose too severe a consequence on a child. For example, when children touch the TV channels against the rules, we do not penalize them by losing TV for the evening. They do lose TV briefly, because time-out occurs out of sight of the TV. We do not want to use consequences that may impose too great a burden on children's egos. Short time-outs often provide more flexibility in use.

Behavior Penalties. Behavior penalties are imposed by adults following certain actions, such as fines, tasks, or loss of privileges. These penalties do not necessarily connect logically to the misdeed. Parents set behavioral penalties according to the child's developmental age and what is most meaningful to the child. Penalties in the family setting may include no TV, no movies on the weekends, no friends over after school, monetary fines, or extra household chores. Time-out is the general penalty recommended for young children when it is not possible to shape the penalty to the nature of the misdeed. As a routine, time-out has other benefits for young children that will be discussed in detail in Chapter Five.

Treatment settings need to design the penalty step in special ways to build in the corrective modifications that allow emotionally disturbed children to complete the discipline process. Our patients need extensive discussion of therapeutically designed behavioral penalties. Patients who are able to participate in treatment are able to use the set behavioral penalties, such as time-out and the penalties built into a privilege system. These techniques are outlined in Chapter Five. When children are unable to cooperate with these interventions, we have to resort to the interventions described in Chapters Six and Seven.

Conclusion

The discipline process is an essential component in the therapeutic management of children. This process describes the ways adults interact with children to teach self-control and adaptive coping with feelings, daily challenges, and stress. Growth-promoting discipline is geared to each child's developmental level of functioning, encourages children to experience and express feelings in adaptive ways, restricts maladaptive behavior, sets reasonable standards and values, models adaptive functioning and self-control, uses a lot of encouragement and praise, and imposes kind and firm negative consequences when children make mistakes and cannot live up to adult expectations. The process also includes the important steps of reparation and forgiveness, which are outlined in the "reactive contract" discussed in Chapter Seven.

PART 2

Practical Ways of Responding to Trouble

Hurt Lion (He's in Pain)

ANGry LioN

CHAPTER 5

Therapeutic Discipline: Modifying the Discipline Process

It should be clear by now that our patients do not have the interpersonal skills or intrapsychic resources to participate in the discipline process unless we modify and add to it. This is what we mean by *therapeutic* discipline.

Therapeutic discipline modifies the normal discipline process to allow the emotionally disturbed child to complete the discipline step of the socialization process outlined in Chapter Four. In therapeutic discipline, adults stand in for missing ego functions and missing skills, make more of the decisions for children, and develop more explicit and simpler routines to assist the child in meeting adult expectations. Expecting emotionally disturbed children to follow the normal socialization process sets them up for failure, just as restructuring this process is focused on ensuring success. We want this process to go well so that children can return to positive relationships with adults and active participation in other aspects of the program. We want them to be able to experience the relief and pride of regaining control and making amends for past troublemaking.

We have previously discussed the therapeutic modifications

163

to empathy (Chapter Two), communication (Chapter Three), and some aspects of discipline (Chapter Four), when designing the interpersonal holding environment of the treatment setting. In this chapter, we illustrate therapeutic discipline by discussing two major interventions: time-outs and privilege systems. A concluding section summarizes the guiding principles for therapeutic discipline.

Therapeutic Use of the Penalty Step

Giving penalties always goes over better with children if there is some acknowledgment of their feelings about the many aspects of the experience. We can acknowledge their motivation, their dislike of the rule, their dislike of the procedure (time-out, quiet room, restraints), or their opinions about the fairness of our actions.

> Michael (age eight) hated to interrupt his playing to report to the nursing station for his safety checks. He grumbled as he left his game and reported to the nursing station.
> When he returned to the activity, Joy (a nurse) smiled and said, "Congratulations for doing your program. I know how hard it is to leave a good game when you're having so much fun."

> Becky (a counselor) knew how much Raoul (age six) hated taking a time-out on a chair. She had to give him a time-out for teasing Andrew, when he accidentally tipped over the toy building Andrew was building.
> She tried to preface giving the time-out with an acknowledgment of this: "I know you hate it, but you're going to have to take a five-minute time-out for teasing Andrew. I hope it goes fast for you."

We also need to praise any cooperation or compliance that a child can produce, even if it is embedded in a lot of troublemaking. For example, Johnny (age eight) was given an award for "taking your time-out in the quiet room with the door closed and not locked." That was the best he could do, and it was an improvement for him. It was important for us to accept it, if we wanted him to feel proud of it.

Children who need extreme measures such as unit restrictions need a lot of positive recognition for complying peacefully when such cooperation involves the unpleasantness of missing an outing or staying inside on a beautiful day. The temptation is often to dwell on the troublemaking that brought about the restriction. But remember that the restriction communicates the penalty for an offense or the need for more safety. In this way, restrictions and privilege systems allow us the simultaneous capacity for clinical flexibility and structured penalties. Once children are complying with the penalty or restriction, we can address their compliance.

Paul (age nine) was restricted to the unit for trying to run away. Most of the other kids were going out for ice cream. Kathy and John (counselors) stayed behind with the kids who remained on the unit. Paul was moping about, complaining that it was unfair.

In a kind and gentle way, Kathy tried to listen and understand his frustration and sense of injustice. "It must be a drag to stay in all day. I know how you love the van trips. It must have been pretty hard to stay in control all day, knowing that you weren't going tonight."

"Yeah, what good did it do me?" Paul whined.

"The report said you were really good during the day. I heard about what a nice thing you did for Maggie when she was having a fit this afternoon."

At this point, John arrived in the room, holding a tray of cupcakes and a container of ice cream. He announced, "We're going to have a party to celebrate Paul's day shift. He's really learning how to not run away when he's feeling frustrated, angry, and unfairly treated by adults. I'm sorry you aren't on the outing, but Kathy and I wanted you to know how proud we are of your new controls and your kindness to Maggie this afternoon."

Kathy and John were able to find and communicate with the "hero" in the "culprit." If this can happen enough times, maybe we can help Paul find the hero in himself, even when he is still causing trouble. The staff translated their understanding of what was hard for Paul into their congratulations for what he was doing right. He was not running away and he was complying with a treatment program that he didn't like one bit.

Time-Outs

Time-outs are our routine behavioral penalty. Short time-outs are assigned following minor trouble, and longer periods are used along with other actions following major troublemaking. Time-outs are recommended in childrearing manuals and clinical behavioral therapy literature for young and school-age children (Barth, 1986; Clark, 1985). Asking children to take time-outs means asking them to remove themselves from a situation until they can act differently or for a specific period of time. The general practice of removing children can help prevent further trouble. For example:

> Heather (age seven) was watching TV with the rest of the kids. She was cranky and rude. Her remarks to Betsy (a counselor) were becoming louder and more provocative.
>   Betsy asked to speak to her in the hall. "I'm sorry you're having a bad evening, Heather. But I'm not going to let you treat me this way. You have a right to your feelings, but I can't let you talk to me this way. I also can't let you interrupt the program for the rest of the kids. I'd be glad to stay here for a minute and we could have a talk, if you think that will help. Otherwise, please go to your room or the quiet room, until you can control your behavior better."
>   "I don't want to go. I'm not bothering nobody," responded Heather defiantly.
>   "Bill (a counselor) is in the kitchen. You can go and help him with the dishes if you want. You're welcome back when you can be polite."

Our most common use of time-outs involves giving a specified period of time out for a misdeed, such as breaking a rule, swearing, teasing, minor poking or shoving, spitting, or throwing food at the dinner table. These time-outs are usually short (five to ten minutes).

Time-outs should involve "physical," not "psychological," separation for children (Maltsberger, 1980). We need to assign time-outs in such a way that children know that they "have done a five-minute bad thing" and that they are not bad people. They are still good people and welcome members of our community (or family when parents give time-outs) after they have completed the time-outs. We need to spell this out to our patients, because they are often more sensitive to feeling rejected than other children who do not share their histories.

> Donna (age ten) grabbed Paul's seat in front of the TV when he went to the bathroom.
>
> Sue (a counselor) said, "Please take a five-minute time-out for grabbing Paul's seat. I hope you take it right away. We're going to have popcorn soon. We'll wait for you, if you take it right away."

One of the great advantages of this disciplinary action is the children's reaction to it. Since it is usually short, time limited, and matter of fact, children do not build up resentment and lasting grudges about it. Children who have grown up with abuse welcome this consequence without physical pain. Children who have grown up with neglect welcome our attention and concern for them. Children who fear parental rejection are relieved to avoid extended periods of parental disapproval and never-ending criticism. The time-out procedure "cleans up" after the trouble-making and allows children (and adults) to begin anew.

Our patients often behave poorly to increase their time-outs with the staff or their parents when they are participating on the unit. They seem comforted by the predictability and non-lethal consequences of this relatively harmless procedure.

Purpose of Time-Outs

Although the term *time-out* typically refers to "time out from rewarding situations" (Clark, 1985; Patterson, 1976), we believe that time-outs also provide multiple opportunities for learning and psychological change. When we use them preventively, we can teach children to anticipate situations and avoid getting into trouble. When we use them following misdeeds, we can teach children the connection between what they do and what happens later.

Time-outs can accomplish the following goals:

1. *Stop or interrupt* maladaptive behavior, which clears the way for exploring different means of meeting needs or expressing feelings.
2. *Remove* the child from the group: decreasing stimulation for the troubled child; decreasing the contagion effect of the child on the rest of the group and the group's behavior on the child (silliness, anger, disobedience, lack of respect).
3. *Deprive* the child of the pleasure of the activity or the group (act as a negative consequence).
4. *Teach* the connections between actions and consequences (cause and effect).
5. *Foster* digestible amounts of remorse and guilt.
6. *Provide* an opportunity to "pay" for the misdeed and wipe out an internal debt of guilt.
7. *Offer* an opportunity to rethink the situation and regain control (cooling-off period or ego repair).
8. *Prescribe* an adaptive coping strategy—that is, taking a break when you feel upset and are about to do something to get yourself in trouble.
9. *Provide* an opportunity to move from intense and negative emotions to calmer and more positive (or neutral) emotions.
10. *Define and circumscribe* adult disapproval (to a single behavior or incident for a specified period of time).

Time-outs can be either aversive or rewarding, depending on what it means to children to be removed from a situation and on how they use the time away. If children want to play a game or finish an activity or see the end of a TV show, they will find time-outs unpleasant.

But certain children will not find leaving an activity or group to be aversive. They welcome the chance to be alone, to be free of the interpersonal demands of other people, to take a face-saving exit from a losing scene, or to regroup their resources in private. This is why children begin to use the time-outs spontaneously as a way of mastering their disappointment or frustration.

Helen (a therapeutic recreationalist) sat down with Donna (age ten) and Lisa (age eleven) to do their nails. She let Donna use the nail-polish first.

Lisa was furious. "You always pick Donna!" She sat pouting and then reached for the red nailpolish (Donna's favorite).

"Please, may I have that until your turn?" Helen asked Lisa.

Lisa glared at Helen and held the bottle tightly. Suddenly she dropped the bottle on the table and ran into the quiet room.

Helen waited a while and then called into the quiet room, "Your turn, Lisa."

As they were starting her nails, Helen smiled warmly, "Great work, Lisa, you're really learning! You got yourself to some place to cool off, instead of staying around here and resenting Donna while she went first. Good thinking! Do you want to try this new color I bought? I've been saving it for something to celebrate."

Lisa grinned shyly and nodded yes.

Time-outs assist children in building the internal structures of self-control and adaptive coping. Behaviorally disturbed children or ego-deficit children need more explicit help with the process of developing self-control than do healthier children, where the process seems to take place with more ease. The predictability and calmness of the routine are at the heart of why it works. The children's knowledge of the "absolute predictability" of time-outs following certain behaviors contributes to the decelerating effect of the time-outs.

The essential advantage of time-outs for our patients is the children's experience that responsible, caring, and fair adults are in charge, rather than their own anger or the punitive anger of out-of-control adults. Children develop internal control as they imitate and internalize the behavior of calm adults, who act as "rational and nonaggressive models" (Clark, 1985, p. 33). With such adults in charge, children can safely experiment with their powerful emotions and develop adaptive strategies for self-control and mastery. The balance of power in the adult-child relationship is returned to a more optimal level of authority, guidance, useful autonomy, and adult-child harmony.

The clinical literature demonstrates that time-outs do

reduce problem behaviors (Barth, 1986; Wilson and Lyman, 1982). This opens the door for children to explore new ways of meeting their needs or coping with stress or intense emotion. Children learn that aggression, whining, and teasing do not get them what they want. When they try more adaptive ways and these new behaviors receive applause and attention and lead to more fun, children are more likely to increase the use of the new ways over the old problem ways.

How to Use Time-Outs

The basic procedure for assigning time-outs should be routine and simple. This makes it easier for staff to uniformly use it and children to learn it. The parameters for designing effective time-out procedures are described by Barth (1986), Clark (1985), and Wilson and Lyman (1982).

Explain Time-Outs. When children first arrive on the unit, we orient them to time-outs before they need to take them. A staff member and the patient's orientation "buddy" explain and show the new patients how they work. Explanations should include why we use time-outs, what a child does to get a time-out, how long it lasts, and what happens if a child does not take a time-out. Use a demonstration when possible:

> Dr. F (a child psychiatrist) and Jimmy (age ten) explained to Paul (age nine) about time-outs.
> Jimmy started to explain, "They give you a time-out when you break a rule or shove someone or tease or throw food or don't listen to a counselor. You sit on a chair in the hall or in the quiet room. You have to sit there for five minutes, or longer if you're really bad. But they tell you how much time.
> "They turn on a timer or use a watch. If you can't take it in the hallway, you can use the quiet room. You can't argue or talk during time-outs. People can't talk to you during time-outs. When you finish, they ask you why you got time. You tell 'em and go back to your group."
> "Shall we show Paul how it works?" asked Dr. F.
> "Okay, you be the kid and I'll be the counselor."

"Ha, ha, Paul. I spilled glue on your model airplane," taunted Dr. F.

"That's teasing, Dr. F," said Jimmy in a serious voice. "Please take your time-out in the hallway. You can fix Paul's model when you get back."

"No, unfair! Paul started it!" whined Dr. F. "He said my picture is yucky."

"Please take your time now," said Jimmy. "If you don't, I'll have to double your time."

Dr. F glared at Jimmy and went to the chair. He sat on the chair and pouted.

After a pretend five minutes, Jimmy said to Dr. F, "Good work, Dr. F! Your time's up! What did you get time for?"

"Teasing," said Dr. F. "But Paul did it, too."

Use Reminders. When possible, help children avoid getting time-outs by reminding them that they are doing something that will result in a time-out if they continue doing it. We can also give "positive cues," such as offering an alternative way to express feelings or get something. If children have started to misbehave, we can clearly warn them that they will receive a time-out if they continue their behavior. Warnings act as cues for children by labeling problem behavior and giving them an opportunity to stop the behavior on their own. This places more control with the children. The reminders, cues, and warnings should be positive and encouraging, not confrontive and unfriendly. A curt, angry warning — for example, "Go to your room, or I'll cancel your pass!" — can incite an already furious and discouraged child. Here are some constructive examples:

Maggie (age six) giggled and spit her carrots onto her plate. Lynette (a nurse) said, "Maggie, remember the rule about playing with your food at the dinner table. Next time, time-out."

"Johnny (age eight), I see your fist, put it here quick!" said Gino (a therapeutic recreationalist), bringing over a sturdy pillow.

"Maria (age twelve)," Gino suggested, "come hold my hand. I don't want to have to give you a time-out for leaving the group."

Connect to a Specific Behavior. Use time-outs as a response to breaking a rule, minor incidences of aggression, teasing, failing to listen or follow directions, swearing, or disrupting meals or activities.

> Mrs. B (a nurse) said, "Jimmy (age ten), please take a time-out for not listening to me."

> Ellen commented, "Donna (age ten), I understand that you're angry with Lisa for teasing you, but I need to give you a time-out for swearing at her. Please take it now. We'll wait for you. Lisa, please take a time-out for teasing Donna. If you take it now, we can wait for you, too."

Be Polite. Calmly, firmly, and politely ask the children to take a time-out immediately following the misdeed. Always describe the reason for the time-out, without humiliation or blame. Avoid judgmental or abstract accusations such as "irresponsible," "inconsiderate," "uncooperative," or "inappropriate." Start time-outs with "please" and thank the children when they comply (if you think they can digest the thank you).

> Raoul (age six) was jumping on the living room sofas during evening meeting. Peggy (a nurse) had given him two warnings, and he continued to disobey.
>   "Raoul, please take a time-out in the hallway for jumping on the furniture," asked Peggy. "Call in to me when you sit down and I'll start your time." (Raoul starts to leave.) "Thank you."

Include Encouragement. When possible, add something encouraging or consoling as you give the time-out. Some children are motivated to do their penalty when they can sense that we have not given up on them because they have caused trouble again. The time-out conveys our disapproval. We can also add our approval and encouragement to the process.

> Heather (age seven) was pulling out grass and throwing it at Maria (age twelve).
>   Sue (a nurse) approached her and quietly touched her arm.

"Please take a time-out for throwing grass, Heather. I know you can do it, because you have done it before outside. Do you want to sit under that tree over there? It was your lucky tree last week."

Do not use encouragement if you think the child cannot accept the good feeling without becoming more disruptive. Remember that some children can resent your compassion in the midst of their guilt or anger.

Oppositional children can object to taking a time-out because it involves participating with "our" rules and plans. Exhibit 4 is an example of helping children make a time-out part of their "own" way of doing things.

Find a Good Place. Use chairs for time-outs when on the unit. Any chair can be used as a "quiet chair." This means that children can easily and quickly get to a time-out place from any location on the unit. Staff do not need to leave other activities to supervise children in time-outs. Determine that the place is free of distractions and danger. Assess whether children need to be out of sight of the group or whether they can take their time-out on a chair next to the activity.

Do not ask children to take a time-out facing the wall or corner. This body position shames children and defeats the constructive purpose of time-outs. We do not emphasize that time-outs need to take place in a "boring" setting, because we assume that time-outs do not work only as a nonrewarding consequence. Time-outs can involve a "state of mind" and a "state of a relationship." In this sense, you can give a time-out in a car or in a public place that does not allow visual or auditory separation from the group. If you think a child is too distracted, it would be better to offer a time-out in a separate place. Use the quiet room if the child needs reduced stimulation and if you anticipate further trouble. Chapter Six provides a more detailed discussion of the use of the quiet room.

Decide How Much Time. Routine time-outs on the unit are five minutes. Time-outs can also be timed according to children's age, conveying our increasing expectations for older children

Exhibit 4. Paul's Star Chart for Managing Things "My Way."

Paul doesn't like people telling him what to do. This makes him very mad! He is working on taking time-outs in his own way.

Paul gets 1 star ✳ = For going to the time-out chair or quiet room on his own.

1 star ✳ = For not talking out loud during time-outs.

1 star ✳ = For coming out of the quiet room when he has cooled off.

Mon	Tues	Wed	Thurs	Frid	Sat	Sun

When Paul earns 12 stars, he can choose an outside activity to play with the counselor of his choice.

to use more self-control than younger children. A seven-year-old is asked to take seven minutes, indicating that we expect the child to have "seven-year-old controls," while a nine-year-old is asked to take nine minutes, because we expect nine-year-old controls. For minor physical violence (pokes, shoves, pushes) or impulsive threats of violence, the standard unit time-out is ten to fifteen minutes.

When a time-out is a part of a reactive contract responding to a more serious incident (see Chapter Seven), the time-out can be longer. In this case, the child, staff, and program need the extra time to cool down and reorganize following a more disruptive situation.

When children refuse to come back after the time-out is up, we should try to avoid what may be the beginning of a new struggle. If at all possible, we can allow them to use the time-out as long as they feel they need it.

Use a Timing Device. Use a timing device (an egg timer or kitchen timer) when possible. The timer's ticking and concluding ring can be soothing and organizing for children. It also asks them to do business with an object rather than a person at a time when they may not be able to handle the person. Children should be able to see and hear but not touch the timer. Our patients are too tempted to reset the time if they are holding it themselves. We also use our own watches or the unit clocks, which are prominently placed in public areas. These are less useful to children who cannot tell time, and we can easily forget to end a time-out. Young children can be given cards that mark each minute of the time-out (five cards for five minutes). Staff collect the cards from the children as they complete the time-out.

Begin Precisely. A time-out begins when the child is in place and is quiet. A child should be *safely* positioned on the chair. We don't fuss whether a child is "properly" (two feet on the ground) seated in the chair. Our criterion is that all the legs of the chair should be on the ground and that the child's body position is safe.

If the child persists in talking or screaming or is not "in" the chair, we emphasize that the time-out does not begin until the proper conditions are met.

> Jimmy (age ten) walked to the time-out chair, complaining that he was being treated unfairly.
>
> "Please stop talking, Jimmy," asked Dr. D (a psychologist). "Remember that a time-out doesn't start until you're quiet. We can talk about it after you've finished your time-out. I'll listen to you then."
>
> Jimmy continued to balance upside down on the teetering chair. He then sat on the chair and tipped it back against the wall.
>
> "Jimmy, please put all four legs on the floor. That'll be safer and your time-out can begin . . . Thanks," responded Dr. D after he reluctantly complied. "See you in five minutes."

If children refuse to start a time-out, we warn them that we will "double" the time if they do not start the time-out within a specified count (usually one through ten). If children become disruptive (yelling, making noises) during a time-out, we will start the time-out again.

Don't Allow Talking to People. During a time-out, children cannot talk to anyone and no one can talk to them. This includes both adults and peers. It is tempting to sputter on about the misdeed, but it prevents the cooling down and reorganizing (for patient and if necessary staff) that we hope are taking place during the time-out.

We also control our talking to the children, because it is "unfair" to take advantage of a "captive" audience. We can discuss the misdeed after the time-out in a dialogue, when children are allowed to talk. The only exception is when adults briefly praise children for doing well during the time-out as a way of encouraging their continued cooperation.

> Dr. G (a child psychiatrist) walked onto the unit and saw Maggie (age six) sitting quietly on a chair in the hall. As he passed Maggie, he commented, "Good work, Maggie, you're really doing a good job!"

No Distractions. Children in a time-out usually do not have toys or games. Exceptions are made for children who are comforted by "transitional objects" such as a favorite stuffed animal or a picture of a special person or place. Other children may be helped by a particular piece of clothing such as a baseball cap, sweater, or jacket. Some children can agree to participate if they have a selected book to read, just for time-outs.

Our time-out protocol encourages any initiative on the children's part to soothe themselves or do the job of regaining control and taking responsibility for their part of a misdeed.

> Maggie (age six) started yelling at Andrew (age seven) for making "weird" sounds while they were watching TV. She probably thought he was making fun of her.
> Allyson (a nurse) asked Maggie to take a time-out in the hall.
> "Andrew was making fun of me. It's unfair. I won't!" yelled Maggie.
> "Please do it now," Allyson softly requested. "I don't want to double your time, because you might miss the best part of the show. Why don't you take 'Taddy' along with you; he can help you."
> Maggie always slept with her stuffed kitty, Taddy, and Allyson had noticed that she brought Taddy to her psychotherapy appointments.

Clarify the Reality. Always conclude a time-out by asking children what they did to get a time-out. This clarifies whether you and they understand the misdeed in the same way. This should be a matter-of-fact step that does not involve an extensive discussion of the incident. When children give an incorrect answer or say they don't know why they got the time-out, calmly remind them of why you gave them the time-out.

> Pam (a social worker) said, "Time's up, Raoul. What did you get your time for?"
> "Michael should have gotten one too. He started it," replied Raoul (age six).
> "I'm sorry. I didn't see that," said Pam. "Can you tell me what I saw you do?"
> "Calling him a jerk. He is a jerk."

"Okay, Raoul. Your time is over. I hope you can avoid Michael
for a while. Do you want to sit next to me in community meeting?"
"Okay."

Congratulate Children for Completing a Time-Out. Completing
a time-out penalty should "clean the slate" for children. Welcome them back "with open arms" and help them return to the
group or activity. Our friendly and enthusiastic welcome conveys our forgiveness and our pleasure that the incident is over
and "paid for."

   Our congratulations and praise point to what the children are doing right, just as the penalty points to what they did
wrong. This sends children back into the program as "winners."
We need to be active in our help during the transition period,
because children may not have forgiven themselves, accepted
their responsibility for the incident, or given up their resentment toward the people involved in the situation. This resentment may include us, the staff, or their peers. *The situation may
be over for us, but it may still be going on for the children.* We should
congratulate them for whatever part or parts of the process they
did well.

"Time's up, Jimmy. Good job! I know you had trouble getting there,
but you did the rest beautifully!"

Discuss the Incident. When feasible or necessary or when children want it, we should have a dialogue with them about the
incident. Often this should occur after a period of time. This
dialogue is different from the simple step of clarification. During the discussion, children can express their opinions, feelings,
and version of what happened.

   Very often children want to justify their misdeeds. We
help clarify that their feelings are legitimate and justifiable, even
if their actions were not. We want to make clear that physical
violence, disobedience, or teasing cannot be tolerated, even if
we agree with the feelings.

"Do you want to talk about your side of the story after lunch? I don't
have time to do it now and I think we should have some privacy,

what do you think?" Diane (a counselor) asked Jimmy (age ten) following his time-out.

"Paul was bragging about his father. He said his foster family likes him better. He's going home after the hospital."

Diane knew that Jimmy's foster family were unable to keep him and that residential placement plans were being made for him.

"I thought there might have been some reason for you spitting at him. Let's talk later, okay?"

Jimmy looked away but nodded agreement.

Give a Count. If children do not go to a time-out, give them a "count" before you add time or double the time-out. A count is when you ask children to do something within a certain period of time, rather than demanding an immediate response. This approach is particularly useful with children who need to maintain some control over the incident and save face. Going in three seconds when we have given them a count of five seconds feels less coercive to some children.

"Jimmy, please go to your time-out before the count of ten. One . . . two . . . three . . . four . . . good! You did it before I got to five."

Don't Keep Adding Time If Children Will Not Go. If children do not start their time-out when you have already doubled the time-out, do not continue to add more time. If they continue to refuse to take the time-out, we tell them to go to the quiet room or their bedroom until they can start the time-out. In this situation, they can choose to begin the time-out while in the quiet room. Otherwise, we end up with absurd time penalties for minor acts. If children are in a bad mood or trying to get into a struggle, they would welcome this opportunity to take control of the time-out and extend the time. They can then feel properly wronged.

Time-outs should be a way of helping children get in control, not a procedure they can shape according to their moods and oppositional goals. If children are not able to participate in the time-out, we help them find a place to be safe and private until they want to or can cooperate again.

Jimmy (age ten) started giggling after he spit the carrots at Paul.
When Diane (a counselor) gave him a time-out, he started yelling
and giggling louder. He was unable to go to the time-out when she
gave him a count of ten.

"Jimmy, I think you need some time in the quiet room. Call
me when you're ready to start taking your time-out. You can take
it in there if you want."

Jimmy ran into the quiet room, laughing hysterically. Ten
minutes later, he had quieted down and yelled out, "You can start
my time now."

Privilege Systems

The privilege system is the safety net of the treatment program.
It involves a series of steps, organized by levels, that articulate
unit behavioral expectations and values into levels of responsibility and freedom assumed by patients. These levels reflect increasing capacities for internal control, good judgment, and
meaningful participation in treatment. The freedom children
are granted on any level is directly related to the kinds of responsibility they are able to assume. Privilege systems communicate feedback to children about their behavior in a direct, non-
personal, and consistent manner. A point system is one form
of implementing a privilege system; it codifies credit for acceptable and adaptive behavior, with the use of points. We can
also count credit by using stars or stickers for younger children
or credit cards for older children.

*In a privilege system, greater freedom is tied to more mature handling
of individual responsibility.* These interventions describe expectations for the whole group of patients. They complement individualized treatment plans that are created for each child. We try
to describe the privilege system with creativity and imagination
in order to interest, engage, entertain, and validate patients.

Format

The privilege system is organized with graduated levels defined
by increasing patient capacity to exercise control, initiative,
responsibility, motivation for change, and success with individual

treatment goals. Each level can be designated by a letter, number, or name. When patients reach a "higher level," it indicates that they are functioning safely and adaptively and are therefore able to manage higher program expectations and more responsibility for their actions. Privileges can include:

- Use of sharp objects
- Decreasing frequency of staff checks
- Access to particular spaces on the unit
- Access to hospital off-unit spaces
- Passes with particular people to particular places
- Telephone access
- Variations in mealtime and bedtime routines

Point systems use total number of points earned in a particular time period. Points can be given for:

- Maintaining good personal hygiene
- Performing duties
- Following schedules
- Participating in treatment
- Attending school
- Assuming responsibilities
- Working toward individualized treatment goals
- Mature peer interactions
- Respectful treatment of staff, visitors, family

Points earned should not be taken away for undesirable behavior. But points can be "frozen" following serious offenses, and penalties for the specific offense can be given.

Empathy and effective communication should be the basis of the "bookkeeping" aspects of the program. Verbal encouragement and praise should accompany point assignment. Solace and problem-solving help should accompany failures. When children lose privileges we try to convey to them that we want to give them the kinds of responsibilities that they can succeed at. We emphasize individual treatment plans to build the skills needed to assume more responsibility.

The following is a list of general characteristics of effective privilege systems:

1. The system should be integral to the total milieu program.
2. Levels and points should emphasize *any effort shown* and *any success achieved.*
3. Patients should be involved in setting up the individualized parts of their own program.
4. Expectations should be specific to minimize manipulations, loopholes, distortions.
5. The program should be implemented consistently.
6. Patients should be able to progress in the programs (not too hard and not too easy).

Goals

There are many advantages to using a privilege system in a treatment setting. Such a system contributes to the stability of the unit by explicitly and consistently stating unit expectations, values, rules, and standards. This reduces unfair and personalized staff responses to individual patients. This approach also teaches consequences of different kinds of behavior by discouraging maladaptive behavior and rewarding behavior that is mature, adaptive, and positive.

The levels in a privilege system systematically summarize a patient's overall functioning across shifts and over a variety of different situations. This helps changing milieu staff keep track of and monitor each patient's level of control and safety. The criterion for each level is explicit, which helps inexperienced or new and part-time staff familiarize themselves with each patient and respond more uniformly. This promotes safety and protection for all patients and staff.

Connecting consequences and behavior can also motivate patients to meet unit expectations and work on individual treatment goals. When patients have individual treatment goals embedded in each privilege, the program helps to keep goals of hospitalization in the consciousness of patients and staff.

Developmental Design

The programs should be developmentally feasible and attractive to children at different developmental levels of functioning. They should be within the children's physical, cognitive, social, and psychological capacities. This means that programs will differ in language, complexity, maturity, level of behavioral expectations, and balance of self-initiation and staff monitoring. When a unit contains school-age (ages five through nine or ten) and preadolescent or younger adolescent (ages ten to thirteen or fourteen) populations, it is usually necessary to have two simultaneous privilege systems for each developmental age.

Preadolescent programs should emphasize personal responsibility for actions, mature problem-solving strategies, and effective and responsible expression of feelings. Detailed point systems can be used. The following is an example that can be used for preadolescent or younger adolescent patients (from a letter to the author by Stuart Koman, June 1989):

Level I (admission level): Am I safe?
Level II: Am I safe and responsible?
Level III: Am I safe, responsible, and invested?
Level IV: Am I safe, responsible, invested, and a role model?
Level V: Am I safe, responsible, invested, a role model, and mature?

Programs for younger children should emphasize positive skill building and "good" and "safe" ways to solve problems and express feelings. Stars or stickers, given more frequently than points, may be more appealing than point systems. The following is an example of a privilege system for younger children (from a personal communication to the author by Joseph L. Woolston, October 1990):

Level I: Try harder
Level II: Beginner

Level III: Moving up
Level IV: Reaching
Level V: Citizen (mostly attained)

Parent Involvement

When possible, parents should be involved in the development and implementation of privilege systems: adding up points, giving privileges, monitoring steps, or making decisions about level changes (Mirkin and Koman, 1985). This helps children and their parents develop better ways to communicate and negotiate with each other. If parents learn how to implement privilege systems while the child is in the treatment setting, they will be better able to carry out similar programs during hospital contacts with the child and when the child is on pass and eventually at home.

Parents can participate directly during the time they spend on the unit during the parent participation program (see Chapter One) or we can involve them through the telephone. The program also extends to visiting on the unit and passes at home or off the unit.

Conclusion

Therapeutic discipline requires us to be creative, resourceful, and patient to help the children learn from their mistakes. We need to pay meticulous attention to what is usually a more spontaneous and invisible process of discipline. We will conclude this chapter with a summary of "commandments" for therapeutic discipline that incorporate our tone and actions at each phase of the process.

We try hard to (our ideals):

• Help the child before the penalty is necessary
• Make good rules and structure with reasonable limits
• Communicate our reasons and limits
• Use the child's strengths
• Convey empathy for feelings and impulses

- Be sympathetic to the child's feelings about the limit or penalty
- Be matter of fact and kind
- Be patient
- Be clear and direct about reason for, duration of, and conditions of the limit or penalty
- Stress that the penalty is for a behavior, not a person
- Discuss alternatives
- Praise any compliance that we can see
- Remain as affectionate and friendly as possible and clinically acceptable to the child
- Accept apologies and reparations
- Forgive (so that the child can learn how)

When we can't follow these guidelines, we will ask for help from our colleagues.

We try hard not to (we are not saints):

- Convey hostility, aggression, anger, impatience, or triumph over our greater power
- Convey disapproval and rejection of the person, not the act
- Act out of revenge
- Act out of anger
- Be humiliating or hurtful
- Blame the child
- Use threats
- Use more force than necessary

When we do these things, we will apologize.

We will never (we have limits, too):

- Physically harm a child
- Initiate or respond to sexual interactions with children
- Be punitive or seductive

When we do these things, we will be put on probation or terminated from our job.

Co Nfused
Lion

CHAPTER 6

Working with the Overwhelmed Child: Rationale and Techniques

In Phase I of therapeutic management, we created the environmental and interpersonal holding environment for all children (described in Chapters One through Five). In Phase II of therapeutic management, we create the clinical interventions for the relationship-resistant, undersocialized, and ego-deficit children who are unable or only partially able to respond to therapeutically designed structure, empathy, communication, and discipline. These children become overwhelmed with intense negative emotions or the expectations and demands of childhood tasks and relationships.

Chapters Six and Seven discuss therapeutic responses to the troublemaking of the overwhelmed child. Chapter Six describes action-oriented techniques required to stop and contain a child's maladaptive and dangerous behaviors: quiet rooms; physical holding; seclusion; mechanical restraints; and psychopharmacotherapy, including chemical restraints. Chapter Seven describes techniques that help children do the psychological work of transitioning back into program structure and relationships following behavioral crises.

During Phase II, children need protection and safety in the form of external controls before they can develop or rebuild internal controls. Seclusion, holding, and restraints are not used as punishments. *They are only used for children who are unable to participate in the normal socialization process (including the discipline and punishment steps) without them.*

Why Children Need Active Containing Interventions

Effective use of physical holding, seclusion, and mechanical or chemical restraint can demonstrate that adults care about children and that there can be control in the arms of another person, within restraints, from a wall, or from a medication, when a child cannot find that control alone.

> Johnny (age eight) threw a chair at Lisa (a counselor). When he refused to go to the quiet room as a consequence for this serious assault, Lisa called two other counselors, Brent and Steve, in order to safely transport him to the quiet room. Once in the quiet room, they physically held him.
>
> While he was safely on the floor in a stable hold, Lisa told Brent and Steve how Johnny could no longer contain his anger and feelings of being left behind after he heard that his grandmother was unable to take him on pass the next day.
>
> When Johnny threw the chair at Lisa, the staff needed to contain what he was unable to contain before they could begin to repair and rebuild. His old maladaptive ways of coping with his pain—anger, assault, and swearing—stood in the way of his developing healthier ways of managing and coping. For Johnny, the crisis caused by his throwing a chair was preferable to his tolerating sadness and anger.

This example illustrates that *treatment starts with stopping and containing behavior before it can move on to recruiting existing resources, building new skills, and developing insight* (the work of Phase III). If we do not intervene effectively, our nonintervention can seem like an intervention to children through the use of projection. Children may attribute their own anger and retaliatory fantasies to us, so that they experience the crisis and subsequent pain and confusion as our doing. Our failure to intervene can fuel children's fears of their own destructiveness or omnipotence. Containment can prevent them from going on to greater violence or destruction, with its subsequent burden of more guilt and shame.

Ambivalent or vacillating responses on our part can increase children's need to test the limits and controls of the setting and the staff. Their behavior is asking who is stronger and more effective. Violent or destructive children create fear in others and are frightened of themselves and adults (Drisco, 1976). Many children become frantic if they succeed in hurting another child or an adult. They fear retaliation based on real and fantasized versions of past hurt.

There are developmental, biological, psychological, and behavioral reasons why overwhelmed children need action-oriented techniques.

Temperamentally, they may have started out from birth with difficult predisposing or inherited characteristics that make it harder for their parents to console them, to aid them in establishing basic routines, to socialize their emotional lability, to help them develop internal controls over impulses, and to assist them in developing adaptive coping behavior and good judgment.

Biologically, these children frequently have attentional problems, hyperactivity, and learning and language disorders.

Neurologically, they may have subtle deficits that distort their experience of the world and cause acute agitation, anxiety, and aggressiveness.

Psychologically, the internal lives of our patients do not have sustaining images of loving people, positive self-concepts, or capacities to regulate intense and troubling emotions. Parents lacking in childrearing skills may not have provided the mix of nurturance and limit setting that fosters the development of internal control, competence, and positive self-esteem and smooths the path for subsequent successful development.

Children who use our active containing interventions have the full spectrum of psychiatric problems, which make them unable to:

- Use external structure constructively
- Attend persistently
- Tolerate frustration, anxiety, and the full range of negative affects: sadness, despair, anger, low self-esteem
- Stop and think before they act and regulate their activity or impulses
- Use language to express feelings or negotiate conflict
- Behave according to the expectations of their setting or the adults in authority

They are less sensitive to consequences or language-based socialization interventions than other children (Barkley, 1987; Forehand and McMahon, 1981; Patterson, Reid, and Dishion, 1992). Some also have trouble accurately perceiving the motivations, feelings, and expectations of the setting and the supervising adults. Therefore, they do not learn from their mistakes in the course of normal socialization.

We must also consider the interaction of these difficulties with the developmental impact of social situational and family history variables, such as poverty, paternal psychopathology and criminality, and family disruption due to death, divorce, or numerous out-of-home placements. As mapped by Patterson and his colleagues (Patterson, 1965, 1975, 1976; Patterson, Cobb, and Ray, 1973; Patterson, Reid, and Dishion, 1992; Patterson, Reid, Jones, and Conger, 1975), some families suffer from negative cycles that have been created over the years. Inherited predispositions to behavioral and emotional problems in these families interact with constitutional patterns of difficult temperaments, family stresses, environmental stressors, and inadequate parenting skills.

In such cases, the basic parent-child relationship, which is the foundation of all later disciplinary action, has not been built to last or to adapt to the changing needs of each developmental period. The relationship channel for therapeutic interventions has been blocked. We need a different foundation on which development of internal control can start to grow again.

Thus, in this model of therapeutic management, the immediate response to a child's crisis behavior is as therapeutic or important as the insight-oriented and skill-building techniques of other phases of therapeutic management. *The patient determines how and when we act or talk.* We think of "active treatment measures" as "differing in degree rather than in kind" from verbal interventions (Susselman, 1973, p. 528): "It is a reflection on the degree of psychopathology and ego interpretation whether the therapist does the interrupting with physical restraint, the most active measure, or whether the patient does it while the therapist observes and verbalizes about the patient's actions. . . . As the patient learns to assume a more active role in intervention, the role of the therapist becomes more inactive."

Separating, restraining, secluding, and medicating are legitimate and necessary responses to aggressive, disruptive, or self-destructive patient distress. As we emphasize throughout this four-phase model, understanding, kindness, psychopharmacotherapy, and talking will not replace the need for active containing interventions if the patient is unable to "make use" of the latter. The therapeutic question is "what and when" rather than "either-or."

Serious mental illness cannot be treated with the more permissive or passive approaches to "acting out" behavior sanctioned by classic psychoanalytic approaches advocated by past milieu therapists (Aichorn, 1935; Bettelheim, 1950, 1955; Redl and Wineman, 1951, 1952). More active measures emerged as legitimate treatment interventions when clinicians began to treat schizophrenic, autistic, or ego-deficit children (Hoedemaker, 1960; Szurek and Berlin, 1973) and severely and acutely disturbed adults (Gutheil, 1982a, 1982b, 1982c). For these children and adults, interpretations of their problem behavior and exploration of their pasts led to devastating regressions, or the children just ran away. Talking and caring fell like seeds on rocks. Treatment programs that do not have use of active containing interventions will need to disrupt the treatment process with transfers and discharges during the intermittent behavioral crises that are inevitable for seriously disturbed children.

In our model, helping children contain and rechannel impulsive and maladaptive behaviors does not replace therapeutic efforts to bring about psychological and personality change; rather, physical containment of symptoms lays the groundwork for positive development and psychological change.

Pros and Cons of Active Containing Techniques

Both clinicians and children have a variety of responses to these interventions.

Clinicians' Feelings About the Technique

Most clinicians are ambivalent about physically or mechanically restraining children. These interventions are distasteful as well as legally and ethically problematic for most of us. In the treatment of severely disturbed children, a fundamental incompatibility often exists between the children's physical, developmental, clinical, and legal rights. Legally, these techniques pose a serious challenge to the most basic tenets of our system of justice, focused as it is on the protection of rights and freedom. The legal issues surrounding their use have been addressed recently in the psychiatric and legal literature (Tardiff, 1984, 1989). Lawmakers and lawyers have been concerned about these interventions, which so clearly impinge on civil liberties.

I remember a psychology graduate student, also a lawyer, who terminated his placement on the unit after two weeks, because he was appalled by the use of seclusion with young children. He viewed it as a flagrant abuse of the child's civil liberties. Unfortunately, he was unable to stay around to learn enough about childhood psychopathology to understand the conditions under which children's clinical needs take precedence over their civil liberties. I wished it had not been his first-year clinical placement.

In fact, our intention is to use those clinical interventions that create the best balance of the child's conflicting needs. In every situation, regardless of the severity of the child's psychopathology or the dangerousness of the situation, a child's individual dignity is always upheld.

Ethically, the use of these techniques seems to run counter to our humanistic intuitions about the proper treatment of children. Like the children we treat, we can fail to distinguish between the caring and noncaring use of physical restraints and seclusion. Over three-quarters of the patients we treat have experienced physical and/or sexual abuse. In fact, it is these traumatized children who often require more physical interventions.

In supervision, Dr. F (a child psychiatrist) told me how awful she
felt when Heather (age seven) screamed out, "You are burning
me! Stop! Stop!" This was during the extended physical holds that
she required, particularly at bedtime.

Heather was in the hospital because her behavior in day
treatment had become too bizarre and disorganized to manage
in that setting. She is sexually and aggressively impulsive with her
siblings and peers.

As a toddler, Heather had been scalded in a bathtub on
many occasions by her psychotic mother, who was apparently trying to "cleanse" her daughter after she was found masturbating.
Dr. F was learning the tragic way in which abused children reenact
their traumas to remember, tell, and hopefully begin repairing.

To Heather, this retelling was an unconscious process. Dr.
F and other staff learned to hold Heather when she needed it and
to help the holding be different this time. We established a routine, using simple words to convey the same message with each
hold: "I will protect your body from harm until you can do it for yourself. Your body does not deserve to be hurt anymore. I am sorry
it was hurt in the past."

Ambivalence about these techniques is stimulated by at
least two aspects of our experience using them: (1) a general
ambivalence about the "nasty" side of mental illness, which is
violence; and (2) the very real unpleasantness we experience
during and after our use of these techniques with struggling children (Lion, 1987). We have to master our ambivalence about
using these techniques in order to treat seriously disturbed children. Childhood pathology is no minor thing. It distorts what
is normal, it poisons what is good, and it destroys positive development while it pathologically preserves patients' fragile
defenses and selves.

Using these techniques is not without personal struggle,
and hopefully, personal growth for therapists. We are not immune to the disappointment, repulsion, and anger we feel when
children do not respond to our kindness and understanding or
when they deliberately hurt us. These incidents are emotionally and physically draining. They challenge our basic beliefs
about ourselves and our patients, as they reveal the uglier and

darker sides of relationships and feelings. We continuously need to struggle with the feelings and thoughts stimulated by these moments.

Children's Reactions to the Interventions

Over the years, staff have questioned whether these active containing interventions cause more trouble than they contain or stop. They point out that with some children, the more you hold and lock, the more they seem to ask for more holding and locking. The adult psychiatric literature also points out that containing impulse-ridden patients can initially cause negative results, because the patients have been robbed of their lifelong pattern of using action to defend against intense emotions (Mackinnon and Michels, 1971; Rosen and DiGiacomo, 1978).

If we saw these techniques purely in behavioral terms, we would conclude that for these children we should discontinue their use, because they are "rewarding" for the children. This viewpoint is widely held among some clinicians, who warn us that some children will continue to act up because they like the "attention," they like the opportunity to "manipulate" staff, and they will not use their own controls, because it is easier to use our techniques to control them.

I agree that some children not only like these techniques, they actively seek them out. However, I am not troubled by this. Some children experience a profound relief that at last there is something bigger than their anger, their anxiety, their fear, or the voices and delusional people that have ruled their lives. When children are unable to rely on relationships with people to help them keep or regain control, they feel less vulnerable when the help is more routine, more mechanical, or less personal.

Restraints and walls cannot strike back or verbally insult a child. They do not ask for obedience and love, which are so hard or scary to give. They do not get offended and stay unforgiving about what is said or done to them. They do not make mistakes. They are not sexual.

The gratification and relief our children feel are rarely conscious, and if they are, our patients rarely express these emotions to us. Just as healthier children rarely thank their parents for limits or punishments given when the children do not follow those limits, our patients rarely thank us for our limits and consequences.

We do have some indication from children about the positive side of their experience of these techniques, however. David Fassler and I asked children to draw pictures about the seclusion experience on the unit. Figures 2, 3, and 4 depict why children go into seclusion: fighting, swearing, and teasing. Figure 5 illustrates "what you do in the quiet room." Finally, Figure 6 depicts "how you feel after coming out of the quiet room." Each child's sequence of pictures usually illustrates the child's awareness of the changing emotions—from mad to sad to happy—during the seclusion process.

**Figure 2. Child's Drawing of Why Children
Go to the Quiet Room: Fighting.**

Figure 3. Child's Drawing of Why Children
Go to the Quiet Room: Swearing.

Figure 4. Child's Drawing of Why Children
Go to the Quiet Room: Teasing.

Figure 5. Child's Drawing of What You Do in the Quiet Room.

Figure 6. Child's Drawing of How You Feel
After Coming Out of the Quiet Room.

A positive experience with these interventions depends on our effective use of them and our explanations of why we use them. Can children understand and believe what we tell them about why we use them? We know that without our explanations, they will develop their own theories about what we do and why. We need to find ways of translating our clinical rationale into the language and cognitive understanding of the children who will use these techniques.

The literature on children's perceptions of aspects of psychiatric hospitalization reveals that children can move from stereotyped views to more accurate understanding as they experience treatment and are given opportunities to discuss their problems or treatment (Roth and Roth, 1984). Active containing techniques require a lot of discussion to distinguish them from their abusive variants in the lives of neglected and abused children. Physical holding can look and feel like a street brawl. Locked-door seclusion is similar to the locked closets of children's nightmares or real traumas of the past. Mechanical restraints look and feel like the belts of past abuse or horror movies. And what is the difference between the calm following medication and the calm following the alcohol and heroin ingested by their parents or the kids down the street?

The active containing interventions require explanations before and after their use, to make them therapeutic for the child. Of course, the words of explanation and understanding may be far away in time and place from the incident. We use the words when the child can listen and use them.

Lisa started a column in the unit newspaper called "Dear Gabby." I was Gabby, because I talk a lot. Lisa's letter to me (Exhibit 5) was written twenty-four hours after an incident in which she used both physical holding and seclusion. My return letter to Lisa is printed in Exhibit 6.

Guidelines for Selective Use of Interventions

State statutes, administrative regulations, and institutional policies and procedures try to arrange active containing interventions along a continuum according to the relative restrictiveness or intrusiveness of the intervention. The assumption is that techniques to be used first are more humane or "less restrictive." However, there is no agreement among clinicians or lawmakers as to the specific ordering of techniques on this continuum.

In our approach, we do not assume that techniques can be graded on a set continuum of restrictiveness. First, the notion

Exhibit 5. Lisa's Letter to Gabby.

Dear Gabby answered by
our boss and our best friend magic.
Why do people hold us down
Why are some people mean and some
nice it confusits me.
Why do they lock us in the Blue
room.
why do the conselers spend
most of their time in the
conferenca room they lock them
selves in there:

           by
           Lisa B.

Exhibit 6. Gabby's Letter to Lisa.

Dear Lisa,

Thank you for your important questions. It is confusing. Even some adults do not see why we need to lock doors on kids and hold the kids down. Especially because the kids are not bad kids. They are really good kids who do bad things.

We lock you up because you deserve help and protection when you can not lock up your kicks, punches, and spitting. When you can use words to tell us your feelings, we know you will not hurt us, the other kids, or yourself. I know you were angry with me yesterday for giving you time. You really wanted to hurt me. Today you and I were friends and you made me a picture for my office. I know you were glad today that the staff did not allow you to hurt me yesterday.

We hold you down so that you can use our controls, when you can not find your own controls. When you find your own controls, we can let you hold down your own anger. Right now you cannot do that because your anger has grown very high and strong and your controls have stopped growing so they are small and weak. The situation looks like this:

LISA'S ANGER

LISA'S CONTROLS

Exhibit 6. Gabby's Letter to Lisa, Cont'd.

We can help you grow your controls so that the situation
will look like this:

LISA'S ANGER

LISA'S CONTROLS

Controls grow when adults give kids lots of *love* with kisses, hugs,
and attention, and lots of _teaching_ with rules, limits, punishments
and timeouts, and lots of _protection_ from meanness and neglect.
You deserve more love, teaching, and protection than the adults
in your life have given you. They tried, but they did not know
what you needed and how to give it. You try too. But you
do not know how to grow and use your controls. I am glad
you and your parents came to the unit so that you and
your parents can learn how to do these things.

The staff goes into the office because we sometimes
get too tired, too frustrated, and too angry when we are
helping the kids. We go into the office to find our controls
and to cool off. This is like when we encourage kids to go
into the quietroom when they need to find their controls.
We do not want to be unfair or stop caring or stop
protecting the kids because we are angry or tired or
frustrated. We will never leave you alone, we will
always ask other staff to take over the kids while
we are resting and cooling off. We do not lock the
door, but we close the door. Sometimes we feel so
bad we cry. Other staff help us feel good and then
we can laugh and work again. We still like the kids,
but sometimes we feel too angry or too sad with
what the kids do.

I hope you know that adults get sad and
angry just like the kids do. I will only hire
adults who have grown big, strong controls, because
the staff are not allowed to lose their controls
when they are working with the kids.

I hope I answered your questions. They were
good questions! Keep asking good questions and
keep growing your controls.

Your friend,
Gabby Cotton

of "restrictiveness" applies more to the restricting of a patient's civil liberties than it does to any changing clinical status of a patient. Second, it is impossible to establish from outside an individual patient whether one intervention is experienced internally as more-or-less negative (or helpful) than another intervention. Which of several limit-setting procedures will be incorporated into an overall treatment plan is determined on the basis of the developmental and clinical status of the individual child and the characteristics of the situation, not on general protocols or staff preferences.

The therapeutic selection of one technique over another depends on the presence and interaction of factors within the child and the situation. The factors within the child include:

- Psychiatric diagnosis
- Ego strength
- Developmental level of functioning
- History and specific nature of trauma if it was present
- History of aggressive or self-injurious behavior
- Phase in the course of treatment

The situational factors include:

- Staffing — number and training of available people
- Location of the incident, on or off unit
- Access to a quiet room or restraints
- Presence of other patients or nonpatients
- Assessment of the risks of different management options

Some children never use either seclusion or restraints, while other children may use a particular intervention or mix of interventions extensively during the course of their treatment.

Developmental considerations would also lead us to select one particular technique rather than another. For example, we recommend physical holding for young children who are still gaining controls within their attachments to adults. Because of their cognitive functioning, younger patients may be unable to comprehend the use of belts for restraint rather than assault. Adolescents, on the other hand, may benefit more from the use of mechanical restraints where they can regain control independent of the adults from whom they also need to separate. Sexual issues complicate the active use of physical holding for older patients and for patients with histories of sexual abuse. Similarly, psychopharmacological interventions are more problematic in families where alcohol and drugs have been abused and are associated in the child's experience with trauma.

Thus, a child's personal history may preclude the use of certain interventions if they will retraumatize the child. For example, children who have been tortured in locked places or with belts or tied to furniture have special needs when they are in need of external limits.

Sequence of Events Leading to Use of Active Containing Interventions

The techniques of this phase are clearly matched to children who are unable to use verbal interventions or self-control. Staff and children usually start off with something minor, and somehow it turns into something major. The ordinary incident occurs when a child is unable to take a penalty or consequence (usually a time-out) given for the infraction of minor rules (Joshi, Capozzoli, and Coyle, 1988). Confusion can arise when we associate the final consequence (use of one containing intervention or another) with the relative insignificance of the initial problem behavior. This sequence does not occur with healthier children and adults in other settings, because the healthier child heeds the warning or more minor limit.

However, in the clinical setting, we adopt a "one-step-ahead" approach." We take seriously lesser forms of aggression and deterioration of behavioral control, such as verbal aggression, aggressive agitation, misuse of property, or failure to obey supervising adults, to prevent escalation toward total loss of control.

If a child swears, is given a time-out, and can take the time-out on a chair, physical intervention techniques will not be necessary. However, many children cannot take time-outs at the beginning of treatment or at particular times during the course of their treatment. When adults confront them with a limit, even if the rule violation was a minor one, they become belligerent, agitated, or deliberately more oppositional.

> Maggie (age six) was watching Friday night movies with staff and other children. Trying to make herself more comfortable, she began to gather the pillows around herself. She and Heather (age seven) had been sharing their space and pillows on the couch. When Heather finally objected to her diminishing share of the pillows, Maggie grabbed all of the pillows and moved to the floor.
> Heather was in tears. Maggie was asked to give half of the pillows to Heather, which she did, calling out, "Heather is a baby! Heather is a baby!" She was given a time-out for teasing. Within thirty minutes, Maggie was in locked-door seclusion after kicking Diane, the counselor.

This was not unusual for Maggie. Described by her parents as unmanageable at home, the staff knew she was unable to live by the rules or accept the negative consequences imposed by adults when she broke the rules. Earlier in the evening, Diane had the foresight to suggest that Maggie and Heather separate the pillows equally and move to separate spaces. As is so often the case, Diane and her co-workers were unable to defuse, de-escalate, or redirect Maggie from her irreversible course of action.

It is important to note that Maggie did not experience the event as we did. In her view, we were favoring Heather just like her parents favored her younger brother. She complained that they never asked if he did anything wrong, always assuming that it was she who caused any trouble. Once we had taken Maggie's perspective into consideration, it became clear that the meaning of these events was not minor to her. Even so, it is crucial to realize that even if we understood Maggie's *feelings,* we still needed to give the same consequences for her *behavior* or "way of telling us about them." *Empathy complements but does not replace limit setting in therapeutic management.*

Avoiding Misuse or Abuse of Control Techniques

The use of these techniques is not always therapeutic. Control techniques are abusive or inadequate when:

- They are used as substitutes for individualized and comprehensive treatment.
- They are used as corporal punishment.
- They are used for the convenience of staff.
- They are used for staff revenge.
- They are not professionally or clinically implemented.

Control techniques are used in a clinically indicated and legally sensitive manner when:

- They are part of a process that promotes the development of internal controls, while maintaining the dignity of the patient.
- They are defined in formalized policies and procedures.
- They are conducted in a consistent manner.
- They are used for predictable reasons.
- They are clinically indicated.
- They are explained to the child before and after their use.
- They are implemented by well-trained, professionally and humanistically oriented staff.
- Their use is supervised and monitored by professionally trained staff.
- They are administered in a safe, attractive, soothing space.

These conditions must exist if treatment strategies of any kind are to be humane and effective with severely disturbed children.

When self-control and judgment are consistently impaired, the process of treatment requires a balancing of civil liberties with clinical and developmental needs. A disturbed child is not benefited and is, in fact, harmed when the treatment setting does not address all of these needs. Table 9 translates our developmental-clinical rationale for the use of these techniques into the language of "rights."

How Do We Implement These Techniques?

Hospital policy and procedure manuals detail the responsibilities of physicians, nurses, and counseling staff during these

Table 9. Patients' Rights for Severely Disturbed Children.

1. The right of children to be protected from the need to interact with people when they are unable to experience people as trustworthy, helpful, or safe.
2. The right of children to be protected from accruing more burdens of shame and guilt from continued violent and destructive acts.
3. The right of children to be protected from hurting themselves during periods of self-loathing.
4. The right of children to experience an adult world as capable of providing external control when their internal controls break down.
5. The right of children to have responsible adults make decisions for them when they are unable to make responsible decisions for themselves.
6. The right of children to receive discipline that is reasonable, constructive, and logical and that does not exceed their capacity to participate in the discipline process.
7. The right of children to another chance at normal socialization experiences with caring and competent adults with whom they can identify.

procedures. Table 10 outlines what should be included in a protocol or policy and procedure for the use of the active containing techniques (Fassler and Cotton, 1992).

In hospitals and treatment settings, the techniques of seclusion and mechanical and chemical restraints require a physician's order and frequent evaluation for the duration of the intervention. Monitoring for physical and psychological side effects is essential to maintaining the proper therapeutic use of these interventions. Detailed protocols help to routinize the procedures across different shifts or individual differences in staff management of crisis situations.

Most protocols include outside scrutiny of these practices through institutional and outside regulatory monitoring processes. Many states require various layers of authorization and clinical review of the use of some of these techniques. These processes can offer helpful feedback on particular incidents and patterns that may not be obvious to the staff who utilize the interventions daily. That is, while the expressed purpose of these reviews is to protect against abuse, they also offer an opportunity to validate a staff's skill in handling a particularly difficult patient or pattern of patients. Once abuse of procedures has not been found, it is hoped that review committees will communicate

Table 10. Protocol Outline for a Control Technique.

---

1. *Policy.* Discusses the philosophy or background of the use of the technique. Includes the purpose or goals of the technique. Specifies the conditions under which the technique can be used and must not be used.
2. *Supportive data or references.* Cites state, regulatory agency, institutional, and departmental laws, regulations, policies, procedures, and protocols; relevant articles and books used to develop the approach; and orientation and teaching manuals and other material.
3. *Content.* Specifies definitions and describes situations (emergency, treatment). Outlines orientation, training, credentialing, and recertification process for use of the technique.
4. *Procedures.* Specifies process of implementation, including *clinical responsibilities* of physician, nurse, counseling staff; *sequence of steps* for implementation; *time constraints* on particular procedures; attention to *patient needs* for dignity, privacy, hygiene, toileting, feeding, drinking, and release periods during the procedure; *documentation* requirements (where, what, by whom, when, authorization); concurrent clinical *tests and examinations* to be administered; time periods and documentation requirements for *staff monitoring* and criteria for observation of physical and psychological side effects of the technique; procedures and criteria for *incident reports; place and equipment* and proper conditions of place and equipment; *criteria and procedure for termination* of the intervention; *steps following the technique* (patient access to complaint procedures, institutional and extrainstitutional review process); process for *reporting of violations* of policy or procedure.
5. *Forms.* Includes copies of hospital seclusion and restraint forms, incident report forms, safety or side-effect checklists, and Department of Mental Health or Public Health seclusion and restraint forms.

---

their finding of relevant and good treatment. The silence of review committees about the discovery of good treatment can stimulate staff doubt, ambivalence, and guilt about their use of these techniques. The goal is a collaborative partnership between the staff and outside regulatory agencies in the best interests of the children.

Active Containing Techniques

Phase II exerts external control through active containing interventions: separation in quiet rooms, physical holding; seclusion; mechanical restraints; and psychopharmacotherapy, including chemical restraints. The message conveyed in these interventions is: *We will be your controls until you can find or grow your own controls.*

During crisis situations, we act to maintain safety as the foundation on which all treatment is built. We can then do the work of other phases: help children redirect their feelings and find alternative behaviors to express their feelings and impulses.

Gutheil's (1978) three general principles for the use of seclusion apply to all active containing interventions. They are:

1. *Containment* to provide reassurance to out-of-control patients by keeping them safe from self-harm and the ward safe from their dangerous and disruptive behaviors.
2. *Isolation* to provide an "oasis" of relief to seriously ill patients who may be experiencing the demands of adult-child and peer relationships in distorted ways, leading to fear, distrust, and anxiety.
3. *Decrease in sensory input* to provide sensory relief to patients who are vulnerable to sensory overload.

We add the *developmental principle* as a fourth principle. It recognizes the immaturity of children who are still in the process of developing inner controls, defenses, and coping and interpersonal skills (Cotton, 1989; Gair, 1984, 1989).

These active techniques protect and control children without hostility or cruelty. When we have done this for a child, we are beginning a new set of experiences and memories of adults who control out of caring and concern. It is a part of the total therapeutic process of helping children make certain fundamental distinctions: children learn to distinguish between safe and unsafe feelings and between caring adults who do *not* lose their controls and caring (or perhaps uncaring) adults who *do* lose their controls. We enlist the parents of our patients to participate in this, as in all phases of treatment with their children. In this way, we can help both the child and the parents develop safe and caring controls.

Quiet Rooms

One of the first steps in active containing interventions is often placing a child in a special room, away from the rest of the population.

The first problem is what to name this room. Do we name it for what happened before a child enters it, such as "hitting room," "out-of-control room," "anger room," or — as the children suggest — the "crazy room" or the "bad room"? Do we name it for what we hope the child will experience or do in the room, such as the "freedom room" (Schulman and Irwin, 1982), "control room," "cool-down room," "safety room," "privacy room," "work room," or "quiet room"?

The problem with each name is that it describes only one purpose of a multipurpose room. Our unit once avoided the issue by naming it the "blue room," after the color of its walls. The neutral name at least avoided a negative, judgmental, or narrow definition of its use (although at least one child thought it was painted blue because it made children cry!).

We decided on "quiet room" because most of the purposes of the room were accomplished when the child became quiet. If I were to name it today, I would probably call it the "work room," because it expresses our philosophy that regaining control or growing controls involves hard work, and it gives credit to the child who does this work. It also labels the positive work that children do when they try to cool down, take a penalty after a misdeed, or remove themselves from a disturbing group experience.

Design. The design of our rooms expresses the multipurpose use of these rooms. We designed a room that would function like children's bodies and egos. At the extreme end of the continuum, the rooms provide protection and control when their bodies are out of control and their egos are not in working order. Design features that accomplish this task include hardwood doors and trim; tamperproof screws; vandalproof lighting; vomit- and urine-resistant carpeting; easily cleaned Kydex-lined walls, which do not give way to scratches, punches, or kicks; low-pile carpet, installed under baseboards affixed with tamperproof screws; thick Plexiglas window covers; windows to the outside lined with Mylar, allowing the child to look out but preventing people from looking in; tamperproof heating, air-conditioning, and air supply vents, located high in the ceiling; metal plates with rounded corners to strengthen hardwood doors; observation windows; soundproofing; and vandalproof door locks.

The room was built for a big temper tantrum. It is a safe place to be, when a child's rage and disappointment hit. It is also a less stimulating space than bedrooms or other treatment spaces. In addition, the room was designed to reflect the changing mood and increasing control that a child will experience in the quiet room. The room invites a return to "normal" with the use of the following design features:

- A neutral color tone to resonate with changing moods, rather than one color to dictate a particular feeling state
- A bench one and a half feet long to sit or lie on
- Carpeting on the floor and bench
- Attractive materials, such as wood panels between strips of Kydex to suggest a small den-type space
- A window looking onto an attractive or interesting scene, which orients the child to time of day, season, and normal activities
- Wall hangings between the Plexiglas and the windows

The quiet rooms are small (forty-six and thirty-five square feet), cozy spaces. They resemble the small spaces that school-age children seek out to construct clubs, tree houses, imaginary homes for their Barbies and stuffed animals, and retreats for themselves when they are feeling overwhelmed by the "big" demands of the "big" adult world.

Michael (age eight) had been accident prone as a young child. On the unit, he made deliberate efforts to hurt himself. He was intelligent and physically competent. However, he was unable to use words to express his feelings. Barbara (a nurse manager) sent him to the quiet room after he had persisted in jumping from the living room window sills and furniture. Behind the Plexiglas wall, this quiet room was decorated with a cloth hanging with small squares depicting different stages of the weather: sun, clouds, rain, thunder, lightning, partly sunny and partly cloudy, and a rainbow.

When Michael calmed down, Barbara went in the quiet

room, sat on the bench, and asked, "Do you feel like this?" (pointing to the thunder-and-lightning scene).

Yes, Michael nodded.

"I saw Paul tease you when you were playing with Heather. I gave him a time-out for teasing. Heather wants you to come back and finish the game with her. Shall I tell her that you'll come back, when the sun comes out? Point to the right picture to let me know when you're ready, okay?"

The panels of the wall hanging allow us to identify and "talk" about feelings to young children who are unable to identify or find words for their intense feelings.

The quiet room is designed to be a less stimulating and less interpersonally demanding setting for children to maintain control when it is tenuous, to not get into bigger trouble, or to regain mastery over their behavior following a behavioral crisis. We encourage children to remove themselves spontaneously to the quiet room when they need it. In fact, many children list the quiet room as their favorite place on the unit.

Multipurpose Use. Unlike many quiet rooms, our rooms were designed to be used by both staff and children during all phases of treatment. At one extreme, the rooms can be locked and used for seclusion. At the other extreme, children can use them for solitary play, private talks with counselors, or homework. Quiet rooms are also used as spaces for staff to do paperwork, receive supervision, interview job applicants, or have lunch and cool off after frantic mornings. Children are initially surprised when they see staff in the quiet room, but we welcome the opportunity to tell them that we like quiet places to do our work and that sometimes we need some time away from people to cool down our feelings.

The multipurpose use of these rooms counteracts the children's perception of the room as the "bad room" for "bad people," where good people do not go. In the same way, we try to counteract the children's self-perception of being bad people, rather than people who do bad things. We want to convey the message: "This room is like your body. It contains good feelings and bad feelings. We built this room to be strong and secure, so that it can hold all the feelings—the big ones and the little ones, the good ones and the bad ones. The room wants to give you the comfort and protection that it feels you deserve all the time. We want to help your body welcome and be kind to all your feelings, just like the room does."

Physical Holding

We base our practice of holding on the role of physical holding in the protection and socialization of young children. When all is going well with development, physical touch conveys a caring, comforting, and reassuring message to the children. And parents hold children when they are too young to hold themselves back in dangerous situations. Young children need to be held when they are upset and in danger of hurting themselves or others. Our arms are the best place for a raging toddler when the screams turn to sobs (Leach, 1988).

Physical holding conveys the message that a person can and will control children when they cannot control themselves. Most children will not work with you on the exploration and expression of intense negative and frightening feelings unless you have convinced them that you are willing and able to provide them with external controls when they lose their internal controls.

Heather (age seven) is psychotic. After years of sadistic physical and sexual abuse, she was removed from her psychotic parents and placed in a foster home. Her foster parents have stayed with her in spite of the unbelievable level of care she requires. She needs time in a hospital when her judgment becomes so erratic that her parents and the staff at her therapeutic day hospital fear for her safety.

These are the times she does not know who she is or who you are and sees things that are not there. She becomes disorganized and disoriented when her feelings become too intense. At these times, the jumble of real and imaginary and good and bad people confuses her and she cannot tell one from the other. She will attack you if she feels that her safety is at stake.

Heather was found in her room, curled on the floor, assuming the position of a dog as she tried to bite her wrists and lick the blood. Jill (a social worker) discovered her and called for help. She was joined by Fran and Becky (counselors).

They placed her face down on the bed. Jill sat on her back and held her arms flat on the bed, while Becky held her legs and feet. Fran held her head to prevent biting and rug burns. They shivered as she voiced louder and more gruesome growls. They knew that she had been locked in rooms with dogs and that her parents had tied them all to bedposts.

Today she struggled for almost an hour. Near the end, her growling turned to rhythmic and quiet sobbing. Jill and Becky were able to soothe her with soft singing, and the physical hold turned into rocking, with Heather in Jill's lap. Fran brought a warm facecloth to wash away the sweat and tears. When it was over, Heather looked perplexed.

This scenario is familiar in our work but out of place in most people's conception of how to soothe a seven-year-old. However, it does occur when parents try to manage a raging toddler in the middle of a temper tantrum. As Leach (1988, p. 326) advises, "To prevent the child from getting hurt or hurting anyone or anything else . . . it may be easiest to keep him safe if you hold him, gently on the floor. As he calms down he finds himself close to you and he finds, to his amazement, that everything is quite unchanged by the storm. Slowly he relaxes and cuddles into your arms. His screams subside into sobs; the furious monster becomes a pathetic baby who has screamed himself sick and frightened himself silly. It is comfort time."

As helpful as it can be for some patients, holding is not for all patients. Many disturbed children cannot bear to be held when they are out of control. Children may have physical and temperamental reasons for experiencing physical touch as noxious and disorganizing rather than comforting and integrating. Some children are noncuddlers from birth, were toddlers driven to greater rages if held during temper tantrums, or have what the occupational therapists call *tactile defensiveness*.

Histories of sexual and physical abuse have left many of our patients with distorted images of adult physical touch. These children will often initially need control and comfort from a nonhuman source, such as the quiet room, either locked or not locked. However, the quiet room cannot be used for self-injurious children, who will bang their heads, bite or scratch body parts, and kick or punch until they have broken bones. These children will need physical holding and mechanical or chemical restraints.

Our unit and many other hospital settings have adopted the hold techniques and training program developed by the National Crisis Prevention Institute (CPI) (Wyka, 1988). CPI teaches the following strategies:

- Verbal and nonverbal techniques to prevent or de-escalate assaultive, disruptive, or out-of-control violent episodes
- Physical personal safety techniques to avoid injury when violent behavior occurs
- Individual and team physical control and restraint strategies and techniques to be implemented when physical intervention is necessary
- Therapeutic techniques to be implemented after physical interventions have occurred

Our physical holding procedures are adopted from the CPI manual: nonviolent and nonharmful physical releases to be used during an attack, individual holds to be used with smaller children, team holds such as that described with Heather, and methods of physically transporting a patient who is being restrained.

Physical holding is usually done by at least two team members. Team interventions are safer for children and staff, are more professional, and are safer from a legal standpoint if patients file abuse charges based on their distorted image of what occurred. One-on-one physical holds can evoke a more confrontational, street fight atmosphere that may stimulate the child to more violence and may bring out more personal defensive maneuvers in staff members.

When a physical restraint is going well, it should have a firm, calm, caring sense about it. Although physical holding is uncomfortable and does indeed hurt in similar ways to physical abuse, we help to differentiate the experiences for the child in *how* we hold, *when* we hold, *why* we hold, and *what* we do following the hold.

Tables 11a through 11d summarize the guidelines for physically holding a child, the formal hold routine, and communicating during and following the hold. When staff members have conducted physical holding with attention to procedural routines and sensitive communication, the children will be more likely to understand and appreciate the process.

Seclusion

Children who cannot comply with an open door (quiet room use) need a locked door (seclusion). Quiet rooms and seclusions are extensions of the parental practice of sending misbehaving children to their rooms. Children who need these interventions do not voluntarily go or stay safely in their rooms. *Seclusion is the place where children complete the discipline process.*

Children use seclusion more frequently and differently than adults on inpatient units (Tardiff, 1984; Valentine, 1984). However, seclusion is not used by all children, and some children will use it more than others. Our study of seclusion for a thirty-month period showed that 40 percent of the children never required seclusion, while 60 percent of the children needed to be secluded at some time during their hospitalization (Millstein and Cotton, 1990). Among the children who used seclusion, about half used it one to five times during the course of their hospitalization (the average length of stay during this study was seventy-five days). The average number of seclusion episodes per child was ten for the children who used seclusion more than once.

In our sample of children, frequent users of seclusion were significantly more likely to have a history of physical abuse, neurological impairment, relatively weaker language skills, assaultive behavior, and a suicide attempt in the six months prior to admission. Our patients who used seclusion also showed more deficits in their capacity to cope with environmental demands

Table 11a. Guidelines for Physically Holding a Child.

---

1. Physical holding is a process. What you do during the hold, why you initiated a hold, how you do it, and what you do following the hold make the hold therapeutic.
2. Remember that the reason you are holding the child is that the child is out of control.
   a. The child has no control over the physical expression of rage. The result could be hitting, kicking, spitting, screaming, swearing, throwing things, or making disjointed and meaningless movements while lashing out at things and people.
   b. The child's relationships with peers and adults have been "functionally" lost.
   c. Talking and reason are ego functions temporarily out of order.
3. Careful ovservation of the cues and warning signals prior to a blowup and quick decision making based on knowledge of the patient, the group, and the setting should guide the decision to hold. A delay in the use of holding can frequently result in injury to the child or others, total disintegration of the milieu, or destruction of property.
4. *Physical holding should not be used punitively.* Do not attempt holding if you are feeling intensely frustrated or angry with a child or are seeking revenge. Transfer the child to another colleague if you become too upset during a holding.
5. Try to minimize the child's experience of physical pain.
6. Follow the formal holding routine. The routinizing of holding helps the child:
   a. Distinguish between the therapeutic procedure, a street brawl, or physical abuse.
   b. Experience the intervention as hospital routine rather than personalizing the experience with one staff member.
7. You will need to tolerate a wide range of intense and unpleasant experiences during and following holding:
   a. The impact of raw hatred and rage.
   b. Physical pain and fatigue.
   c. The narcissistic hurt caused by the loss of the relationship you thought you had with the child and the loss of the power you thought you had over the child.
   d. Natural disgust with aggression and pain.
   e. Fear of serious bodily injury.
   f. Fear of counterattack fantasies.
   g. Shame over physically restraining a young child.
8. The key to keeping the holding therapeutic is your capacity to *not take the child's behavior or words personally.* This helps you remain nonpunitive, calm, firm, and as available to the child as possible.

Table 11b. Formal Hold Routine.

1. When you assess a child to be out of control, do *not* attempt a partial hold, because the child can easily strike back from the unrestrained limb.
2. Use at least two staff members when possible.
3. One staff member may attempt to hold a young or small child, depending on the aggressiveness of the child and the strength and training of the staff member. Do not attempt to hold a child unless you feel reasonable confidence that the hold will be safe for all involved.
4. Designate a leader of the hold who will assess the situation and delegate actions.
5. Follow precise routines for posturing of adult and child, formal sequence of events, and the use of neutral tone of voice and choice of language.
6. Use no counteraggression nor more force or discomfort than is necessary to achieve the goal of safety. Ask the child if one position is more comfortable than another. If the child is more agitated when consulted, talk among staff about ways of making the child more comfortable. Try pillows and blankets to cushion positions. Use cool washcloths to wipe away sweat and soothe a child. These efforts convey caring.
7. Attempt to hold the child out of sight of other people to protect the child's privacy as well as to reduce any need to play to an audience.
8. Inform the child that you will release the hold as soon as you think the child is back in control.
9. Use the routine release sequence, which specifies staff actions and child responses and gives increasing amounts of responsibility for self-control: release one leg, the other leg, one arm, the other arm, the torso.
10. During the release, congratulate the child for calmness and control at each step.
11. Stay with the child after releasing the hold until the child is capable of maintaining control without help.

Table 11c. Helpful Talking or Helpful Silence During the Hold.

1. At each step during this process, assess whether silence or talking is more therapeutic. The guidepost should be: which approach soothes or incites? And remember that you also have the audience of other patients.
2. Try to match your verbal interactions and affectionate physical contacts with what the child can take and digest on a moment-by-moment basis.

**Table 11c. Helpful Talking or
Helpful Silence During the Hold, Cont'd.**

3. Describe your actions concretely as you are doing them. Address staff partners, if directly addressing the child results in too much agitation.
4. Repeat often, as simply as possible, the generic reason for holding (for example, "I will be your controls until your controls return").
5. Use diversionary talk about superficial topics to distract, soothe, or calm the child.
6. Delay the discussion of emotionally relevant observations, dynamic interpretations, connections with life events, and precipitating events, unless you have some indication from the child that this discussion will be helpful. Most situations require delay. Each child's response will be quite individual (never preach responsibility now).
7. Do not enter into any arguments that the child's delusional system may suggest. Remember that the child is stripped of cognitive functions, leading to distortions of reality, motivations, and relationships.

Table 11d. Communication Following the Hold.

1. *Communication with the child.* Attempt to convey the following points to the child orally or in writing or pictures:
   a. "Do *not* feel guilty about what you did or said during your outburst, because you were not in control."
   b. Assure the child that the behavior during the outburst will not be punished: "We will not punish you for your outburst. You were not in control. What you do at times like that makes no sense, and we know it."
   c. Be low key and introduce to the child the idea that these control problems can be mastered by growing better controls.
   d. Stress that *your job is to help the child master these problems.* Emphasize that you have known and helped other children who have had this problem and that they have been able to grow controls for their strong feelings.
   e. Stress that these are big problems that require hard work. Stress that the child *deserves* help with them.
   f. Try to plan for future outbursts by devising anticipatory plans with the child about what both of you can do when the child is out of control. Assess when the child is ready to listen to and learn from your observations and dynamic interpretations of the holding experience. This will help the child develop a more realistic understanding of the experience.

Table 11d. Communication Following the Hold, Cont'd.

---

2. *Communication with other patients about the holding incident.* Remember that these incidents can be very upsetting to the other patients, particularly when they stimulate their fears and memories from the past.

   a. Assess and respond to the other children's perceptions of the incident.

   b. The group or particular children may need an explanation of the holding and an opportunity to discuss their feelings about it.

   c. There are times when the frequency and intensity of holding incidents (or restraints) precipitate a group dynamic of "kids against staff." When this occurs, a group meeting with all children and as many staff as possible should be held.

3. *Communication with colleagues.* Seek collegial and supervisory support and help! These experiences can be extremely disturbing to staff. They are always upsetting. The staff involved in holds are usually drained and often disoriented after an intense crisis. They will need validation from their colleagues or supervisors that they "did the right thing" or "the best they could have done under the circumstances." In some cases, staff meeting discussions are needed beyond individual support.

---

and internal needs. They showed marked lack of frustration tolerance, inability to handle limits set by staff, and confusion about what is expected of them when they are emotionally upset (Millstein and Cotton, 1990).

There are some children who will find seclusion more soothing than other control techniques, because they distort interactions with adults when they experience intense anger, frustration, or disappointment. The discomfort and pain, inevitable in physical holding and mechanical restraints, feed into their feelings and thoughts that we are deliberately hurting them. It is as if they welcome the walls and locked door, because they protect them from us. For example, Lisa (age eleven) asked for seclusion when she was in the middle of a limit-setting struggle with a staff member, especially if the staff member was a male. She explained to us that she knew that a male staff member could not hurt or sexually touch her if "he was behind a locked door." In this way, children experience the locked door as keeping us out, just as we see the locked door as keeping the children in.

Seclusion creates a "physical" separation for the children and for us. But it does not (and never should) create a "psychological" separation. We designed the quiet room with a Plexiglas window to my office and an intercom system. Children in seclusion can choose to have the window open or the system turned on. In this way, they can talk to staff (or family members) but still have the safety of the locked door. Talking to us from this vantage point helps children regain perspective on who is angry with whom and what staff are likely to do to them. The window to the room and the microphone convey our concern to children in a way that they can hear and use.

The open window to my office and the microphone also offer other opportunities to relate to children who need the locked door and cannot relate to staff in more traditional ways.

Paul (age nine) had been in seclusion since he had thrown a chair at staff earlier that morning. Tonight was visiting night. Paul was anticipating that he would be the only child without parents on visiting night. He stated that he wanted to spend the rest of his life in the quiet room with the door locked.

When I heard him banging on the walls, I opened the window and turned on the intercom, "Oh it's you, Paul. Sorry to see that you're having such a bad day. Would you like to watch me do my work, while you do yours? I'll leave the door open. I'll need to close it if you bang, because the noise disturbs me. Let me know if you want me to close the window. You're entitled to your privacy."

Paul settled down on the bench and watched me intently until he fell asleep. Staff unlocked and opened the door. They put a pillow under his head and covered him with a blanket. He spent most of the morning in the quiet room but did not need seclusion again until the evening during the visiting hour.

We did not hold Paul, because we felt that he wanted to be alone while he tried to live with the reality that he could not be with the adults that he really wanted.

Seclusion can be an essential step for some children in the process of learning control through the experience of control. However, children do not enter these spaces or stay in these spaces without staff escort, staff monitoring, or locked doors. The locked room al-

lows them to save face with peers and reduces the need to im-
press or struggle with a peer and adult audience. They need
the locked door because they cannot stop themselves from returning to these groups.

Six-year-old Raoul was hyperactive and incapable of
listening to staff or taking his time on a chair. The following
incident occurred after he had been on the unit for three days:

Joanne and Vivianne (counselors) were leading an art group.

Joanne observed Raoul grabbing the paintbrush from another patient (Donna). "Raoul, you'll need to take a five-minute time-
out for grabbing Donna's paintbrush. Please take it over there,"
said Joanne, pointing to a chair at the other end of the room. "I'll
save your project and get you a paintbrush while you're taking your
time-out."

Raoul ran to the other side of the table with Donna's paintbrush in his mouth.

"Maybe you should take your time-out in the quiet room.
It may help you do the time-out, so you can finish your picture before we need to go," Joanne continued.

Raoul started to tear up Michael's picture, which was dry-
ing on the counter.

"You can't get me. You can't get me, bitch!" screamed
Raoul.

"I'll need to help you get to the quiet room. Please help me
help you," replied Joanne.

Joanne and Vivianne walked up to Raoul and needed to
physically hold and escort him to the quiet room. When he got to
the quiet room, he was swearing and flailing at them. They laid
him on the bench and quickly left the room. Raoul leapt up and
rushed toward the door, which they had closed.

"Raoul, please sit on the bench and finish your time-out,"
said Joanne. *"If you need the door locked to help you do this,* I
can lock it. I'll wait here for a minute to see if you can calm down
with the door closed. Vivianne, you can go back to the group. Be
sure to thank the kids for helping us help Raoul by being so quiet
and getting out of the way when we walked by."

"Open the door, you bitch!" yelled Raoul.

"I'll open it after you've calmed down and when you've
started taking your time-out," Joanne replied.

Raoul resumed swearing and started pushing and banging on the closed door.

"I think you need the *help of the locked door.* I'm locking it now. I'll unlock it when you stop swearing and pushing on the door," said Joanne, holding the door closed and then locking it.

After four minutes, Raoul went over and laid down on the bench. He stopped swearing and looked quietly out the window.

"Good work, Raoul. I started your time-out." After five minutes, she unlocked and opened the door. "I have your paintbrush and picture ready. Your time's up. What did you get your time for?"

"Grabbing and tearing the picture."

"That's half right, Raoul. You got time-out for grabbing the paintbrush. I didn't give you more time-out for tearing the picture and swearing. I know it's hard for you to listen to us and take your time-out. We can help you with this problem. I'm going to tell your team that you need help taking your time-out. Maybe we could start a star chart?" asked Joanne.

This incident is typical of those involving young children who have poor self-control, histories of inadequate parental discipline practices, and biological vulnerabilities such as hyperactivity. Our experience has been that seclusion experiences are shorter, which means that children calm down quicker and return to the program faster than when we start a physical holding. The average length of seclusion experiences is relatively short for young children (Garrison and others, 1990; Millstein and Cotton, 1990). A study on our unit showed that the average seclusion episode was about fifteen minutes. Physical holding episodes usually are much longer, and mechanical restraints are longer still. In the incident just described, Raoul returned to the group after ten minutes, in time to finish his painting.

We build on the positive aspects of the seclusion experience. For example, the following sequence of clinical expectations could be the basis of a therapeutic program for Raoul. We would first reward Raoul for a shorter time in seclusion, then reward him for getting to the room without staff escort and staying in the room with a closed but not locked door. After that, we would reward him for spontaneously removing himself to the quiet room and taking his time-out with the door open, then for spontaneously removing himself to the quiet room *before* he loses control and staying in the quiet room until he has calmed down. Gradually, more "normalized" variants of the same coping skill can be introduced.

Children who are leaving for homes or residential treatment centers without quiet rooms and seclusion worry about staying in control and being safe without these interventions, which have been so helpful to them. We have helped children build "portable" quiet spaces out of sheets, which they retreat under to "find their controls." We have suggested quiet corners or quiet time with music and earphones. These are the concrete manifestations of the working ego we hope to help construct eventually inside the child. This final stage is the product of a longer developmental process for normal children and a long-term treatment goal for disturbed children. The hospital work usually only starts off this process.

Mechanical Restraints

Mechanical restraints are used less in elementary school–age treatment settings than on adolescent units. We do not use mechanical restraints on our unit. We feel that for developmental reasons, it is hard for children in this age range to comprehend the harmless use of belts, metal beds, and other professionally designed mechanical restraints. Another consideration is that mechanical restraints affirm the children's fear that no person can control them when they are unable to control themselves (Schulman and Irwin, 1982). Thus, we rely more heavily on seclusion, physical holding, and chemical restraints.

However, I include a section on mechanical restraints, because I now think there have been children treated on the unit over the years who could have benefited from this technique. There are developmentally understandable reasons why mechanical restraints may be soothing and effective during some phases of the treatment of young children and adolescents. There are also some types of disturbed children that we do not treat who benefit from mechanical restraints. We are unable to treat certain aggressive psychotic patients who are clearly stimulated and provoked by physical holding and who are too self-injurious for the use of seclusion. Our unit does not accept court-referred patients, but forensic treatment settings have described the need and therapeutic benefit of restraints for this population (Maier and others, 1987). Mechanical restraint devices are also essential treatment tools with mentally retarded and neurologically impaired patients where verbal interventions and relationships will not control violence when the patients become overwhelmed with impulses or feelings. In these patients, the violence remains unpredictable.

The pediatric and psychiatric crisis management literature describes a wide variety of restraint devices: leather cuffs and belts, soft ties, vests, posey jackets (canvas restraining jackets), mits with lock buckles or waist straps, head straps and helmets, protection sheets, simple sheets, papoose boards, safety coats or "body bags," or cold wet packs (Tardiff, 1984, 1989).

New devices are developed and old ones jettisoned when the newly designed restraint suggests a more humane treatment. For example, the use of Utica cribs (metal wire boxes) and restraint chairs has been discontinued in favor of camisoles (canvas modified restraining jackets) or leather muffs, mitts, anklets, and wristlets (Ventura, 1974). Recently, I was consulted by a unit that was designing a restraint chair because it would be less restrictive and more humane than existing restraint devices. Actually, it sounded much like the device on view at Colonial Williamsburg in America's first mental hospital.

The most frequently used restraint technique is four-point restraint, which uses belts to immobilize the patient's arms and legs. This can happen on mental health–designed beds or portable stretchers. Physicians and nurses are trained to position the child safely in restraints. During the course of the restraint, they must also observe the child carefully for medical side effects, such as urinary retention, fecal impaction, dehydration, adverse physical reactions to concurrent medications, pressure sores, or any injury or disability. Nursing protocols include the necessary clinical examinations and tests routinely conducted and documented in the patient's chart. Ambulatory restraints called *preventive aggressive devices* (PADS) were developed for use on secure units in forensic centers. They serve as intermediate management techniques for patients who are out of seclusion but are still considered dangerous by staff (Maier and others, 1987). Pediatric settings have developed safe and effective restraint devices for medical examination and treatment of young children. Papoose boards allow for total body or selective body part restraint. Psychiatric units can use these boards for treatment of toddlers with hyperactivity, histories of physical and sexual abuse, and neurological impairments.

Mechanical restraints are indicated for older children and adolescents. For developmental reasons, physical holding can prolong dangerous situations (for example, see Drisco, 1976). Older children are moving away from physical and psychological dependence on adults. Physical holding could feel too childish and contradictory to their attempts to "act their age."

During a consultation to an adolescent unit, I met a thirteen-year-old girl who was in four-point restraints. She taught me something about the need for mechanical restraints in some situations:

"In my hospital, we believe that physically holding children is kinder and more normal. We do not use mechanical restraints. What do you think would be better for you?", I asked while sitting with the staff member who was observing her.
"Belts," she mumbled immediately.
"Why?" I asked.
"Belts don't make mistakes," she answered.
"What do you mean?" I queried.
"I could get hurt if I struggled with a person. The belts are stronger than me when I struggle."
"Anything else?" I wondered aloud.
"Yeah, I don't want no fucking counselor on top of me."

The clinical rationale for the use of restraints with adolescents is also a developmentally based concept that sees restraint as a specialized technique that is a symbolic extension of parental holding (Marohn, Dalle-Molle, McCarter, and Linn, 1980). Marohn and his colleagues illustrate the positive use of restraints with adolescents, who are able to experience calm and soothing in the middle of their most violent feelings.

Psychopharmacotherapy

In hospitals and medically supervised treatment settings, we can use psychopharmacotherapy to alter biological factors leading to, prolonging, or complicating impulsive and severely maladaptive behavior. Most of our patients receive medication. Pediatric psychopharmacology is an integral part of therapeutic management of aggressiveness; agitation; anxiety; problems with attention, memory, and activity; depression; mania, psychosis; sleep and eating disturbances; seizure and tic disorders; and enuresis (Campbell and Spencer, 1988; Green, 1991; Lewis, 1991; Lewis and Volkmar, 1990; Meltzer, 1987; Popper, 1987a, 1987b; Shaffer, Erhardt, and Greenhill, 1985; Stewart, Myers, Burket, and Lyles, 1990).

We also use psychopharmacological interventions during behavioral crises. Doctors' orders can be written into the patient's treatment plan for the use of psychotropic medications to prevent predictable problem behaviors or the greater deterioration of a child's functioning once trouble has begun. These medicines are called *PRNs* ("as occasion arises"). PRNs are used most frequently for acute agitation, anxiety, and aggression.

Treatment Procedure. A careful diagnostic evaluation precedes the use of psychotropic medication. The effectiveness of medication is best monitored by continuous, skilled observation within the comprehensive therapeutic management plan. Child psychiatric and nursing expertise ensures that a developmental approach will be used in this treatment modality, as in all treatment modalities.

Pediatric psychopharmacotherapeutic treatment, according to Lewis and Volkman (1990, p. 406), requires the following:

- a careful preparatory work-up;
- careful monitoring;
- a thorough knowledge of the pharmacology and pharmacokinetics of the drug being considered;
- an understanding of the variations encountered during the different developmental phases throughout childhood and adolescence;
- and a knowledge of the indications, contraindications, and side effects for each drug, as well as drug interactions.

Special pediatric psychopharmacological expertise is needed for children in hospitals and treatment centers, because these are the children who have most likely been poor responders to routine psychopharmacotherapy. Children who simultaneously carry one or more psychiatric diagnoses prove to be special challenges to this treatment modality. For example, antipsychotic medication for distorted thinking may complicate the presentation of depressive symptomatology or lower a child's threshold for seizures.

Parents and legal guardians are included in all stages of the decision to use psychotropic medications. We discuss the indications for use and problems with side effects of particular medicines with both the children and their parents. We obtain parental consent for use of specific medications. According to Dalton and Forman (1992, p. 104), parental and child discussions (when applicable) should include:

- Rationale for the chosen drug
- The desired results
- How this therapy fits into the larger treatment plan
- Methods of administration
- Potential side effects
- Positive and negative reports in the literature
- The physician's own experience using the specific medication

Chemical Restraints. When psychotropic medicines are used in emergency situations, they are called *chemical restraints.* Chemical restraints are used to control assaultiveness, destructiveness, and self-injury. PRNs and chemical restraints are used when less invasive treatments have failed to alleviate the crisis behavior. PRN usage varies greatly from clinician to clinician and has not been adequately studied (Popper, 1990; Vitiello, Ricciuti, and Behar, 1987). In emergency situations, we inform parents as soon as possible after medication has been administered.

We use psychopharmacotherapy in combination with other techniques of therapeutic management.

Staff Training and Support for All Active Containing Interventions

To use the control techniques of this phase, staff need training and orientation to specific skills, clinical supervision and support from each other, and clinical and administrative sanction from the leaders of the unit. The effective use of these techniques requires that the staff can reflect on their own feelings and reactions to their participation in this phase of treatment and their feelings about the children and what they do to need this kind of help. This can occur in orientation programs, individual and group supervision with peers and senior clinical staff, clinical group discussions, staff meetings, and modeling of these techniques by staff at all clinical levels.

In our setting, staff of all disciplines receive orientation, training, and practice in the use of control techniques. They have the opportunity to use them during their participation in the milieu, co-leading groups or supervising mealtime and bedtime routines. This means that staff at all professional levels share a common experience with these techniques. If the techniques are utilized only by milieu treatment staff, skepticism and conflict can develop among staff members about their valid clinical use (Lion, 1987), resulting in dysfunctional staff relationships. A common philosophy of management builds staff unity, which in turn enhances the safety on the unit. The children, who are so sensitive to power structures and struggles, need a unified approach to the use of these techniques by all clinicians.

Staff are also encouraged to discuss management options with each other, even when this has to occur in front of the child.

Although they may be discussing differences of opinion, these collaborative discussions convey the joint working efforts of the entire staff to the children.

> Dr. Z (a psychologist) was standing outside of the locked quiet room door. Donna (age ten) had been placed in seclusion after her predictable pattern: swearing in group, failing to take a time-out, going to the quiet room, starting new personalized swears directed at Dr. Z, and pushing the door into his face.
>
> Dr. Z called Ruth (a counselor) over and started discussing his concern that he was unable to help Donna because he was too angry at her. Dr. Z also thought that Donna was too angry at him to calm down. Ruth suggested that she take over and give both Dr. Z and Donna a chance to cool off.
>
> Dr. Z and Ruth both knew that Donna had listened to her alcoholic father swear abusively at her mother when he was drunk. She was angry at men and had little respect for them. She allowed Ruth to come into the quiet room and was able to complete her time-out for her. Ruth helped Donna write a letter of apology to Dr. Z.
>
> Here is the good-night note Dr. Z wrote Donna in return:

> Dear Donna,
>
> Thank you for your note. It made me feel much better about what happened this afternoon. I know you don't mean what you say sometimes, but it really gets to me. I'm only human and it was so hard to take that from you. I've never allowed anyone to talk like that to me. I know you wouldn't like it either.
>
> I guess it's hard not to give back what you saw adults give out. Please try to remember that I'm trying very hard to be a different kind of adult for you. I'm glad Ruth was there for both of us. Next time, maybe we should ask for her help before we get into such trouble.
>
> Have a good day tomorrow! I'll see you tomorrow night. Try to think of something fun to do in group. You always have such good ideas!
>
> Your friend,
> Dr. Z

It feels so good when we can turn the possibility of a nasty exchange into such a reparative process for both children and staff. When staff ask other staff for help in this way, the children are frequently surprised, suspicious, and anxious. They may never have seen adults work together like this. They may fear the tension or confuse the request as a sign of weakness. The constructive use of staff relationships can be experienced quite differently as children observe the full process.

Conclusion

We see from this discussion that containment can prevent children from going on to greater violence or destruction, with the subsequent burden of more guilt and shame. Preventing children from hurting themselves and others can curtail a negative escalating cycle. When children are physically controlled by nonaggressive adults in professionally designed ways, we give them the opportunity to experience nonabusive, caring adult physical containment. We help them to value and protect themselves in order to develop their self-esteem and capacities for inner control.

exsausted lion

CHAPTER 7

Postcrisis
Therapeutic Management:
Picking Up the Pieces

The focus of this chapter is the "cleanup" or rebuilding operation that follows behavioral crises. All troublemaking children
need to be helped with how to get back from the trouble. *The
art of transitioning children back into the milieu is as important therapeutically as removing them from the milieu.* How this is done can
make the difference between their peaceful reintegration or escalation to similar or worse trouble. Treatment planning in this
phase needs to design a pathway for the "way back" for children and staff returning from the battlefield of behavioral crises.

   This chapter examines the reactive contract. The components of the reactive contract translate the separate psychological
steps needed for the "return journey" into required actions for the
child and staff. These actions include negative consequences, reparative words and acts, and anticipatory plans for better future
coping. We emphasize again that negative consequences (or punishments) are used for teaching and psychological development.

The Therapeutic Opportunity of the Postcrisis Period

There is a unique postcrisis therapeutic opportunity, which includes, but goes beyond, limit-setting responses to troublemaking.

Once trouble has been contained and stopped, the new challenge is how to make something positive out of the experience, so that children and staff can restore what had been, move ahead, and, most important, learn from the experience. Careful structuring of treatment at this time can:

- Take advantage of the therapeutic opportunity for children to learn from their mistakes and develop psychologically
- Prevent the development of negative cycles of staff-patient interactions that lead to further behavioral crises
- Manage the emotional aftermath for both staff and children

Treatment settings frequently do not explicitly address the postcrisis treatment phase, naively assuming children and staff will just "get back to normal." Other programs create unrealistic protocols that do not take into consideration children's developmental and clinical status during these times. For example, some protocols require young children to apologize immediately following a disciplinary action, ignoring the inevitable resentment children feel at these times. Intense negative feelings and continued ego deterioration often make it impossible for children to acknowledge their part in the trouble immediately. Protocols may exclusively focus on punishment or safety needs of children and staff, ignoring needs for reparation.

Both patients and staff are often burdened by intense feelings after a major behavioral incident. These emotions can cause staff to withdraw or become overinvolved with the children who have just run away from, hit, or lied to them. Effective protocols need to address the postcrisis psychological needs of both children and staff: regulating intense negative affects, such as anger, guilt, shame, resentment, and repulsion; controlling wishes for revenge and fears of retaliation; and negotiating repair and reparation. Unattended to, these feelings can lead to negative cycles once crises begin.

Two images come to mind about the subjective experience and tasks of this phase: cleaning up the mess or picking up the pieces and putting them back together. Messes describe the strong affective component of the children's subjective experience. The mess metaphor conveys images of blood, poop, urine, sweat, and throw-up, with scenes of overturned furniture, torn paper, bruised or bloody bodies, smeared walls, broken toys, and contraband matches and knives.

> Lisa (age eleven) was crying softly after another blowup. She was sitting with Gino (a therapeutic recreationalist) after several other staff members had asked Gino to take over the care of Lisa. They needed a rest after secluding and physically holding her when she started to bite herself. Lisa's rage seemed to swell at the mere sound of their voices or sight of their faces.
>
> "Lisa, I'm here to help you feel safe again . . . safe with yourself and safe with us," Gino told her. "I don't know exactly what happened, but you heard Fran and Stephanie (counselors) ask for help. I'm glad they asked."
>
> "Fuck them!" Lisa screamed.
>
> "I think you're all too mad to help each other now. I'm here to help you all cool down and feel safe again. When you're ready, I brought a wet washcloth for your face. I can get you some juice if you're thirsty."
>
> Lisa sighed with relief and reached for the washcloth. "Look at my shirt. It's a mess. My hair's a mess." Looking down at her hands, she started to sob harder and harder. "Why do I always make such a mess! My whole life is a mess."
>
> "Joe (her uncle, the man who had sexually abused her) said I would make a mess of Ma's family if I told and he was right. My grandmother isn't talking to Ma, because she's pressing charges against her own brother. We're never invited to go there any more, even for Christmas. I know it's me. I bet they would ask Ma if I wasn't around . . . " Sobbing interrupted Lisa's burst of talking.

Gino used Lisa's metaphor in his response to her:

> "What a mess! No wonder you feel so discouraged all the time. Like yesterday, when you didn't even want to try to write a story about what you want to change in yourself. You've learned how to make messes. And you've learned how to take full credit for the messes other people make.
>
> "You've come to the right place. Our job is to help children learn how to clean up after a mess. Then we can help you avoid making more messes. When you're ready, let's start your contract."

Just as the mess metaphor directs us to the violence and feelings of the past, picking up the pieces points us to the feelings and tasks of the present and future. Images of Humpty Dumpty and jigsaw puzzles come to mind, capturing the more cognitive and behavioral side of the rebuilding process. Picking up the pieces vividly captures the process of fragmentation that psychotic children experience when overwhelmed by feelings during these crises.

> Seven-year-old Heather had been scalded in bathtubs and locked in closets as a toddler by her psychotic mother. Barbara (a nurse manager) noticed her walking into the freestanding closet in her bedroom. She went in, closed the door, and emerged minutes later. Barbara thought that she was seeking peace in this small, contained space. The closets had been childproofed with air holes and no hooks or poles to prevent suffocation or hanging.
>
> Later that day, staff and children noticed a disgusting smell emanating from Heather's room. Heather started screaming, kicking, and punching when Barbara began searching the room and opened the closet door.
>
> Barbara gasped. She saw what Heather had been desperate to conceal. Heather had created a bathroom in the closet. The closet was bare except for a box of hospital tissues taped to the wall and a wastepaper basket filled with urine and feces.
>
> Although Heather was not able to describe the meaning of her private bathroom practices, we pieced together the connection between these behaviors and early abusive situations with her mother, when she had been locked in closets for long periods of time. Heather's reenactments of her past were her way of remembering. The closet ritual was Heather's desperate attempt to put the pieces of her past together into a bearable reality, binding her anxiety and fear.

Our efforts in this phase of therapeutic management are designed to help children put their lives back together without resorting to distortions of reality, retreats from helping adults, or impulsive acting out.

Reactive Contracts

In the sense in which we are using the term, a contract is a systematic form of communication between children, staff, and their families. Contracts appeal to school-age logic, which focuses on concrete behaviors, concern about fairness, and legalistic balancing of good and bad. In the behavioral literature, this approach is known as *contingency contracting* (Barth, 1986; Dardig and Heward, 1981; De Risis and Butz, 1975; Hersen and Van Hasselt, 1987).

Why Do We Use Reactive Contracts?

Milieu treatment planning uses two major types of behavioral contracts: reactive contracts and proactive contracts. *The reactive contract is our primary response to the immediate clinical needs of the children and the staff following a behavioral crisis.* Proactive contracts develop preventive plans for the future. They translate the deficit identified during the child's troublemaking into a new skill or coping strategy that the child can use when next faced with the same emotions or stresses. Proactive contracts are at the heart of the work in Phase III of therapeutic management, discussed in more depth in Volume Two of this book.

The protocol for a reactive contract ritualizes a process and provides a prewritten script to guide staff-child interactions. It prescribes what specifically needs to happen between the child and staff following a behavioral crisis. The tone is matter of fact and businesslike, helping to control the destructive expression of negative emotions that can permeate child-staff relationships at these times. The component parts of the reactive contract are based on the final steps of the discipline process described in Table 5, which outlines teaching with negative consequences and providing opportunities for reparation, accepting, and forgiving.

Since crisis management usually involves unilateral decisions made by staff, the contract format allows children to return to more active participation in their treatment by individualizing the components of their contracts, such as specifying which penalties they will receive, for how long, and under what circumstances. The contracting process acts as an external ego for disturbed children, helping them to make amends for their troublemaking. Without blaming or judging, contracts point out children's responsibility in the cleanup operation and suggest potentially more adaptive behavior in future crises.

Reactive contracts also prescribe staff responses to the children. Since the specific content of each contract is unique to the child and to a particular situation, contracting requires staff to stop and think imaginatively about this child, this situation, and the most resourceful way to make something therapeutic out of the incident.

We have found various ways of explaining the contract to children — that is, of translating the contracting process into meaningful steps for them. This is one of my favorites:

> Sue (a counselor) knew that Raoul (age six) loved baseball. He had only been on the unit for three hours when he hit her during a tantrum over returning a toy to the cabinet. Raoul was sent to the quiet room.
>
> Sue came into the quiet room with a blank contract and some juice after Raoul had calmed down.
>
> "Don't worry, Raoul," she said. "We have a way of helping children after they make mistakes, like you did with me." Choosing a matter-of-fact tone, she continued, "Let's drink some juice and I'll explain to you about contracts. We're going to make one just for you. After that, you can come out and join the rest of the kids."
>
> "I don't want to do that stupid thing," responded Raoul.
>
> "Please give it a chance. It's kind of like a baseball game. The contract has things for you to do. Each thing is like a base. When you get through all the bases, you can make a home run!"

Contract Format

The same format is used for all reactive contracts. We printed the blank contract sheet on hospital stationery to borrow status and underline the "businesslike" nature of the work.

The general features of an average contract are:

- Dates and conditions of the beginning and ending of the contract
- Text of the contract (substance of the agreement)
- Signatures of agreement by the child and "witnessing" adults
- Conditions if the contract is not fulfilled

The text of the contract reflects what should happen inside a child and between children and their environment in order for them to move beyond the present trouble they have caused. In other words, the components of the text represent the "psychological" bases to get "home." These components are:

- Description of the troublemaking
- Provision for reparation
- Specification of penalties or negative consequences
- Suggestions for rechanneling
- Educational assignments

We elaborate on each of these items below. In our discussion, we occasionally refer to a sample reactive contract (Exhibit 7), which was developed by Stacy (a counselor) and Johnny (age eight), following Johnny's serious assault on both staff and children.

Description of the Troublemaking. The first sentence of a contract starts with the word *I* and is followed by a confession. *Think carefully about what you ask children to confess to.* The description of the trouble is our initial chance to describe the trouble in a way that helps children understand what they have done (and clarify what they have not done) and acknowledge their part of the responsibility for an incident.

We need to describe these incidents in ways that are *digestible* and *comprehensible* for children. If our words are too judgmental, children may not be willing to acknowledge their part in the incident. If we use jargon or unfamiliar words, young children may feel disconnected from unknown behaviors, not responsible, or confused by contracts that ask them to confess to "vandalism" or "assaultive" or "inappropriate" behaviors. If we become too dramatic, children may like the new status of being dangerous and powerful. We must be specific and clear and use words that are in the children's vocabulary, which means they describe events within the children's experience.

Useful descriptions of troublemaking involve an extensive discussion of what may be obvious to us, but not so obvious

Exhibit 7. Johnny's Contract for Assaulting Paul and Stacy.

New
England   **Ruble 2 B**
Memorial
Hospital   **CONTRACT**

                                    May 10
                                    (DATE)

I _Johnny_ understand that hurting
(NAME)

people is against the rules on Ruble 2-B and not a
safe way to tell people that I am angry. Because
I sat on Paul's legs and hurt him and then
punched Stacy in the arm and scratched her in
the eye, I will need to do the following:

☐ 1. Take 20 minutes of time-out in the quiet room.
☐ 2. Do Paul's chore after supper
☐ 3. Do a chore for Stacey
☐ 4. Write an apology letter to Paul
☐ 5. Write an apology letter to Stacy
☐ 6. Punch the punching bag in the quiet room (2min)
☐ 7. Miss snack outing
☐ 8. List 3 ways to safely tell people I am angry
     1._____ 2._____ 3._____

IF I DO NOT OBEY THIS CONTRACT

    I will be unable to rejoin the group and
watch T.V. with them.

                    SIGNED: _J O HNNY_
                WITNESSED BY: _Stacy_

THIS CONTRACT EXPIRES:
                    When done

to children. Johnny's contract begins as follows: "I Johnny understand that hurting people is against the rules of Ruble 2-B and not a safe way to tell people that I am angry. Because I sat on Paul's legs and hurt him and then punched Stacy in the arm and scratched her in the eye, I will need to do the following . . . "

While Johnny's behavior was a serious assault against a staff member, we avoided the word *assaultive* in order to help Johnny recognize the incident and yet not become so overwhelmed with guilt or fear that he couldn't perform reparative acts. We described the actual behavior (sitting on Paul's legs or punching Stacy in the arm and scratching her in the eye), as we observed them. We described the impact of the behavior (hurting Paul), as we understood it. We invoked the "structure" or rules of the unit. Johnny was able to tolerate the size and seriousness of his behavior when it was described in this way. By making this experience more "digestible" to him, we encouraged him to work for forgiveness. *"Digestible" troublemaking is also more "forgivable" troublemaking.* Children experience relief when they think that they are able to make up for their mistakes and return to the good graces of people they love and depend on.

Contracts criticize behaviors, not persons, by avoiding reference to feelings, moods, or vague descriptions of temperamental and personality characteristics. Behavioral descriptions of troublemaking explicitly tell children what is wrong in how they act or how they say something, not who they are or what they are feeling. We described the impact of the behavior to help Johnny redefine the incident and see it as we see it. We cannot expect children to do the repair steps that are next if they do not agree with us about what happened and what was wrong with it.

Spelling out the specific sequence of events connects to the children's memory of the incident and helps them accurately reconstruct their own actions. Frequently, the intensity of the feelings following a behavioral crisis leads to distortions of the events and sequence of the incident. School-age children are concrete, and they reason from the particular to the particular. We need to calmly help the child reconstruct what happened in specific ways.

Provision for Reparation. To make reparation means to make amends for wrongdoing and to repair or restore a relationship, a self-concept, or the environment to a previous state. Reparation contributes, while troublemaking destroys. *Reparation is the children's ticket to return to the good graces of a person, group, or institution, and to restore their own positive feelings (self-esteem) about themselves.* Reparation involves reparative acts that complement reparative words (apologies).

During initial or acute phases of treatment, we cannot totally stop our patients from making trouble, but we can help them do the repair work after the troublemaking. This is particularly important for disturbed children, who make a lot of trouble and easily become discouraged after they have "messed up" once again.

The opportunity to make amends is a crucial step in building the children's sense of mastery over the whole discipline process. Reparation is the "antidote" or buffer to the experience of guilt or remorse (Faber and Mazlish, 1980). Children are more motivated to improve their behavior and learn new ways to deal with their feelings once they have learned to lessen the internal burden of guilt through reparative acts.

The positive impact of a cycle of troublemaking, apology, and return to normal is reflected in the children's sense that they can do something about the mistakes they make or the trouble they cause. Eventually, we hope the process will be internalized so that the children can spontaneously ask themselves "What can I say and do to make amends?" following the misbehavior.

Reparation can counteract what disturbed children usually do following troublemaking. For example, many children get worse after they have started to break rules and lose control. They "throw in the towel" and quit the fight to be good. Johnny's tendency was to withdraw and become overly critical of himself after he had lost control.

A vivid example of the staff's intuitive reliance on reparation following trouble occurred when a staff member was hurt by a child's slamming a quiet room door in her face:

Ralph (age twelve) looked terrified as he noticed the spurt of blood running down the counselor Diane's face. He started to run away.

"Stop," yelled Diane. "You did this and I expect you to help me now. Get a paper towel and I'll turn on the cold water. I'll wait in the quiet room with you until I can send a staff member to help you finish your time-out for not listening.

"I'm going to the emergency room. I hate needles. I think it's only fair for you to do an extra chore if I have to get a shot. Also, you'll need to keep the other kids posted on what is happening. I'll call you from the emergency room."

Ralph mutely did what Diane told him to do. He was too overwhelmed with fear to object.

When a reactive contract was written, Ralph was required to do a chore for every stitch Diane had and for the tetanus shot. He announced at the evening meeting that Diane had gone to the emergency room, where she had six stitches and one tetanus shot, and that she would not be back at work today but would be tomorrow. His contract included an apology to Diane and an essay about safe things to do when he felt angry with counselors in the future. His stepmother and father were called and told about the incident. Part of his contract was talking to them about what had happened.

Diane knew that if Ralph had been left alone, he would have been overwhelmed by his own harsh conscience and his fears of retaliation. Ralph's family needed help to find words that were firm and clearly disapproving of what he had done, yet not an angry tirade about what a bum he was. They wanted to add a weekend chore to the contract, and we agreed that this was a good way of emphasizing their disapproval of violence and their support of our disciplinary actions. The staff-child-family clinical team was in collaborative action.

Reparation and forgiveness are reciprocal processes. They are at the heart of the healing process of the reactive contract. Staff and parents need to accept apologies and reparative acts and then forgive the child. In this way, the apologizing child learns the lesson that apologies can rebuild relationships and make you feel better about yourself.

Accepting apologies and communicating forgiveness challenge even the most empathic staff member. Often, staff and
parents need some training in their role in the apology (accepting and forgiving), if a child is to experience making an apology as satisfying and meaningful. Children who have been neglected or abused are too often alienated from this reparative
process. They feel entitled to mistreat others as they have been
mistreated in their lives. They either have not received apologies from adults who have wronged them, or adult apologies
were followed by further neglect and abuse.

Verbal apologies begin a dialogue about what happened.
They help to make the offended person more open to renewing
a relationship.

An apology does not have to be profound or complicated.
Apologies can take many different forms, depending on the children's developmental level and skills. They can be pictures drawn
by children, pictures chosen by children from magazines and
pasted into collages, letters dictated to staff members or helpful
peers, or letters written by children themselves. Letters are used
more often or in addition to interpersonal apologies. Our patients may not be able to trust that the adult will listen and accept the apology. Their only experience may have been with
adults who continue to berate them or physically punish them.
Apology letters can also be written with the support and help
of other staff members.

Apologies should go to anyone or any place affected by children's troublemaking: other children, staff, hospital administrators (vandalism or noise), hospital maintenance crew (plugging
toilets, breaking windows), housekeeping staff (smearing food,
urinating on bathroom walls), hospital telephone receptionist
(swearing into the phone), or parents (rudeness during visiting).

Our patients have written or telephoned to places outside the hospital: to a Howard Johnson Motor Lodge that gives
us time in their pool, for creating noise and a mess with towels;
to the Science Museum, for disrupting a show; and to department stores, for stealing. Maggie (age six) had to write to the
crew of the USS *Constitution* when she had a temper tantrum
and had to be physically restrained on the gangplank.

Many children need to be taught the skill of making a good apology. We give the following advice to children learning to apologize. Each question reflects a different component of an apology:

1. Why don't you start with "I'm sorry for . . . "?
2. What are you sorry about? What did you do?
3. Can you say what upset you?
4. How else could you tell someone about being upset in the future?
5. What could you do with these feelings in the future?

Apologies should always contain the first two components. The remaining three are optional, because they require insight and some psychological capacity for relationships. We do not expect this of children before they can participate in the reparative step. However, including all of these components allows you to use the apology experience to its full teaching and therapeutic potential: providing insight into the feelings and situations that arouse anger or frustration, developing alternative adaptive ways of telling negative feelings or solving similar problems in the future, or learning ways to rechannel the feelings in the future.

Reparative actions go one step further than words, by doing something concrete toward restoring and repairing (making amends). As Faber and Mazlish (1980) point out, "Sorry means behaving differently" or "sorry means making changes." Staff can say "I'm glad to hear you're sorry. That's the first step. The second step is to ask yourself what can be done about it." Reparative actions have additional power to purge shame. For children (and parents) who come from families where talk has been cheapened by broken promises and unfulfilled commitments for change, they can teach that feelings of guilt and embarrassment can be translated into constructive action.

The key to reparative acts is to turn the situation around, so that children who are disruptive and destructive become active contributors to the community, the environment, and their relationships. Reparative activities allow children to stay involved or return to a constructive, active involvement in a program or relationship.

Our process of reparation is similar to what behaviorists (Barth, 1986; Herbert, 1987; Ollendick and Matson, 1978) refer to as *overcorrection*. Overcorrection requires that children correct the consequences of their misbehavior by restoring the environment to a former state (*restitutional overcorrection*) or "overcorrect" it to an improved or better-than-normal state (*positive practice overcorrection*). Like reparative acts, overcorrection allows children to practice positive behaviors that are incompatible with the behaviors that got them in trouble to begin with. Although overcorrection can be used as an "aversive" technique (Herbert, 1987), we never use it in this way.

When choosing a reparative activity, we rely heavily on general acts of cleaning and repairing. There is a concrete, psychological connection that makes sense to young and school-age children between making a mess (causing trouble) and cleaning up after the mess. The key is to keep children close to the person or place where the trouble occurred. When possible, the reparative act should prescribe a behavior that is the opposite of what the children did to get themselves in trouble. In this way, they can begin to practice contributing, where they had only taken away; or building, where they had always destroyed. We use fines, chores, repair or replacement programs, or extra favors as reparative acts. Table 12 lists the common reparative acts that we have used over the years.

We try to prescribe reparative acts that connect concretely to the misbehavior. This makes great sense to the child. Johnny's contract (Exhibit 7) included doing chores for Paul and Stacy, which could include drawing a picture for Stacy or making Paul a cardboard road for his cars. Table 13 provides several examples of typical problem behaviors and associated reparative acts.

Specification of Penalties or Negative Consequences. Chapter Four introduced the five possible kinds of penalties. In a behavioral crisis, a child's behavior has already outstripped the usefulness of ignoring or reprimands. Reactive contracts incorporate natural or logical consequences and behavioral penalties. In some cases, a penalty is also a reparative act (when breaking a toy is followed by fixing or replacing the toy); in other cases, the

Table 12. Common Reparative Acts.

On the unit

Wash chairs, tables, windows, walls, floors (vary the number according to the
seriousness of the misbehavior).

Clean quiet room walls and windows.

Clean out the snack refrigerator and organize its contents.

Dust furniture.

Wash out trash baskets.

Polish brass or chrome.

Clean or organize the contents of toy boxes.

Fix up games — put pieces together, tape boxes, stack games neatly in cabinet.

Straighten the art supply cabinet or library.

Organize the marker bucket (put caps on markers, test markers, and throw
away dried-up markers).

Wash the kitchen cabinets, counters, refrigerator, stove.

Vacuum upholstered chairs and sofa.

Fold unit laundry.

Repaint a piece of furniture or equipment.

Draw a new welcome-to-the-unit sign.

In and for the hospital

Pick up trash or plant flowers on the hospital grounds.

Draw a picture for the lobby.

Build a pencilholder for the receptionist.

Write a poem for the hospital newsletter.

Bake cookies for hospital administrators.

For staff in general or for a particular staff member

Make out the "Who's Working Today" sheet (secretarial chore).

Bake a snack for the day or evening shift.

Help staff with cleaning up or preparing for an activity.

Redo the unit rule book.

For the community of peers or one particular peer

Help a younger child complete a task or chore or play a game.

Do a child's chore for a set time period.

Read a bedtime story to a younger child.

Draw a poster to teach about a rule, safety procedure, or activity.

Draw picture of the child's favorite hobby or animal for the bedroom wall.

Build a suggestion box.

Help maintenance staff repair the damage.

For nonhospital settings

Make an advertising poster for the restaurant or theater in which the child
broke the rules.

Make a poster warning against shoplifting for a store in which the child stole
something.

Pick up trash in a park or recreational area.

Write safety suggestions.

Write an article for a local newspaper about the store, restaurant, or recreational
facility.

Table 13. Connecting the Reparative Act to the Misbehavior.

Hurting children
Do a chore for them or sit with them at the doctor's office.
Help them do their homework or read a story to them.
Hurting staff members
Bake them a cake or draw them a picture.
Do a chore for them or help them wash their car.
Call them at home and report about their health to the other kids and staff.
Disrupting the unit at bedtime
Read a bedtime story to the younger kids.
Make hot chocolate for the children the following night at bedtime snack time.
Breaking something on the unit
Repair or pay a fine toward replacement.
Repair, clean, or organize the unit toys or equipment.
Causing trouble in the van on an outing
Clean the van.
Help revise or copy the van schedule.
Running away
Do a chore for the staff member who took the time to find you.
Make educational posters about running away for the unit door.

---

penalty is only a negative consequence (time-outs or unit restrictions) and does not involve contributing or undoing the damage.

The penalties in the reactive contract represent time-limited and confined statements of adult disapproval. The reparative and penalty steps finish off children's debt for their troublemaking in the discipline process. Without negative consequences and reparative acts, children build up enormous debts inside until guilt or avoidance need to become ways of living if the children's sense of self-esteem is to survive. On completion of the reactive contract, children should be able to feel that they have "paid for their sins."

Pick penalties that are reasonable, clear, brief, and understandable to the children. The "punishment should fit the crime" and children's developmental level. We use brief periods of time-out for minor offenses; loss of special activities or privileges if the offense is likely to occur while doing these; or unit restrictions (staying on the unit for specific time periods) for running away, disruptive behavior in the milieu, and extreme impulsive outbursts. Young children can learn from brief time-outs and what appear to be "light" penalties.

If the penalty is not reasonable, it will exceed the children's tolerance and may "backfire," diffusing guilt and regret and sometimes creating a self-righteous sense of being wronged in the children. Children with weak controls, faulty consciences, and poor self-esteem need the punishment step to be explicit and externally set, with a beginning and a clearly defined end.

The description of the penalty in the contract should state:

• The task, fine, or loss of privilege
• How well the task must be done
• Who the task will be done for or with
• How many tasks should be done or how long the activity should be carried out

Penalties can be passive, such as taking a time-out, or active, such as doing a physical activity. Some children do better with active penalties, such as punching the punching bag, push-ups, jumping jacks, sit-ups, or riding the exercise bicycle. The effectiveness of the punishment lies in the children's connection of the penalty to their behavior and in the children's perception of the total process.

Whenever possible, we try to let the penalty communicate our disapproval and surround it with our support and praise for the children's participation in the rest of the process. The penalty "pays for the crime," leaving room for the staff to give the children credit for something else — the making of amends. Without such praise, our patients can easily lose their motivation to complete the penalty and move on to trying to improve their behavior. They are easily discouraged and too likely to give up during the reparation and penalty work.

> When Raoul (age six), who has a history of fire setting, was found with a lit match on the unit, he was put on a unit restriction, which meant that he could not go off the unit for twenty-four hours. Unfortunately for Raoul, that evening was Halloween and the entire unit was going out trick or treating. Raoul stayed back and completed his contract.

Mid-evening, two staff members surprised Raoul with a
"mock trick or treating" on the unit. He was allowed to put on his
devil costume and go from room to room, trick or treating. Staff
members, equipped with candy, moved from room to room to receive him when he came to trick or treat.

Meetings with unit and hospital administrators are also
included as penalties. For example, all contracts for vandalism
include meeting with the unit director, who sets a fine for the destruction of unit property. In some cases, the child and the director will call various hospital departments to determine the cost
of replacement or repair. The child's fines are usually a very
small proportion of this cost but a meaningful depletion of the
child's monetary resources. The money is sent (along with a letter
of apology) to the hospital administrator who signs the work-
order requests for repairs.

Suggestions for Rechanneling. Rechanneling refers to the process
of substituting adaptive behaviors and words for old behaviors
and words that have proved maladaptive. We take every opportunity to introduce other ways of communicating strong feelings
or getting something, even during our initial contracts with our
patients. Reactive contracts introduce the notion that there are
safe and less costly ways to say the feeling or get what you want.
*We expect our patients to think of alternative ways of communicating
and acting before we expect them to use alternative ways.* Examples include talking and listening rather than starting a fistfight, going
to one's bedroom rather than running off the unit, writing feelings of self-loathing in a journal rather than cutting one's body,
or negotiating for something rather than stealing it. A child's
initial reactive contract emphasizes generating substitutes and
listing alternative behaviors, rather than requiring the child to
practice them. The long-term goal of therapeutic management
is to teach these alternative ways of communicating feelings,
solving problems, and getting what one wants and needs.

Substituting behaviors makes the important point that the
original feeling or activities are "okay," but the thing, place, or
way of saying it needs to change. The capacity to use substitute
activities and people is a process akin to sublimation — through

which children manage and express their internal conflicts, wishes, and drives by doing activities that express them in ways acceptable to the children, their parents, and other children and adults who make up their world. The capacity to sublimate or accept substitute gratifications is one of the stabilizing character- istics of healthy personality development (Freud, 1965).

Our patients do not have a repertoire of safe and accept- able ways of expressing negative feelings, resolving internal conflict, solving problems, or coping with disappointment and frustration. Perhaps they started off in life temperamentally as children who were initially less easy to distract and rechannel. Or it may be that the adults in their lives did not have the skills and resources to model and teach strategies to rechannel. By the time we meet them, their parents describe them as stub- born and persistent in their troublemaking. We need to start with the beginning steps of rechanneling to help both parents and children experience some success in developing and prac- ticing new skills.

There are stages in how to develop safer, more adaptive ways of dealing with the world. First, we teach children to iden- tify in themselves a set of feelings or beginning behaviors that signal trouble ahead. Second, we welcome their commitment to try something new. We actively discourage children from say- ing and writing in apologies that "I will never do this again." We want to make words mean something in all the work we do; therefore, we discourage the use of words that make promises that cannot be kept. I would rather hear a child make another kind of commitment: "I will *try* not to kick the wall again. I will *try* to kick my mattress instead."

Third, we treasure (quietly, which means we do not make a big deal of it) the children's recruitment of our help to keep out of trouble. This means they no longer think that we are the trouble; they know that the potential trouble to be made is in themselves. We can infer in their request that they are ready to make a change. This is the motivation for treatment that we need to continue into later phases of therapeutic management.

Exhibit 8 is a letter written by Johnny (age eight) to our hospital vice president that incorporates an apology component with a rechanneling effort.

Exhibit 8. Johnny's Letter of Apology.

Dear Ms James Brewer,

I sorry breaking one of the chains that I broke because I throwed it against the wall. And the Next time I won't throw chains I throw snowballs.

Johnny,

Ruble 2b,

P.S. My conslr says I shold say I will try. but I don't want to throw then anymore

The rechanneling step uses the empathic formulation. We need to have some idea of what children were trying to do, how they felt when they committed the offense, or what adaptive skill or coping strategy was missing. Rechanneling suggestions work well when:

- They match the troublemaking.
- They satisfy the inner wishes and longings that prompted the troublemaking.
- They communicate the feelings that the trouble was trying to express.

For example, in Johnny's contract for assaulting Paul and Stacy (Exhibit 7), he was asked to "list three ways to safely tell people I am angry" in the future. His contract did not expect him to practice these ways yet but focused on the task of listing "three ways" to feel something, tell something, or do something differently.

The substitute behaviors focus on the misbehavior as a maladaptive solution to a missing problem, a missing skill, or an unsafe way of telling someone what you are feeling. Therefore, if anger is the problem, children need to think up alternatives to expressing it. In Exhibit 7 Stacy was helping Johnny see more constructive ways of handling his anger in the future. The rechanneling step tells Johnny that he has a right to feel angry, as we encourage him to pay attention to what he can do for himself now and later on.

With young children, we avoid abstract words to describe feelings and stay close to the concrete behaviors that express them. We make contracts to address "punching" feelings, not "angry" feelings, for the young child who punched a counselor. We can also make contracts for "spitting," "kicking," "biting," "throwing," and "smashing" feelings when upset children react with these behaviors. A concrete description of the problem behavior also guides the choice of the "channel" in the rechanneling phase. Thus, children who bite themselves can make a contract to "bite a washcloth when I have biting feelings"; punchers can "put my punching feelings in the punching bag"; kickers can "put my kicking feelings in a soccer ball" (or Nerf [foam rubber] ball when inside); spitters can "put my spitting feelings into blowing bubbles."

We believe that there are feelings behind the troubling behavior, and we want children to make that connection. There is, of course, the added advantage that we do not have to name a feeling if we do not know what it is or what the child calls it. Thus, we can do this work for children we do not know very well or have just met briefly in shelters and short-term treatment facilities.

The rechanneling step requires our clinical imagination. Lisa (age eleven) swears a lot. Her contract suggested that she make a private swear book in which to keep her swearwords. This alternative does not give too much power to the word. It emphasizes that the context of swearing is what gets you in trouble.

Andrew (age seven) stole Michael's (age eight) baseball cards in order to be accepted by the group of kids who were trading cards. His contract included a suggestion about ways of earning money on weekends to purchase his own cards.

If a contract addresses a child's touching another patient's private parts, the rechanneling step could suggest other ways of being a good friend to the patient. If the sexualizing was considered a way of communicating about sexual abuse, the patient could write a story or draw a picture about an animal who touched (or was touched by) other animals.

We often have to provide the ideas for children at this phase. They may not have been exposed to models of nonviolent, adaptive, and effective strategies for expressing and coping with strong feelings and wishes. When Stacy met with Johnny to complete his reactive contract (Exhibit 7), he could not think of any way of safely telling someone that he was angry. She helped him formulate the following suggestions:

1. I will try to scratch the rug in the quiet room instead of someone else's skin and eyes.
2. I will try to yell my anger in the quiet room with the door closed.

Therapeutic management requires that we both contain the behavior and rechannel the troublemaking impulses. Limit setting alone will not give children assertive and satisfying alternatives to troublemaking in the future.

Educational Assignments. Whenever possible, we add an educational component to the reactive contract. It underlines our philosophy of learning from mistakes. Educational assignments on contracts help children learn more about our values, the reasons for certain rules or routines, and the impact of the troublemaking behavior on other people or on the community. If children have disrupted the unit in the morning, the contract asks children to review the unit rules for morning routine. We ask children to learn the privacy rules when they violate them.

Contracts also include writing essays on topics such as "why bringing a screwdriver on the unit is unsafe," "why hitting people is wrong," "what is the importance of privacy rules?", or "why listening to counselors at the science museum is important." Young children dictate stories or answers to the counselors and draw pictures. The unit bulletin boards display this work. Children can add pages to the unit rule book that give more detail about adult expectations for certain behavior at a particular group or outing. Sometimes their own words make more sense to each other than our more abstract descriptions.

> Older Kids' Group is a free-time activity that the ten- to twelve-year-old patients attend three afternoons a week. Jimmy (age ten) was complaining about Joyce (a social worker), who had given him several time-outs prior to Older Kids' Group. There was some question whether he should attend, because the group was meeting outside. Emmy (a nurse) decided to take him, hoping a new set of people could help turn around his bad day.
>
> However, his complaints became more emotional and he tried to enlist other children in a plan to "boycott" Joyce the next day. Emmy told him that he needed to stop revving up the kids against Joyce. She warned him that he would need to leave the group if he could not be more constructive in his discussion of his complaints.
>
> Jimmy stopped talking and started to poke his arms with twigs when he was challenged. He was brought back to the unit, and his reactive contract for the incident included listing acceptable ways to complain:
>
> 1. Tell Joyce what you don't like.
> 2. Write a suggestion for the suggestion box.
> 3. If you can't talk to Joyce, write a letter and tell her what she is doing wrong.
> 4. Listen to Joyce's side.

The educational component of a contract teaches children the language of a helping community or family when we show them that improving their behavior will help others as well as improving their own lives.

When children's hospital-based troublemaking would have resulted in more serious negative consequences if it occurred in the community—for example, court or jail involvement— we add penalties to educate children about these more serious negative consequences. Children who pull the fire alarm or light

matches are required to meet with the town fire marshal. A
police officer (specializing in juvenile offenses) met with one boy
who was exposing himself to visitors on the unit.

Ralph's (age twelve) father and stepmother arrived on the unit to
take him for his Saturday pass. Ralph was taking a time-out in the
quiet room for teasing his roommate. Suddenly Ralph streaked
down the corridor, nude from the waist down. He was laughing
hysterically and shouting obscenities. He was fat and quite tall for
his age. His nude body made quite an impression on the visiting
parents and on the children who were in the corridor preparing
to go on passes.

His contract for this event (Exhibit 9) reflected our concern
about what may be becoming a pattern for Ralph. He had exposed
himself to girls in a school bathroom prior to hospitalization. Ralph
was embarrassed about his looks and frequently got into fights
because he was teased about his weight. He had found a way to
control when and where people would laugh at him.

We arranged for a meeting with Ralph's father, a unit staff
member, Ralph, and a town juvenile police officer. The officer explained that in Massachusetts, children over the age of seven are
legally accountable for obedience to the law and may be arrested
and charged with delinquencies and brought before a Juvenile
Justice or a District Court Justice for trial or disposition. Ralph was
told what would happen if he exposed himself to a girl sunbathing
in the park.

The officer emphasized that the police want to help kids,
but they also have a job to protect other people from pranks that
may frighten or insult them, even if the kids did not mean to hurt
anyone. The officer encouraged Ralph to use his intelligence and
sense of humor to have fun in safer, more considerate ways.
Ralph's reactive contract also included the following provision:
"Read unit joke book. Tell a joke at community meeting each day
next week."

Exhibit 10 provides an example of another reactive contract—for threatening to throw a chair. In Table 14, we summarize the components of a reactive contract.

Exhibit 9. Ralph's Contract for Streaking.

New
England   **Ruble 2 B**
Memorial
Hospital   **CONTRACT**

August 26
(DATE)

I,. _Ralph_
(NAME)

understand that I was unfair
to the kids and their visitors on the unit this morning
by running around without my clothes. I was also
unfair to myself. I will

☐ 1. Take 30 min. in the quiet room.

☐ 2. Clean and organize the visiting cabinet.

☐ 3. Write a letter of apology to the kids and their
visitors. (Post on Notice bulletin board)

☐ 4. Cook snacks for next visiting night.

☐ 5. Read unit joke book. Tell a joke at community
meeting each day next week.

☐ 6. Meet with Officer Casey from the Stoneham
police department about what would happen
if I did this in the park.

☐ 7. Write an essay on the laws about nudity
in public places.

☐ 8. List 3 other ways to prepare for a difficult
home visit
1. ___
2. ___
3.
IF I DO NOT OBEY THIS CONTRACT
I will not go on outings with the group and
I will have supervised weekend passes (can't go out of
my house).

SIGNED: _Ralph_

WITNESSED BY: _Kelly_

THIS CONTRACT EXPIRES: ___

When done

Exhibit 10. Donna's Contract for Threatening to Throw a Chair.

New
England
Memorial
Hospital

Ruble 2 B

CONTRACT

<u>June 27</u>
(DATE)

I, <u>Donna</u>
(NAME)
threatened to throw a chair. I know that throwing a chair is very dangerous and will not be accepted on this unit. Because of my unsafe behavior, I will

  ☐ 1. Meet with Dr. Cotton.

  ☐ 2. Write an apology to the staff.

  ☐ 3. Write an apology to the kids.

  ☐ 4. Pay a fine for breaking a chair. (Dr. Cotton and I will determine the amount)

  ☐ 5. All chairs will be removed from my room for 24 hours.

  ☐ 6. Wash 10 chairs.

  ☐ 7. write an apology letter to the security guards.

  ☐ 8. I will wait in the quiet room until my meeting with Dr. Cotton.

  ☐ 9. 24 hour restriction to the unit.

  ☐ 10. Write an apology letter to Vice President Mr. Bruer.

  ☐ 11. After unit restriction is up, I will throw my throwing feelings into 25 snowballs.

  ☐ 12. I will meet with my mother and my doctor about this incident.

IF I DO NOT OBEY THIS CONTRACT

I will need to start a transition program for Safety.

SIGNED: <u>Donna</u>

WITNESSED BY: <u>Pam</u>

THIS CONTRACT EXPIRES: when done

Table 14. Summary of Components of a Reactive Contract.

---

1. *Description of the troublemaking.* Establish reality. Be specific. Do not use jargon or judgmental language. Make the description "digestible" to children. Describe the impact of the act or rule violated.

2. *Provision for reparation.* Verbal apologies help children make amends to people and the community. Apologies start to rebuild relationships. Children write, draw, or dictate their apologies. Reparative acts are the children's ticket to return to the community. Construction replaces destruction and reengages children with the community. Reparation dilutes shame and guilt and builds self-esteem.

3. *Specification of penalties or negative consequences.* Be explicit, concrete, and understandable to children about the punishment or negative consequences of their actions.

4. *Suggestions for rechanneling.* Suggest substitute behaviors. Validate the children's feelings and introduce the idea of adaptive, safe ways to express these feelings. Rechanneling helps children distinguish their feelings from their actions and imagine new solutions to old problems. This is a future-oriented and "just think of" or "try to do" step. Do not ask children to say they will never do the problem behavior again.

5. *Educational assignments.* Teach the information needed to avoid trouble again — for example, rules, philosophy of the organization, and legal or ethical consequences. Emphasize the impact of the action through learning, writing, or presenting a talk on it.

Impact of Behavioral Crises on Others

Behavioral incidents reverberate throughout the unit and affect the staff and other children, as well as the troublemaking child. Table 15 lists the pieces in the child, in other children, and in the staff that need to be "put back together again" to repair the negative impact of the behavioral crisis.

Both staff and patients may be burdened by intense feelings of anger, guilt, shame, resentment, disappointment, repulsion, and fear of retaliation after a major behavioral incident. Unattended to, these feelings can lead to reverberating negative cycles once crises begin. We use all the existing therapeutic forums for patients and administrative meetings for staff to put the pieces back together.

Table 15. Pieces to Be Put Back Together Again.

In the troublemaking child
    Self-concept, self-esteem, and self-control
    Relationships with staff
    Relationships with peers
In other children
    Self-concept, self-esteem, and self-control (when group contagion has occurred)
    Relationships with the troublemaking child
    Relationships with staff
    Relationships with other children
In the staff members
    Self-concept and self-esteem
    Relationships with the troublemaking child
    Relationships with other children
    Relationships with each other

Impact on Patients

Participating in and observing violence and intense conflict are particularly complicated for children who have experienced extreme interpersonal conflict and physical violence.

Types of Responses. Behavioral crises in the present reawaken memories of past conflicts. Reliving past feelings only intensifies the wide range of negative feelings toward the adults involved in the current struggle. Children are always affected by these incidents, whether they participated, were physically hurt or teased, or merely observed. Patients have reported feeling various combinations of anger, guilt, responsibility, fright, or helplessness.

The children who participated in the event directly will receive their own reactive contracts. However, other children may feel responsibility for the incident through their own egocentric thinking or pathological personalizing of conflict. Other children feel guilty because they failed to protect a friend or favorite staff member, did not prevent the incident from occurring, or added to the trouble. Other children will feel less safe because the treatment setting feels suddenly out of control.

The milieu program uses the daily community meeting or specially convened meetings to review the behavioral incident.

We encourage children to ask questions and articulate their own version of the events. These versions often contain distortions of the sequence of events or staff motivations during the incident. Once they are verbalized, we are better able to correct the distortions. This often involves restating the purpose of restraints or seclusion. These discussions often involve serious patients' questions, such as the following: Why couldn't you control the situation? Will it happen again? Do we hate the trouble-making children? Will we get rid of them? Will we quit and go away? What will we do to children who hurt us? Do we blame them? and on and on.

Individual psychotherapy is one arena for children to discuss what such an incident evokes in them about their past lives, their own controls, the controls of adults from their past, and questions they have about our capacity to keep them safe and use our own controls. Younger children will use their play to dramatize and try to master their concerns. Milieu therapists use the private moments throughout the day or expressive milieu groups to allow children to discuss (play or draw) their feelings and reactions. They may bring the subject up while they assist children during mealtime, bed, or bathtime routines.

The use of tighter group management structures helps to return the group's sense of comfort in the setting. We also acknowledge children who were able to stay in control during the trouble. We let children know that we consider this their way of cooperating with the adults in charge. We clarify that we don't expect children to prevent or control the incident, but we clearly expect them to not contribute to the trouble. We will throw a pizza party or play a special video to reward their cooperation and create a calmer mood.

It is sometimes necessary to cancel activities or outings because we are concerned about continuing disruption or violence. We explain why we are making any changes in the routine. We do not "blame" the troublemaking child. The point of all milieu programming is to get back to normal.

When Johnny (age eight) was in the quiet room, Stacy and Stephanie (counselors) met with the children to discuss Johnny's attack on Stacy.

"I'm sorry to report that we will not be going on snack outing tonight," said Stephanie. "But we can make popcorn on the
unit and watch a special video." The children were very angry with
Johnny.

"Are you mad at Johnny?" Michael (age eight) asked Stacy.

"I'm mad about the kick and I'm mad about the scratching," Stacy responded. "My eye hurts. I don't like it when people
attack me."

"Are you gonna get back at Johnny?" asked Maggie (age
six).

"No," said Stacy. "I feel sorry for Johnny. His temper is always getting him in trouble. Some people can't ever forgive him
after something like this, but I'm a good forgiver."

"I'm not gonna forgive him," said Paul (age nine). Johnny
had also attacked him.

"Well, I can't work here if I can't forgive. It wouldn't be fair
to the kids. Kids who come here make a lot of trouble. They need
us to forgive them so we can help them not make the same mistake again. Johnny did the best he could. I'm going to stick around
and help him do much better."

Group Contagion. Behavioral crises generate a great deal of psychological contagion. The younger or more disturbed the children are, the more likely they are to be swept up in the trouble.
As Redl and Wineman (1951, p. 103) describe it, "The mere
visualization of acted-out behavior itself becomes the stimulus
that gives intensity to a previously dormant urge, or throws the
ego's watchfulness overboard, or does both."

Group contagion accounts for the occurrence of riots on
inpatient child units, when individual children act more destructively than we would predict from their individual psychopathology. We later called our worst unit crisis the "Saturday
night massacre." We needed to call hospital security because
almost every child was joining in on the trouble.

Paul (age nine) began the trouble. He was unable to sleep and
started making animal noises, which woke up his roommate. Meg
(a counselor) entered the room, asking Paul to be quiet. When he
continued to make noises, she asked him to go to the quiet room.
He refused and started to kick and push Meg. As she fell to the

floor, her back hit the corner of Paul's bureau and she was unable to get up.

Since it was 1:00 in the morning, Ginny (a nurse) was the only other staff member on the unit. She rushed to Paul's room in time to see Paul jump on Meg's back. He was now screaming for the other children to get up and help him. Ginny ran to call hospital security, the usual procedure in such emergency situations.

Children swarmed into the hall and started throwing pillows and trash cans at Ginny, who was trying to pull Paul off Meg. Paul's excitement turned to suspicion and fear. He started accusing Meg of attacking him, gloating hysterically over her injuries.

When additional staff arrived and restrained him, Paul boasted of his strength and threatened to do it again when he was released from seclusion. The other children were terrified. Most children had joined the fray. Even Michael, a timid child, had thrown his wastebasket at the security guard.

Paul continued his bravado through the next day. He bragged of his attack and made fun of Meg and Ginny, who were "too stupid and weak" for him. Staff were horrified and repulsed by the stories of the children's sadism and continued glee. Many staff could not believe that individual children, including Paul, were capable of being so mean.

Administrative and supervisory staff were called onto the unit to help staff manage the children. Tension and mixed feelings of anger, disgust, and fear continued for most of Sunday. Special meetings were held with the children and staff to manage their feelings about what happened the night before.

Riots are fed by group contagion, which can stimulate memories of similar scenes in the past for some patients, who then relive their feelings about what they did or didn't do. Some children suffer from their sense that they failed to protect a parent or sibling from abuse by another parent or sibling. Their attempt to strike out at staff and defend a child may be an effort to do now what they are ashamed of not doing in the past. At other times, the contagion leads to plots or actual aggression toward the child who has caused the trouble. They punish "the aggressor" in the present, as they were unable to punish the aggressors in their past. They also imitate the harsh and abusive punishments that they have received in the past.

In some cases, children identify with the staff and want to punish the child for hurting "their" counselor or doctor. Other times, fear predominates following crises — fear that the staff cannot control the kids or fear that the staff will hurt the kids like the other adults in their lives have done to them. Individual and group relationships need to be examined and repaired in the aftermath of unit crises.

Impact on Staff

Putting the pieces back together includes therapeutic management of the staff as well as the children. Relationships with treatment staff can be impaired during and following behavioral incidents. Children's strong negative emotions can cause staff to withdraw or become irrationally overinvolved with the child who has just run away, hit, or lied. Staff reactions may vary along a range of strong feelings, including anger, helplessness, shame, guilt, fear, and confrontation with their vulnerability. The staff's capacity to cope maturely with intense and corrosive feelings determine the nature and depth of treatment in other phases, since inadequate management of these feelings make real treatment impossible.

Even more seasoned staff members can become unhinged by behavioral crises. The incident itself is always a stimulus for questioning our competence, our motives, our commitment to our work, and our feelings about working with each other. Even with proper orientation and continuous inservice training, staff can feel ashamed that they were unable to prevent or contain a behavioral crisis. They may take this "personally" and feel that it reflects badly on their therapeutic management abilities. The children's sense of helplessness is mirrored by the staff's realization of their helplessness in the face of extreme psychopathology.

The situation is further complicated by our feelings toward the child involved. Feelings of helplessness and shame can quickly convert to anger with a child for successfully disrupting staff members' sense of their own goodness and competence. I have often heard in meetings and supervision the growing image of a child as an untreatable monster who should be given "more structure" or transferred somewhere else. While that may be a legitimate option, we need to monitor whether our own feelings are distorting our understanding of what a child needs, or whether we have, in fact, underestimated a child's pathology or overestimated our own capacity to give this child the most useful clinical setting.

The problem is further complicated when these incidents are caused by the "less likable" patients. There are always some patients who we will never be able to connect with or like as much as others. It is much more difficult for us to be objective about our interactions with these patients. We should question our actions, since we will have a harder time controlling our negative reactions in these situations.

We cannot help feeling angry when a child's troublemaking has seriously disturbed the unit's peace and orderliness. When we are involved in serious behavioral crises, we need the opportunity to review and recover from the personal aftermath of a behavioral incident.

Collegial Support. The first line of defense or recovery is collegial support. *The capacity of the staff to nurture discouraged and enraged children and parents is largely a function of their capacity to give and receive such nurturance from each other.* After being insulted, spit on, hit, scratched, sworn at, and otherwise abused, milieu staff know how good it feels to receive a validating comment, pat on the back, short note, or telephone call. The supportive conversation can be for the staff what the life-space interview is for the child or supportive parent-group conversations are for parents.

The informal network of support created by caring and respectful staff members starts with how they treat each other, particularly during times of stress. Staff members depend on each other to help soothe hurt feelings, calm burning rages, repair injured self-esteem, and understand what happened. Following behavioral crises, staff acceptance of each other makes possible the necessary learning situations to improve treatment. Therefore, understanding and listening should precede analytical reviews of the situation. After we have empathized with, accepted, and supported the staff member's feelings (even if we do not agree with their actions), we can hold the necessary discussions about what happened. Eventually, we can discuss what we could have done differently.

I have seen the same imaginative efforts exerted to support a colleague as I have described in the treatment of the children. With some humor and a belief that what helps distressed patients can also help distressed staff, we often borrow from our treatment techniques to concretize our collegial support.

As Clare (a nurse manager) was leaving one night, she noticed the mother of eleven-year-old Lisa reading Ruth's (a counselor) "feeling wheel." The wheel was similar to what we create for the children. Ruth's colleagues had made her a wheel to help acknowledge a particularly hard day at work. She was given stars when she was able to point the wheel's arrow to what she was feeling (sad, happy, angry).

Many of Ruth's closest colleagues were leaving and she was feeling frustrated with her work with a rather unlikable child (eight-year-old Johnny) who had thrown a chair at her that morning. When Ruth had tried to work with Johnny later that day, he had warded off Ruth's affection with obnoxious personal attacks on Ruth's body.

Clare asked Mrs. T what she thought of the wheel. She was curious and surprised.

Clare explained that we used feeling wheels with children when they were feeling stuck or lonely with their feelings. We thought they helped children identify and share their feelings. The program also told children that we were interested in their feelings and wanted to hear about them. Clare described how they thought this would help a fellow staff member who had had a bad day. Mrs. T smiled and got the point.

Administrative and Supervisory Support. Milieu staff work side by side and have the greatest opportunities to comment on and assist each other's work. However, administrative and supervisory staff are also crucial during postcrisis periods. The participants in a milieu incident will look and listen for approval or disapproval from the people who are supposed to know the most about the treatment process (the unit supervisors and leaders). They will also notice and be disappointed by indifference.

In fact, there are many reasons why the most professionally sophisticated clinicians may *not* be the best judges of the situation. As with the parent who returns to the family at night, it is very common to underestimate the stresses of being with children all day and to overestimate the capacity of supervising adults to remain patient, empathic, and effective in their interactions with children. Many administrative staff have never worked as milieu therapists; for that matter, some have never spent a full shift in the milieu. They may feel that their brief interactions with children are typical of all milieu interactions. But this position does not take into account that children perceive milieu counselors and nurses differently than they perceive unit leaders, doctors, social workers, and other nonmilieu clinicians. Milieu therapists do not have the fancy titles, authority, credentials, and training that the other nonmilieu clinicians have. Our patients, like most children, are very attentive to differences in status and power.

Nonmilieu administrative and supervisory staff should spend periods of time in the milieu. They need to be attuned to what they do not know as well as to what they do know. They need to affirm the unique stresses and demands on milieu therapists in a behavioral crisis. Unless it is clear that misconduct has occurred, they need to provide immediate attention and validation to staff involved in a crisis situation.

The most frequent mistake made by administrative and supervisory staff is to voice their disapproval (subtle or direct) of how the situation was handled: "too much screaming," "voices too loud," "too punitive," "not empathic," "too permissive," "failure to understand the child," or "failure to set 'appropriate' limits."

Although their observations may be correct and may be important to review at some later point in time, the immediate aftermath of a crisis is not the time to start with this message and teaching. The motivation to teach is too often confused with the critical message. The criticism is incorporated by the upset staff, and the learning message does not get through. To remedy this approach, we only need to think about our therapeutic communication style with the patients when they have misbehaved. Just as we always give a child credit for trying, we need to start with our acknowledgment, appreciation, and respect for what the staff went through.

Cohesive milieu treatment depends on the unit leadership and supervisory staff for understanding and support of the realistic stresses and strains of therapeutic management of severely disturbed children. Informal and formal structures of supervision and clinical teaching consist of individual supervision, group supervision combining day and evening staffs, weekly inservice education based on selected milieu management topics, clinical case conferences, daily clinical rounds, and yearly milieu staff retreats. These forums stress the need to develop realistic goals for therapeutic management, based on an appreciation of each child's psychopathology and potential for change and development. We review and adapt these goals for individual patients and for the group of patients following a behavioral crisis.

Dramatic incidents can occur during hospital and residential treatment of severely disturbed children when leaders of these facilities need to provide special inspiration and guidance. In my experience, these incidents usually involve violence, death, or other tragedies. When a child's mother admitted her eleven-year-old child and then killed herself three days later, the clinical team members were overwhelmed with guilt and anger toward the mother for not allowing them to help her. They were also overcome with feelings of horror and sadness for the child's plight.

Violence characterizes most of the incidents on our unit that require the greatest amounts of support and respectful attention from staff at all levels. When the violence results in physical injury to children and staff, the healing is more complicated and requires careful attention. When a staff injury occurs, the entire staff should be notified and the clinical director, nurse manager, and other clinical and administrative supervisors should make a point of reviewing major incidents and connecting personally with the staff members involved. These connections are supportive but they are also informative for the unit leadership, who may become aware of clinical needs in staffing patterns, physical space repairs or changes, orientation or training, supervision, group dynamics, clinical leadership, program philosophy, or treatment planning.

Exhibit 11 is the letter I wrote following the "Saturday

Exhibit 11. Letter Following the "Saturday Night Massacre."

Dear Staff,

This has certainly been a week of death and violence - a baby and the frightening nightmare of last weekend. I wanted to tell each of you how proud I am to work with such a devoted and competent staff. I also wanted to reaffirm with you our common goal. "Everyone" wants to be a "therapist" and "work with people." When I hear someone say in an interview "I love kids", I shudder. I shudder because that statement in no way prepares a person to manage, emotionally bear, or live through the events of last Saturday night.

There are many complex fears and feelings in the aftermath

Exhibit 11. Letter Following the "Saturday Night Massacre," Cont'd.

of such violence and sadism. We must all continue to support each other and particularly the staff who were working last weekend. We must help them with their memories of being hurt and helplessly watching as their fellow workers were being attacked. They must face the complex task of trying to relate to the children who wreaked such havoc - the same children who will - out of their own disturbing memories - brag of their crimes, threaten each other and staff with future violence, and taunt the very same staff who had tried so hard to protect and help them.

After last weekend - we all must share the shattered illusions that children are innocent, lost sheep who only need love and affection. That may have been somewhat true for each child when they were born - but

Exhibit 11. Letter Following the "Saturday Night Massacre," Cont'd.

now they are people who have been loved in certain ways and now they are the products of how they have been loved and treated. It is a frightening view into man's potential to see the sadism that can be developed in children through neglect, abuse, and constant devaluation and lack of positive support.

It is an amazing feat that we perform by walking in the door each day to face the darker sides of what all people can become. But this is what we set out to do. Last week end reminded us that our work is not pretty or comfortable or happy - but it is always important, rare, very human, and frequently profound. Through it - I firmly believe that we become more human ourselves. What other job offers the opportunity to touch nobility and ugliness in ourselves and in our patients on a daily basis?

Exhibit 11. Letter Following the "Saturday Night Massacre," Cont'd.

I am reminded of my Christmas toast last year and I would like to share it with you once again:

"You who sit there in utter misery, look up and show your friend your face. There is no darkness bears a cloak so black as could conceal your suffering. Why wave your hand to warn me of the taint of blood? For fear your words pollute me? I am not afraid to share your deep affliction with you..." Euripides

This is our task. It is not easy. I do love and respect you all.

— Nancy Cotton

---

night massacre" described earlier. This letter was mailed to all staff, including part-time and on-call staff. The death referred to in the letter was the miscarriage of a staff member. The letter directly addresses the raw sadism of the incident and the day following the incident. It incorporates the events of Saturday night into our philosophy of treatment and our basic motivation to do this work.

Conclusion

Our primary response to serious troublemaking is to pay attention to the therapeutic opportunity in the postcrisis period. We use reactive contracts to pave the children's way back into the program and relationships. Reactive contracts are prewritten scripts that cover the psychological steps for reparation and repair.

Behavioral crises have an impact on troublemaking children, the other children on the unit, and the staff involved in containing the trouble and helping with the rebuilding process that follows limit setting. Therapeutic management pays special attention to the emotional aftermath of these incidents. Like property, activities, sleep, and mealtimes, self-concepts, self-esteem, and relationships have been broken. The cleanup operation involves simultaneous repair of both staff and patient pieces.

Happy Lion

Epilogue: Taming the Inner Lions

If the core of therapeutic management is interpersonal interaction, what is its effect on the staff? We have described what it is supposed to do for the children. It is designed to contain, engage, heal, and teach emotionally disturbed children and their families. It is not designed to have a specific effect on the staff who do it. The physical and emotional impact of working with disturbed children, however, is profound. We are often not prepared for the disruption such work causes in our sense of self, our current and past relationships, and our assumptions about what it is to be a child, a parent, a human being.

The more I describe this work, the more I wonder why people do it. Living with disturbed children can be exhausting, frustrating, depressing, and frightening. Most of us do not come to work in the morning looking for this set of experiences or the intensity of emotions they elicit. I have looked for answers in my personal experiences with these children and their families and my sharing of my colleagues' experiences over the years. The story can't be told without examining the impact of this work on the worker. Genuine treatment is a hard, intimate, emotional, and challenging undertaking. Our personal lives become tools to be used in this process, and those lives in turn are transformed by their involvement in other people's lives.

First, it is impossible to detach one's personal life from this work. When we are knee deep in the lives of these children, we find ourselves confronting our own childhood and the parents, friends, and successes and failures that helped form who we are today as people and as therapists. We reach back into these experiences to find treatment responses. In some cases, we are helpful when we imitate what our parents said or did with us, as we respond to a child's trouble in the present. At other times, our responses are unhelpful or miss some crucial interpersonal piece needed by our troubled patients, just as the parents or adults we are imitating missed that piece in our own development. Our feelings about our own parents can also interfere with our capacity to give our patients' parents the respect and empathy they deserve.

There are times when we surprise ourselves. We respond with more intense emotion than we had anticipated. Reflecting back on the incident leads us to childhood disappointments, fears, and yearnings that had long been buried. In comforting or disciplining a child, we can feel a deeper satisfaction coming from our meeting some need within ourselves for such comfort or external control.

One of the more disturbing experiences in this work is when we discover that what we find in our patients and their families is also in ourselves. We will need to acknowledge and welcome these feelings. As we encounter aggression and sadism, we can feel our own. As we confront a child who is out of control, we can feel our own potential for loss of control. Comforting the sadness in a child reawakens memories of our own childhood sadness. Soothing loneliness revives experiences of loneliness. Trying to help a child cope with greed or the wish to be the center of attention can remind us of our greed for things, food, or attention. Rechanneling anger and frustration will reawaken our own past resentments and disappointments.

We meet ourselves in the depths of our patients' negative

feelings and painful memories. Most of us have made uneasy compromises with this side of ourselves. The constant bombardment by painful and disturbing feelings and memories can leave us vulnerable. Our old compromises may not work in this less civilized world of wounded children and families.

There is opportunity as well as potential trauma in this work. We can greet the reemerging parts of ourself with more compassion and perspective than we did before. As we experience old feelings and memories, we can transform them for ourselves, just as we are trying to help children transform them in themselves.

We can also run from the opportunity. We can block these feelings, memories, or experiences by closing them off. However, *what we cannot feel in ourselves, we cannot treat in others*. We can treat our patients as we treated ourselves and as others treated us when we were frustrated, angry, overwhelmed, sad, and lonely. If we have been punitive to ourselves, there is a risk that we will become punitive to our patients. If we are unforgiving of our own parents, we may not be able to forgive our patients' families or help the children forgive their own families. If we are frightened of our own anger, we may not be able to let children keep and control their anger in a safer way. If we are repulsed by our own sadism, we may become repulsed by the sadism in our patients. If we fear loss of meaning, feelings of despair, or nagging criticism from self-doubt or dislike, we will find it hard to listen to these experiences in our patients.

If we can join and listen to our patients in these darker sides of the spirit, we will find that there is a new opportunity to heal, contain, and teach our own spirits. *The lion's den contains lessons for us as well as for our patients and their families*. As our patients are helped to befriend or tame their inner lions, we are also greeting our own inner lions. In my supervision of others, I watched and helped staff members soothe, give, accept, and put in perspective troublesome feelings, thoughts, and memories. When all was going well, I noticed a parallel process between our patients' therapeutic journey and our own feelings, memories, and spirit. When we could experience and then share our own dark sides, we could notice that our work became easier and more effective. Our sense of our own selves was expanded and made more whole. Children, parents, and staff wrestled with unruly anger, painful sadness, aching yearnings, frightening memories, relentless self-criticism, and debilitating helplessness. These experiences were made livable and transformed through inner acceptance, safe expression, and shared perspective.

Let's conclude our journey with the following story, which tries to illustrate lessons to be learned in the lion's den.

Sam and Molly were tired, frustrated, and hungry. They tumbled into Molly's kitchen and smelled newly baked chocolate chip cookies. They poured some cold milk, stacked up some warm cookies, and sat down at the kitchen table to talk about the day's work.

Sam and Molly were lion tamers. They had been best friends since they took this job last year. They met at the lion's den. Sam and Molly had a lot in common. They loved lions and hated to see the lions confined to the den. They wanted to see them out running in the woods, where they belonged. The zoo had many acres of land in which the lions could roam, but first the lions had to be trained.

A year ago, the chief lion tamer, Ron, and his assistant, Fredda, came up to them one day while they were visiting with the lions in the cage.

"You're here a lot," Ron said to them.

Sam looked at Molly. Molly looked at Sam. They both looked at Fredda and Ron.

"We need some assistants," said Fredda. "Would you like to apply for the job?"

"Sure, but I have no experience training lions," Molly said. "I've read books about them and I visit lions whenever I can, though," she interjected.

"I love lions, but I don't have any experience either," Sam said.

Ron looked at them seriously and then smiled. "What do you like about them?" he asked Sam.

"I like the way they growl and look so strong. I like the way they take such good care of the baby lions. Lions like to play, too. I saw them batting the ball around yesterday. They broke the ball into pieces. I must admit, sometimes I'm scared of them."

"I think they're beautiful," said Molly, "but I think it's sad when they can't go out of the den. I hope you don't mind me saying that."

Ron kept smiling. "We're worried that they'll hurt someone or run away and not be able to take care of themselves. What would you try to do for them?"

Molly gulped and then spoke up. "I think we should teach them to be strong and good to themselves and other lions. I think we should teach them how to take care of themselves, or they will always need to be in a cage or need to have us around. How will they grow up?"

"I want to teach them how to be friends with all the other animals in the woods and kids even," said Sam. "They could have more friends if they didn't frighten all the other animals and kids who come to visit them."

"Those are good ideas. You sound like just the kind of trainers we need," said Ron. "We look for things other than experience when we're hiring our staff, because we're always looking for better ways to train lions. Right now, we know how to keep them safe and keep them from hurting other lions. But we want to do a lot more for them!"

Ron was getting excited as he spoke. "We want to teach them to tame their anger, share their sadness so it gets lighter to carry, accept and forgive themselves so that they can like themselves more, learn how to be a good friend so that they don't feel lonely all the time, and *have more fun!* It's hard work, but we're going to try our hardest. Do you want to join the team?"

"Sure," said Sam.

"I really want to be a lion tamer!" said Molly.

That was a year ago. Ron and Fredda were right. This was hard work. Each lion was so different from every other lion. What helped one lion was no good for the next lion. Although Sam and Molly still liked lions and were glad to be lion tamers, they both felt sobered by the experience.

Sam noticed that Molly seemed particularly discouraged today. She hadn't said a word on the ride home. He looked over and noticed tears forming in her eyes.

"What's wrong, Molly?" asked Sam.

"Nothing," Molly replied, and then she really started crying.

Sam went over and gave her a hug. She cried for a long time and then became quiet.

"I have to tell you what I did today. I'm so ashamed of my-self," started Molly. "I squeezed Jimmy the lion really hard when I was leading him back to the den. He had attacked Michelle in the fields and was saying some pretty mean things about her and me."

"Yesterday he called me a 'fucking whore' because I gave Johnny the lion a hug. I know he was jealous, but he didn't stop there. He whispered stuff about me to the younger lions and now they're calling me names, too. They were impossible to train in school this morning. We had to cancel the class and the afternoon outing to the woods."

"Jimmy has a gigantic temper. What did you do to him?" asked Sam.

"I'm so sick of him!" Molly burst out. "He's been here longer than any of the other lions. He's a swine. He doesn't want to tame his anger. He likes to hurt other lions. He doesn't even feel bad after he paws you. Yesterday he ran away. I had to chase him into the woods and tackle him. He just laughed when he saw me limp-ing back to the group."

"I wish I'd seen it. I could've helped you. I was across the field yesterday."

"I should've asked for help. I guess I didn't want to admit that he had gotten to me. I'm just as bad as they are. I thought I loved lions. But I hate Jimmy. I didn't realize until I squeezed him and I wanted to smash him down on the ground. I didn't, but I wanted to, and I'm afraid I might do it next time. I hate him! I hate him! I never want to see him again!"

Molly started to cry again. Sam felt so bad for her. He didn't know what to do or say. Then he remembered Michelle, a very young and angry lion who had been in the training program when he first started his job. Sam knew what it was to hate a lion, be-cause he hated Michelle. It didn't start off that way.

At first, she was his favorite lion. They used to have long talks, and sometimes Sam was the only lion tamer who could help Michelle calm down. One day it all changed. She started a riot in the den. She incited all the other lions to roar and run around wildly, throwing the furniture and tearing the paper off the walls. Sam and Gino (another lion tamer) had had to physically hold her and carry her to the quiet cage.

When she bit him, he yelled at her. He told her that the riot was all her fault and blamed her for the broken furniture and the bruises on her roommate's paws. Gino had to silence him and take over the situation. What he really remembered was how she kept smiling when he was yelling at her. She calmly said to him, "You think you're so great, better than the lions. Well, you're not. You're just like my parents. You blame me for everything."

Two weeks later, Michelle left the den. She and Sam had never discussed their yelling match. He had never apologized. She hadn't either. They avoided each other. Sam felt ashamed when he thought about it. He had talked to his supervisor (Sue) about this incident, but he had never told any of the other lion tamers about it.

"You know, Molly, we aren't any better than the lions. Michelle was right. And I don't think we should try to be," Sam said. He then told Molly his story.

Molly calmed down as she listened to Sam. She was surprised. She thought Sam was one of the best lion tamers in the lion's den. He was so kind and understanding toward the lions. He always seemed to have some creative plan to help even the most difficult lions.

"Gee, Sam, I didn't think it would be like this. I wanted to help the lions tame their anger and solve their problems. I didn't realize that I had some taming to do inside myself. I thought all the anger was in the lions—not us," said Molly.

"Me too. I never thought I could be that mean. The lions count on us to be different. They need us to have more control and not to fight back," Sam said.

"I think we're more like the lions than we thought we were," said Molly.

"You bet we are," said Sam. "That's what Clare and Sue (lion tamer supervisors) have been trying to tell us. Sue told me we have our inner lions, too. But we are different because our inner lions are more tamed. But she told me that I may discover some new inner lions and may need to do some taming while I'm working here. She said that's what happened to her."

They both sat quietly for a long time.

"What are you going to do, Molly?" asked Sam.

"I think I'll talk to Clare about it. But I think I better tell Jimmy that I'm sorry. I think I can also tell him that I've tamed that lion that got out of control yesterday. He might be worried about it coming back. He's met some pretty mean lion tamers in his short life."

The next day, Sam picked Molly up on the way to work for the evening shift. They had a plan.

When they arrived at the lion's den, Sam went right over to Jimmy.

"I have a letter for you," he said.

"What?" Jimmy asked, looking surprised. "From who?"

"From Molly. She wanted to tell you something, but she didn't know whether you'd listen."

"I'm not talking to her," said Jimmy. "She's mean."

"Will you let me read the letter?"

"Okay, but I'm not talking to that bitch!"

Sam read:

Dear Jimmy,

I'm sorry for squeezing you. I'm sorry for getting so angry with you. Sometimes I have to tame my inner lions, too. I had a good talk with them last night. I hope you will give me another chance tonight. I'm sure I can handle it. If we need help, Sam said he would help us.

Your friend,
Molly

Jimmy listened quietly with his back to Sam and his head in his hands. When Sam was finished, he turned around and said, "Can I have that?"

"Sure," said Sam.

Later that evening, Jimmy asked Molly for some help with his homework. When they were finished, she helped him brush his mane, untangle his tail, and get into bed. With gratitude and satisfaction, she tucked him in and left him to sleep soundly through the night. They were friends again until the next battle . . . but she felt humbled and better prepared for the next one.

THE END

(and Good Night!)

Appendix

A. The People: Patients

The following descriptions are more detailed accounts of the children who have appeared in this book. As I noted in the preface, each child is a composite of actual patients. I have changed the identifying details for each patient to protect the confidentiality of the real children and families involved. Any similarity to actual people is purely coincidental.

Michael

Michael is an eight-year-old "wimp," according to his father and peers. He whines and yells when he becomes upset at home and at school. The children make fun of him, and we are worried that his alcoholic father hits him when he starts this at home. He was admitted to the hospital because he started to threaten to hurt himself with a knife when he didn't get his way at home. He has a history of persistent accidents and has had many visits to the local emergency room for minor injuries.

His mother is psychologically fragile and was hospitalized for suicidal ideation during Michael's hospitalization. His father works as an inventory clerk for the military and has un-treated alcoholism. Michael is cute and physically competent. The staff initially liked him, but his whining and passivity didn't wear well after a while. He is frequently the brunt of jokes by other kids on the unit.

If you came onto the unit, Michael is the attractive (in a waiflike way), skinny kid with the big intelligent eyes who is watching or sitting on a time-out chair, pouting and trying to peel paint from the wall.

Paul

Paul is nine years old and "tough." His biological mother left town when he was a baby. His father is in jail for armed rob-bery. Both parents were drug and alcohol abusers and lived chaotic lives before Paul was taken from them permanently when he was seven. After several foster families, Paul was placed in a preadoptive foster family two years ago. The first year went well, but he started to be hard to manage within the last year.

He was always a bit of a loner, but he began to spend almost all of his time alone. At home he was oppositional, re-fused food during meals, was often obnoxious on family outings, and began to run away. He was admitted to the hospital after spending three nights away from home. His parents still do not know where he was during this time.

Although plans are for him to return home, the parents have expressed worries about adopting Paul. They are startled by his newly displayed anger. He works hard in school, though he has a minor learning disability and has been on medication for attentional problems.

If you came on the unit, Paul is the well-built, lively boy who is arguing with the counselor who is looking fed up. Paul's body is always moving. He is articulate but gets louder and an-grier when he can't change the counselor's mind. If you came at night, he might be crying softly to himself in bed. He would deny it, if you tried to comfort him.

Heather

Heather is seven years old. She has been in day treatment, but her behavior became too disorganized and bizarre to manage in that setting. She is sexually and aggressively impulsive at home and in day treatment. At the time of admission, she was unkempt and smelled of urine. She is psychotic most of the time, helped in the past by psychotropic medication. However, she began to develop side effects, and her doctors and her adoptive parents are concerned about her long-term need to be on these medications.

Her early history is a nightmare of sexual and physical abuse. Her biological mother scalded her in bathtubs, locked her in closets for days, left her unattended in her apartment as a toddler where she ate toothpaste to survive, and allowed changing boyfriends to sexually abuse her. It is believed that her mother was also seriously mentally ill. Nothing is known about her biological father.

Heather's adoptive mother is intensely involved with her and totally committed to making her better. She fights frequently with her husband about Heather. The adoptive father is a kind and hard-working man who is frustrated because their lives are so dominated by Heather's troubles. He wonders how long they can keep this up.

When you observe the unit, Heather is almost always holding the hand of a counselor or playing alone in her room or contained in the quiet room. She is skinny and waiflike, with awestruck blue eyes and long, scraggly blond hair. The staff all dream about her. She haunts us. We work hard not to do things for her when she can do them for herself. The other kids are frightened by her weirdness, disgusted by her hygiene, and jealous of the special treatment given her by the staff.

Ralph

Ralph is twelve years old. He is fat and coarse. He was admitted because he attacked the principal of his school during a lecture on his disruptive behavior in science class. He had been disciplined and suspended frequently during the last six months. He had been picked up by the police for stealing and disturbing the peace at a local shopping mall. He lives with his biological father and stepmother and a two-year-old half sister.

Ralph's biological parents had fought frequently, and both abused alcohol. His mother left the family when Ralph was four years old. He lived with his father and various foster families before his father remarried three years ago. Ralph has lived with this new family for one tumultuous year. His stepmother believes that he cannot return home. His father is torn but also thinks that they cannot control him at home. The plans are for residential treatment with active family involvement.

You could never miss Ralph. He is very unattractive and seems to revel in it. He wears tight, ill-fitting clothes and struggles over washing and brushing his teeth. He loves to "gross out" the girls. When he is angry, he completely loses control and strikes out at anyone in his path.

Jimmy

Jimmy is ten years old but looks and acts much younger. He is not very smart and has a severe learning disability. He cannot read or do simple arithmetic problems. Jimmy's impulsiveness has raised serious questions about whether he has neurological deficits, and he is receiving a complete neuropsychological evaluation. He was returned from a recent foster placement because he was unmanageable. He alternates between angry tirades against adults and peers and serious attacks on himself. He articulates that he is "no good" and tells about all the people who have "dumped" him to prove it. His biological mother died when he was three years old, after abandoning him to his abusive, alcoholic father. She died in a car crash, driving to the West Coast with his younger sister, who was also killed. After sustaining several years of neglect and abuse at the hands of his father, he started a series of foster placements that never worked out. His caseworker is looking for a residential placement for him.

You can spot Jimmy immediately on the unit. He sits or

stands as if he doesn't deserve the space. He never makes it through an activity, because his anger or frustration overwhelms him and he acts up. He demands staff time and then wrecks it, if they seem to be having too good a time. Jimmy is a challenge, and staff are counting (guiltily) the days until his discharge. He dissolves into tears when he is held and cries for his mother. After an outburst, he can rest in your arms and cry himself to sleep.

Maria

Maria is twelve years old. She was admitted for suicidal thoughts and increasing withdrawal in school. She is a good student and seems much older than her age. She mothers the younger patients and is very responsible. Staff love and identify with her. Her biological mother is schizophrenic and alcoholic. She lives on the street or in shelters in Maria's city neighborhood. Maria passes her on the street, but her mother rarely recognizes her. After several years of foster placement, Maria was granted her wish to live with her father and his old and dying mother. Her father is an isolated and well-meaning man who is considered odd but harmless by his neighbors. He works temporary jobs as a security guard in local factories.

Maria's school counselor was concerned about her constant talking and writing about beautiful and peaceful deaths. Maria has pretty much brought herself up.

Maria is tall and thin. She has a bad complexion, which she tries to hide by keeping her long, scraggly hair in her face. She is always clean and neatly dressed. You would notice her most often talking to the female staff. They love her, and everyone (including me) dreams of adopting her.

Johnny

Johnny is eight years old and is considered the chief troublemaker on the unit. He lives with his maternal grandmother and various aunts and uncles. His father is in jail. He killed Johnny's mother when Johnny was six months old. Johnny has been a behavioral problem for most of his life. His relatives say that he is much like his father. He has a severe learning disability and cannot read. He is well liked by some peers, who let him lead them into trouble at school and in the neighborhood. He steals money from his grandmother and stole a bike from a child across the street. He is very aggressive, and the school believes he is too dangerous to return. He is unable to fall asleep and disrupts the unit at bedtime.

You will always find Johnny on a time-out chair or in the quiet room. Staff appreciate what a hard life he has had, but they are frequently frustrated and angry at his troublemaking. He continually expresses his disinterest in treatment, but he participates in some groups with zest and interest.

Raoul

Raoul is six years old. He has a close relationship to his mother, who calls the unit several times a shift. Raoul is very small for his age. He is hyperactive, sets fires, gets easily disorganized and frustrated, and has a "big" temper. His tantrums were a major problem in his brief but unsuccessful attempt to go to school. He never wanted to go to day care or preschool. He steals toys from other kids and doesn't know how to play cooperatively with his peers. His mother lives with a boyfriend who is willing to become involved in treatment, but he does not know what to do. Raoul's mother has been called overprotective by outpatient therapists. His biological father has never been involved in his life. His mother says she did not know this man and currently does not know his whereabouts.

Raoul is dark and very small. You would notice his big brown eyes and his thumb, which is always in his mouth. He avoids other kids and likes to sit by himself. He would watch TV all day if given the choice. Staff treat him as if he were four years old, and he doesn't seem to mind.

Donna

Donna is an attractive and feisty ten-year-old. She is a natural leader, so the kids like her and look up to her. She lives with her mother and two younger sisters. Her father and mother are separated. He lives in the neighborhood with his mother and has trouble keeping jobs as an unskilled laborer. Donna set a major fire in her apartment, which was half of a two-family house. Her family is facing eviction and is unable to rent another apartment in the neighborhood after her name appeared in a newspaper article describing the fire she set.

She has refused to attend school regularly for the last two years, and her mother is worried about her increasingly tough behavior at home. She swears, talks back, has physical fights with her sisters, and will not talk with her mother about her changes in behavior. She also refuses to go to therapy at the community mental health center in her neighborhood. The family has been attending family therapy, where she is silent or disruptive.

Donna is either the life of the party or the party wrecker. She is athletic and very bright. When she is cooperative, she can contribute and enjoy the groups on the unit. The staff like her and easily forgive her when she is difficult, because she is sincerely repentant and great fun at other times.

Lisa

Lisa is eleven, but she dresses and looks like a teenager. She has the loudest voice on the unit. She is aggressive and easily frustrated. She can strike out at kids or staff and has a history of cutting herself and biting her lips until they bleed. Lisa lived with her mother and younger sister until she revealed that she had been persistently sexually molested by her mother's brother during his visits to her home. She was placed in foster homes after this disclosure. Although her mother believes her and supports her, the rest of her extended family has called her a liar and defended her uncle. She and her mother have been ostracized by the family. Court appearances have been required, because her uncle is being prosecuted for sexual abuse.

Lisa was admitted because she was unmanageable at home. Her mother is committed to learning how to parent her and feels guilty about not detecting the sexual abuse earlier. She admits that she probably did not want to know. She and Lisa are preparing for Lisa to go to residential treatment, where the mother plans to be very involved.

Lisa is a unit challenge. She argues, fights, and devalues milieu staff when she is not getting enough attention. But she is equally difficult to manage when she is getting attention. She can't seem to handle close relationships and adults asserting authority. She often reminds us that adults are weak or cruel. She will loudly point out when staff raise their voices or seem to be too harsh. She seems to be jealous of the attention that younger children receive and accept. Lisa makes us all think about where some of these children have been.

Andrew

Andrew is seven. He lives with his parents and is an only child. His parents are concerned about but confused and overwhelmed by his behavior. Although he was toilet trained briefly, he soils or wets his pants at home and in school. He is also a behavior management problem at home or in school. He is so loud and disruptive in public that his parents have stopped bringing him to restaurants, shopping malls, and even playgrounds. His parents became alarmed when neighbors accused him of torturing their cat. He was admitted when he ran away after they confronted him with this information.

Andrew is slightly overweight and a messy dresser. He can be seen playing by himself with superhero toys engaged in fierce battles. He fights with other kids over who should go first in the line at the door and makes fun of kids who are taking their time-outs. He is very curious about what cars the staff drive and where they go at night. He doesn't like to talk about his feelings or his actions after a disruption on the unit.

Maggie

Maggie is six years old and lives with her parents and a younger brother. Maggie rules the house. Her parents moved out of their bedroom when Maggie demanded more space. She is a terror at family gatherings, and her parents bribe her with toys and food to behave. Her screaming tantrums have caused neighbors to call police for disruption of the peace. She is forbidden to play with most of the neighborhood children. Her parents are alternately amused and alarmed by her antics. Her teachers are not amused, and she spends long periods of time in the principal's office. She started a fire in a school bathroom after being kept in for recess. She seems to never regret her actions, and she is immune to criticism. Although the children on the unit like her, they are afraid of her tantrums. Staff find her funny and impossible. She is bright and articulate and has great ideas in unit projects. But she is impossible if she does not get her way or the attention she feels she deserves. Staff wonder whether she ever cries.

Maggie looks like a female Dennis the Menace. Her twinkling eyes, freckled face, and carrot-colored hair shoot through the unit on her troublemaking missions. She is not mean, but she is unruly and lacks any ability to wait her turn. She is a real challenge, and some staff are fed up with her.

B. The People: Staff

The following is a list of the staff who worked on the Children's Psychiatric Unit at New England Memorial Hospital during my stay as the director of the unit (1977-1987). They include staff counselors, nurses, social workers, occupational therapists, recreational therapists, expressive therapists, educators, psychologists, pediatricians, psychiatrists, and all the trainees in these fields. The work described in this book is a synthesis of their questions, suggestions, and creative interventions, as well as their unbounded energy, enthusiasm, and commitment to their work. The clinical vignettes actually happened. But I have changed names and pertinent facts in order to fully conceal the identities of children and staff involved.

Michael Abbruzzese
Betty Adelsberger, R.N.
Mirna Aeschlimann, M.D.
Sarah Allen
Lonnie Anostario
Melissa Antul

Alexander Asch, M.D.
Judith Asci, R.N.
Susan Austrian, M.D.
Susan Ayers, LIC.S.W.
Keith Baber
Marlene Baim

Mitchell Bakst
Betsy Barnett
Richard Barnum, M.D.
Jean Barstow, R.N.
Jane Bartolomi, R.N.
John Batista
Catherine Bauer, M.D.
Julie Beck-Goss
Karen Belanoff
Melissa Belz
Brenda Bemporad, Ph.D.
Barbara Bennett
Sue Bent, R.N.
Richard Berlin, M.D.
Liz Bezdighian
Barbara Bidwell, R.N.
David Binder, M.D.
Peggy Booth, R.N.
Ginny Bouley, R.N.
Sue Bowler
Mary Lou Bracciotti
Michael Brady, R.N.
Elizabeth Braun, R.N.
Karen Braunwald, Ph.D.
Julie Breskin, Ph.D.
Nick Browning, M.D.
Judy Bunn, R.N.
Stephen Burnham
Eileen Burns, R.N.
Jean Campbell
Sandy Caponi
Mario Carcamo, M.D.
Dan Carella
Mary Carlson, R.N.
Jody Carner, R.N.
Susan Caron
Linda Carter-Ake, R.N.
Margret Casey, R.N.

Trish Caven
Susan Childs
Debbie Clark, R.N.
Joyce Coccia
Brenda Cogan
Brent Cohen
Glenda Collis, R.N.
Joyce Colman, LIC.S.W.
Pamela Corrigan, R.N.
Linda Cotagno, R.N.
Rocco Coviello, R.N.
Pat Cronin, R.N.
Sue Curtis, R. N.
Jackie Cvinar, R.N.
Ruth D'Agostino
Stan Dalton, M.D.
Brenda Daly
Vivian Davidovich
Tony Degregorio
Ruth DeLisio
Ginny DelSignore
Pat DeMeule, R.N.
Virginia Demos, Ed.D.
Laurie Dennhardt
Gino DeSalvatore, MTRS
Marylou Desmond
Clare DeZengotita, R.N.
Peg Dickerman, LIC.S.W.
Lehanna DiLibero
Katie Dillon, R.N.
Kathi Dimarchi, R.N.
Rita DiStefano
Catherine Donovan, R.N.
Gary Donovan, M.D.
Judy Dueker
Ginny Eagan, R.N.
Rochelle Eckstein
Emme Edge

Tricia Edmonds
Sheri Eisenstadt
Nancy Ellis
Ginger Ellmyer
Ann Epstein, M.D.
Alex Erickson, R.N.
Caryl Fairbanks
David Fassler, M.D.
Jamie Feldman, M.D.
Helen Finch
Tricia Finigan
Daniel Fitzgerald, M.D.
David Foster, M.D.
Mary Lee Garant, R.N.
Katie Garate
Olga Gashugni, R.N.
Jack Genakos
Kathy Geraty
Ronald Geraty, M.D.
Beth Gilmore
John Gould, M.D.
Katherine Grimes, M.D.
Bonnie Grissop
Charles Gunnoe, Ed.D.
Sarah Hale, R.N.
Bob Hallett
Dorothy Hanks, M.S.
Della Hardy
Stacy Harris
Beverly Harron, L.P.N.
Julie Hassett
Joanne Heineck
Stephanie Hill
Donnagene Hofmann
Fred Holmes
Ruth Hornstein
Kay Horrigan, R.N.
Paul Howes

Barbara Hubbard
Marie Hunt
Deborah Hutchinson
Joan Jablow
Jim Jacobson
Becky Jacques
Cheryl Jacques, R.N.
Joan Jordan, R.N.
Steve Kanofsky
Ellen Kantrovitz
Pat Kenneally
Debbie Keohane, R.N.
Stephen Kerzner, M.D.
Jackie Keshian, R.N.
Bill King
Walter King, R.N.
Jim Kirk
Kathy Kurras
Jan LaBazzo, R.N.
Dennis Lantry, R.N.
Joanne Lapo
Meredith Laufer
Allyson LeBlanc, R.N.
Ben Leder
Joy Libby, R.N.
Pat Linneman, R.N.
Betsy Locke
Peggy Loscalzo
Maria Luciani
Tammy MacAllister
Beth McCabe, R.N.
Margo McClendon
Edward McClung
Ann McDonald
Martha McDonald
Betsy McLaughlin
Bev McNaught, R.N.
Doreen McNeil

Peggy McNeil, R.N.
Betty Malewicz
Allegra Manacher
Lisa Mancini
Susan Manheim, Ph.D.
Joseph Marotta
Cathie Ann Marquese
Lisa Maselli
Andrea Masterman, Ph.D.
Neo R. Mathabe
Linda Mazie
Sharon Mendlesberg
Leon Michaud
Eric Miller
Neil Miller
Hope Misail
Sandi Mitchell, R.N.
Cathy Mitkus
Sue Moran-Barry
Joyce Mucci
Rowena Nash
Jody Newton
Betty Nicholson
Francis Nicoll
Joan Nikonchuck, R.N.
Andrea Nugent
Robert O'Berry
Mark O'Connoll
Bonnie Ohye, Ph.D.
Paul Organ, M.D.
Abigail Ostow, M.D.
Julie Palm
Allen Palmer, M.D.
Susan Parry, R.N.
Chris Patterson
Janice Perates
Donna Petengil, R.N.
Ann Marie Pino

Elliot Pittel, M.D.
Sue Polevy
Lee Ann Powers
Adele Pressman, M.D.
Pam Quinlan, LIC.S.W.
Gail Rappaport
Paula Rauch, M.D.
Laurie Raymond, M.D.
Wendy Reich
Janet Rice
Donna Richardson
Wendy Ripley
Sam Rofman, M.D.
Deborah Rosenman
Diane Rubin
Jean St. Pierre
Jody Sakakeeny, R.N.
John Sardella
Maureen Savage, R.N.
Audry Scalfo
Carol Scally
Susan Schieb, R.N.
Jill Schlanger, LIC.S.W.
Paul Schnellor, M.D.
Bryan Schultz
Jodi Schwebel
Raquel Selig
Rebecca Shahmoon
Kathie Sherman
Paul Shiebler
Alan Shields, M.D.
Debra Siciliano
Jan Siedelman, R.N.
Ron Siegel, Ph.D.
Jane Simpson, R.N.
Mathew Sisson
Amy Slutzky
Mary Smallis

Maureen Smith-Wojcik
Lynn Stanley
Heidi Steele
Leslie Steenstra
Ginny Steinberg, R.N.
Ron Steingard, M.D.
Barbara Stephens, R.N., M.S.
Ami Stern
Andrea Stern, M.D.
Lorna Stockbridge, R.N.
David Stoler
Karen Stoler
Mel Stoler
Colleen Stone, R.N.
Joyce Sullivan
Sue Sussman, R.N.
Liz Taylor
Lynette Taylor-Schmidt, R.N.
Karen Teitelbaum
Lisa Tiabi-Goss
Cathy Tingley
Barbara Tocco, R.N.
Liz Tomlinson, M.D.

Molly Torra
Phil Troped
Laura Trulli
Steve Tryder
Ann Twohig, R.N.
Amy Utoft, R.N.
George Velmanchos
Suzanne Vienneau
Alice Viola
Pam Voith
Connie Wall
Ellie Weintraub, R.N.
Beth Weisblatt, R.N.
Gail Williams
Stephanie Williams
Susan Williams
Peter Wintheisen, R.N.
Pat Wood, R.N.
Patricia Wright, M.D.
David Zoll, Ph.D.
Fredda Zuckerman-Match,
    LIC.S.W.
Karen Zwinakis

REFERENCES

Adessa, S., and Laatsch, A. "Therapeutic Use of Visiting in Residential Treatment." In G. Weber and B. Haberlein (eds.), *Residential Treatment of Emotionally Disturbed Children.* New York: Behavioral Publications, 1972.

Aichorn, A. *Wayward Youth.* New York: Viking Penguin, 1935.

Alt, H. *Residential Treatment for the Disturbed Child.* New York: International Universities Press, 1960.

American Academy of Child and Adolescent Psychiatry, Committee on Rights and Legal Matters. *Policy Statement: Corporal Punishment in Schools.* Washington, D.C.: American Academy of Child and Adolescent Psychiatry, 1988.

American Academy of Child and Adolescent Psychiatry, Task Force on Adolescent Hospitalization. *Model of Minimum Staffing Patterns for Hospitals Providing Acute Inpatient Treatment for Children and Adolescents with Psychiatric Illnesses.* Washington, D.C.: American Academy of Child and Adolescent Psychiatry, 1990.

Barkley, R. *Defiant Children: A Clinician's Manual for Parent Training.* New York: Guilford Press, 1987.

Barth, R. P. *Social and Cognitive Treatment of Children and Adoles-cents: Practical Strategies for Problem Behaviors.* San Francisco: Jossey-Bass, 1986.

Beck, J. C., Macht, L. B., Levinson, D. J., and Strauss, M. "A Controlled Experimental Study of the Therapist-Administrator Split." *American Journal of Psychiatry,* 1967, *124,* 467–474.

Becker, W. C. Parents Are Teachers: A Child Management Pro-gram. Champaign, Ill.: Research Press, 1971.

Berlin, I. N. "Developmental Issues in the Psychiatric Hospitali-zation of Children." *American Journal of Psychiatry,* 1978, *135,* 1044–1048.

Bettelheim, B. *Love Is Not Enough.* New York: Free Press, 1950.

Bettelheim, B. *Truants from Life.* New York: Free Press, 1955.

Bettelheim, B. *A Home for the Heart.* New York: Knopf, 1974.

Bettelheim, B., and Sylvester, E. "A Therapeutic Milieu." *Amer-ican Journal of Orthopsychiatry,* 1948, *18,* 191–206.

Campbell, M., and Spencer, E. K. "Psychopharmacology in Child and Adolescent Psychiatry: A Review of the Past Five Years." *Journal of the American Academy of Child and Adolescent Psy-chiatry,* 1988, *27,* 269–279.

Caudill, W. A. *The Psychiatric Hospital as a Small Society.* Cam-bridge: Harvard University Press, 1958.

Caudill, W. A., Redlich, F. C., Gilmore, H. R., and Brody, E. B. "Social Structure and Interaction Processes on a Psy-chiatric Ward." *American Journal of Orthopsychiatry,* 1952, *22,* 314–334.

Clark, L. *SOS! Help for Parents.* Bowling Green, Kentucky: Par-ents Press, 1985.

Cohen, R. E., and Grinspoon, L. "Limit Setting as a Correc-tive Ego Experience." *Archives of General Psychiatry,* 1963, *8,* 74–79.

Coppolillo, H. P. *Psychodynamic Psychotherapy of Children: An In-troduction to the Art and the Techniques.* Madison, Wis.: Interna-tional Universities Press, 1987.

Cotton, N. S. "The Developmental-Clinical Rationale for the Use of Seclusion in the Psychiatric Treatment of Children." *American Journal of Orthopsychiatry,* 1989, *59,* 442–450.

Cotton, N. S., and Geraty, R. "Therapeutic Space Design: Planning an Inpatient Children's Unit." *American Journal of Orthopsychiatry*, 1984, *54*, 624-636.

Critchley, D. L., and Berlin, I. N. "Parent Participation in Milieu Treatment of Young Psychotic Children." *American Journal of Orthopsychiatry*, 1981, *51*, 149-155.

Dalton, R., and Forman, M. A. *Psychiatric Hospitalization of School-Age Children.* Washington, D.C.: American Psychiatric Press, 1992.

Dangel, R. F., and Polster, R. A. *Parent Training: Foundations of Research and Practice.* New York: Guilford Press, 1984.

Dardig, J. C., and Heward, W. L. *Sign Here: A Contracting Book for Children and Their Parents.* Bridgewater, N.J.: Fournies, 1981.

De Risis, W. J., and Butz, G. *Writing Behavioral Contracts: A Case Simulation Practice Manual.* Champaign, Ill.: Research Press, 1975.

DeSalvatore, G. "Therapeutic Recreators as Family Therapists: Working with Families on a Children's Psychiatric Unit." *Therapeutic Recreation Journal*, 1989, 23-29.

DeSalvatore, G., and Rosenman, D. "The Parent-Child Activity Group: Using Activities to Work with Children and Their Families in Residential Treatment." *Child Care Quarterly*, 1986, *15*, 213-223.

Dinkmeyer, D., and McKay, G. *The Parent's Handbook: Systematic Training for Effective Parenting.* Circle Pines, Minn.: American Guidance Service, 1976.

Dinkmeyer, D., and McKay, G. *The Parent's Guide: STEP/Teen.* Circle Pines, Minn.: American Guidance Service, 1983.

Drisco, J. W. "Memo to Institution Staff: Physical Involvement with Children—A Therapeutic Intervention." *Journal of the Child Welfare League of America, Inc.*, 1976, *55*, 469-477.

Dumas, L. S. *Talking with Your Child About a Troubled World.* New York: Fawcett Columbine, 1992.

Erikson, E. H. *Childhood and Society.* New York: Norton, 1950.

Erikson, E. H. *Identity and the Life Cycle.* New York: Norton, 1980.

Erikson, J. *Activity, Recovery, and Growth.* New York: Norton, 1976.

Faber, A., and Mazlish, E. *How to Talk So Kids Will Listen and Listen So Kids Will Talk.* New York: Avon Books, 1980.

Faber, A., and Mazlish, E. *Siblings Without Rivalry.* New York: Avon Books, 1987.

Fantuzzo, J. W. "Effects of Adult and Peer Social Initiations on the Social Behavior of Withdrawn, Maltreated Preschool Children." *Journal of Consulting and Clinical Psychology,* 1988, *56,* 34-39.

Fassler, D., and Cotton, N. "The Use of Seclusion in the Psychiatric Treatment of Children: Results of a National Survey." *Hospital and Community Psychiatry,* 1992, *43,* 370-374.

Forehand, R. L., and McMahon, R. J. *Helping the Noncompliant Child: A Clinician's Guide to Parent Training.* New York: Guilford Press, 1981.

Fraiberg, S. H. *The Magic Years.* New York: Charles Scribner's Sons, 1959.

Freud, A. *Normality and Pathology in Childhood: Assessments of Development.* New York: International Universities Press, 1965.

Gair, D. S. "Guidelines for Children and Adolescents." In K. Tardiff (ed.), *The Psychiatric Uses of Seclusion and Restraint.* Washington, D.C.: American Psychiatric Press, 1984.

Gair, D. S. "Psychiatric Restraint in Children and Adolescents." In R. Rosner and H. I. Schwartz (eds.), *Juvenile Psychiatry and the Law.* Washington, D.C.: American Psychiatric Press, 1989.

Garrison, W. T., and others. "Aggression and Counteraggression During Child Psychiatric Hospitalization." *Journal of the American Academy of Child and Adolescent Psychiatry,* 1990, *29,* 242-250.

Ginott, H. G. *Between Parent and Child.* New York: Macmillan, 1965.

Ginott, H. G. *Between Parent and Teenager.* New York: Macmillan, 1969.

Glenn, H. S., and Nelsen, J. *Raising Self-Reliant Children in a Self-Indulgent World.* Rocklin, Calif.: Prima, 1989.

Gordon, T. *P.E.T.: Parent Effectiveness Training.* New York: Wyden, 1970.

Green, W. H. *Child and Adolescent Clinical Psychopharmacology.* Baltimore, Md.: Williams & Wilkins, 1991.

Grisanti, M. L., Smith, D. G., and Flatter, C. *Parents' Guide to Understanding Discipline: Infancy Through Preteen.* Englewood Cliffs, N.J.: Prentice Hall, 1990.

Gutheil, T. G. "Observations on the Theoretical Bases for Seclusion of the Psychiatric Inpatient." *American Journal of Psychiatry,* 1978, *135,* 325-328.

Gutheil, T. G. "On the Therapy in Clinical Administration, Part I: Introduction and History; Administration and Its Relation to Psychotherapy." *Psychiatric Quarterly,* 1982a, *54,* 3-10.

Gutheil, T. G. "On the Therapy in Clinical Administration, Part II: The Administrative Contract, Alliance, Ultimatum, and Goal." *Psychiatric Quarterly,* 1982b, *54,* 11-17.

Gutheil, T. G. "On the Therapy in Clinical Administration, Part III: Administrative Applications of Space and Time; Countertransference and Resistance; Summary and Conclusions." *Psychiatric Quarterly,* 1982c, *54,* 18-25.

Harper, G. "The Empathic Formulation." Unpublished manuscript, Children's Hospital Medical Center, Harvard Medical School, 1991.

Harper, G., and Geraty, R. "Hospital and Residential Treatment." In R. Michels and J. Cavenar (eds.), *Psychiatry.* Philadelphia: Lippincott, 1987.

Hartup, W. W. "Peer Interaction and Behavioral Development of the Individual Child." In E. Schopler and R. J. Reichler (eds.), *Psychopathology and Child Development: Research and Treatment.* New York: Plenum, 1976.

Hartup, W. W. "Peer Relationships." In P. H. Mussen (ed.), *Handbook of Child Psychology,* Vol. 4: *Socialization, Personality, and Social Development.* New York: Wiley, 1983.

Havens, L. *Making Contact.* Cambridge, Mass.: Harvard University Press, 1986.

Hendren, R. L., and Berlin, I. N. *Inpatient Care of Children and Adolescents: A Multicultural Approach.* New York: Wiley, 1991.

Herbert, M. *Behavioral Treatment of Children with Problems: A Practical Manual.* San Diego, Calif.: Academic Press, 1987.

Hersen, M., and Van Hasselt, V. B. *Behavior Therapy with Children and Adolescents: A Clinical Approach.* New York: Wiley, 1987.

Hoedemaker, E. D. "Psychoanalytic Techniques and Ego Modifications." *International Journal of Psychoanalysis,* 1960, *41,* 1-3.

Hoffman, L. (ed.). *The Evaluation and Care of Severely Disturbed Children.* New York: Spectrum Publications Medical & Scientific Books, 1982.

Hornik, H. W. "Introduction to the Northampton Center for Children and Families." Unpublished manuscript, 1987.

Joshi, P. T., Capozzoli, J. A., and Coyle, J. T. "Use of a Quiet Room on an Inpatient Unit." *Journal of the American Academy of Child and Adolescent Psychiatry,* 1988, *27,* 642–644.

Kalogjera, I. J., Bedi, A., Watson, W. N., and Meyer, A. D. "Impact of Therapeutic Management on Use of Seclusion and Restraint with Disruptive Adolescent Inpatients." *Hospital and Community Psychiatry,* 1989, *40*(3), 280–285.

Kashani, J. H., and Cantwell, D. P. "Characteristics of Children Admitted to an Inpatient Community Mental Health Center." *Archives of General Psychiatry,* 1983, *40,* 397–400.

Kendall, P. C., and Braswell, L. *Cognitive-Behavioral Therapy for Impulsive Children.* New York: Guilford Press, 1985.

Leach, P. *Your Baby & Child from Birth to Age Five.* New York: Knopf, 1988.

Lewis, M. (ed.). *Child and Adolescent Psychiatry: A Comprehensive Textbook.* Baltimore, Md.: Williams & Wilkins, 1991.

Lewis, M., and Volkmar, F. *Clinical Aspects of Child and Adolescent Development.* (3rd ed.) Philadelphia: Lea & Febiger, 1990.

Lickona, T. *Raising Good Children.* New York: Bantam Books, 1983.

Lion, J. R. "Training for Battle: Thoughts on Managing Aggressive Patients." *Hospital and Community Psychiatry,* 1987, *38,* 882–884.

McGoldrick, M., Pearce, J. L., and Giordano, J. (eds.). *Ethnicity and Family Therapy.* New York: Guilford Press, 1982.

Mackinnon, R. A., and Michels, R. *The Psychiatric Interview in Clinical Practice.* Philadelphia: Saunders, 1971.

Maier, G. J., and others. "A Model for Understanding and Managing Cycles of Aggression Among Psychiatric Inpatients." *Hospital and Community Psychiatry,* 1987, *38,* 520–524.

Maltsberger, J. "Seclusion and Restraint." Unpublished manuscript. Boston, Mass., 1980.

Marohn, R. C., Dalle-Molle, D., McCarter, E., and Linn, D.

Juvenile Delinquents: Psychodynamic Assessment and Hospital Treatment. New York: Brunner/Mazel, 1980.

Mayer, M. F., Richman, L. H., and Balcerzak, E. A. *Group Care of Children: Crossroads and Transitions.* New York: Child Welfare League of America, 1978.

Mehrabian, A. *Nonverbal Communication.* Hawthorne, N.Y.: Aldine de Gruyter, 1972.

Meltzer, H. Y. (ed.). *Psychopharmacology: The Third Generation of Progress.* New York: Raven Press, 1987.

Millstein, K. H., and Cotton, N. S. "Predictors of the Use of Seclusion on an Inpatient Child Psychiatric Unit." *Journal of the American Academy of Child and Adolescent Psychiatry,* 1990, *29,* 256–264.

Mirkin, M. P., and Koman, S. L. (eds.). *Handbook of Adolescents and Family Therapy.* New York: Gardner Books, 1985.

Nelsen, J. *Positive Discipline.* New York: Ballantine Books, 1987.

Noshpitz, J. D. "Notes on the Theory of Residential Treatment." *Journal of the American Academy of Child Psychiatry,* 1962, *1,* 284–296.

Noshpitz, J. D. "The Psychotherapist in Residential Treatment." In M. F. Mayer and A. Blum (eds.), *Healing Through Living.* Springfield, Ill.: Thomas, 1971.

Noshpitz, J. D. "Toward a History of the Role of Milieu in the Residential Treatment of Children." *Family and Child Mental Health Journal,* 1982, *8,* 5–25.

Ollendick, T. H., and Matson, J. L. "Overcorrection: An Overview." *Behavior Therapy,* 1978, *9,* 830–842.

Parmelee, D. X. "The Adolescent and the Young Adult." In L. I. Sederer (ed.), *Inpatient Psychiatry Diagnosis and Treatment.* (2nd ed.) Baltimore, Md.: Williams & Wilkins, 1982.

Patterson, G. "Responsiveness to Social Stimuli." In L. Krasner and L. P. Ullmann (eds.), *Research in Behavior Modification.* Troy, Mo.: Holt, Rinehart & Winston, 1965.

Patterson, G. *Families: Applications of Social Learning to Family Life.* Champaign, Ill.: Research Press, 1975.

Patterson, G. *Living with Children: New Methods for Parents and Teachers.* Champaign, Ill.: Research Press, 1976.

Patterson, G., Cobb, J. A., and Ray, R. S. "Direct Intervention in the Classroom: A Set of Procedures for the Aggressive Child." In H. E. Adams and I. P. Unikel (eds.), *Issues and Trends in Behavior Therapy.* Springfield, Ill.: Thomas, 1973.

Patterson, G., Reid, J. B., and Dishion, T. *Antisocial Boys,* Vol. 4: A Social Interactional Approach. Eugene, Oreg.: Castalia, 1992.

Patterson, G., Reid, J. B., Jones, R. R., and Conger, R. E. *A Social Learning Approach to Family Intervention.* Eugene, Oreg.: Castalia, 1975.

Perry, S., Cooper, A. M., and Michels, R. "The Psychodynamic Fomulation: Its Purpose, Structure, and Clinical Application." *American Journal of Psychiatry,* 1987, *144,* 543–550.

Popper, C. W. "Child and Adolescent Psychopharmacology." In R. Michels and J. Cavenar (eds.), *Psychiatry.* Philadelphia: Lippincott, 1987a.

Popper, C. W. *Psychiatric Pharmacosciences of Children and Adolescents.* Progress in Psychiatry Series. Washington, D.C.: American Psychiatric Press, 1987b.

Popper, C. W. "PRN Medications and Chemical Restraint." *American Academy of Child and Adolescent Psychiatry Newsletter,* Summer 1990, 7–8.

Redl, F. "The Life-Space Interview-Strategy and Techniques." In F. Redl, *When We Deal with Children: Selected Writings.* New York: Free Press, 1966a.

Redl, F. *When We Deal with Children: Selected Writings.* New York: Free Press, 1966b.

Redl, F., and Wineman, D. *Children Who Hate: Disorganization and Breakdown of Behavior Controls.* New York: Free Press, 1951.

Redl, F., and Wineman, D. *Controls from Within: Techniques for the Treatment of the Aggressive Child.* New York: Free Press, 1952.

Robbins, L. *Deviant Children Grown Up.* Baltimore, Md.: Williams & Wilkins, 1966.

Roff, M. "Childhood Social Interactions and Young Adult Bad Conduct." *Journal of Abnormal and Social Psychology,* 1961, *63,* 333–337.

Roff, M., Sells, S. B., and Golden, M. M. *Social Adjustment and Personality Development in Children.* Minneapolis: University of Minnesota Press, 1972.

Rose, S. D., and Edleson, J. L. *Working with Children and Adolescents in Groups: A Multimethod Approach.* San Francisco: Jossey-Bass, 1987.

Rosen, H., and DiGiacomo, J. N. "The Role of Physical Restraint in the Treatment of Psychiatric Illness." *Journal of Clinical Psychiatry,* 1978, *39,* 228-233.

Rossman, P. G., and Knesper, D. J. "The Early Phase of Hospital Treatment for Disruptive Adolescents." *Journal of the American Academy of Child Psychiatry,* 1976, *15,* 693-708.

Roth, E. A., Roth, L. H. "Children's Understanding of Psychiatric Hospitalization." *American Journal of Psychiatry,* 1984, *141,* 1066-1070.

Schulman, J. L., and Irwin, M. (eds.). *Psychiatric Hospitalization of Children.* Springfield, Ill.: 1982.

Selman, R. L. *The Growth of Interpersonal Understanding: Developmental and Clinical Analysis.* San Diego, Calif.: Academic Press, 1980.

Selman, R. L. "The Development of Interpersonal Competence: The Role of Understanding in Conduct." *Developmental Review,* 1981, *1,* 401-422.

Selman, R. L., and Demorest, A. P. "Observing Children's Interpersonal Negotiation Strategies: Implications of and for a Developmental Model." *Child Development,* 1987, *55,* 288-304.

Selman, R. L., Jaquette, D., and Lavin, D. "Interpersonal Awareness in Children." *American Journal of Orthopsychiatry,* 1977, *47,* 264-274.

Shaffer, D., Erhardt, A. A., and Greenhill, L. L. (eds.). *The Clinical Guide to Child Psychiatry.* New York: Free Press, 1985.

Shapiro, T. "The Psychodynamic Formulation in Child and Adolescent Psychiatry." *Journal of the American Academy of Child and Adolescent Psychiatry,* 1989, *28,* 675-680.

Silberman, M. L., and Wheelan, S. A. *How to Discipline Without Feeling Guilty.* Champaign, Ill.: Research Press, 1980.

Simon, E. "Parent-Child Activity." In L. Hoffman (ed.), *The Evaluation and Care of Severely Disturbed Children.* New York: Spectrum Publications Medical & Scientific Books, 1982.

Siskind, A. B. "Stages of Residential Treatment: Clinical and Milieu Considerations." *Family and Child Mental Health Journal,* 1982, *8,* 26-39.

Small, R., Kennedy, K., and Bender, B. "Critical Issues for Practice in Residential Treatment: The View from Within." *American Journal of Orthopsychiatry*, 1991, *61*, 327–338.

Smith, J. M., and Smith, D.E.P. *Child Management: A Program for Parents and Teachers.* Champaign, Ill.: Research Press, 1976.

Spivack, G., Platt, J. J., and Shure, M. B. *The Problem-Solving Approach to Adjustment: A Guide to Research and Intervention.* San Francisco: Jossey-Bass, 1976.

Stanton, A. H., and Schwartz, M. S. *The Mental Hospital.* New York: Basic Books, 1954.

Stechler, G., and Halton, A. "The Emergence of Assertion and Aggression During Infancy: A Psychoanalytic Systems Approach." *Journal of the American Psychoanalytic Association*, 1987, *35*, 821–838.

Stewart, J. T., Myers, W. C., Burket, R. C., and Lyles, W. B. "A Review of the Pharmacotherapy of Aggression in Children and Adolescents." *Journal of the American Academy of Child and Adolescent Psychiatry*, 1990, *29*, 269–277.

Strayhorn, J. M. *The Competent Child.* New York: Guilford Press, 1988.

Susselman, S. "The Use of Physical Restraint: Its Relation to Other Forms of Psychotherapeutic Intervention." In S. A. Szurek and I. N. Berlin (eds.), *Clinical Studies in Clinical Psychoses.* New York: Brunner/Mazel, 1973.

Szurek, S. A., and Berlin, I. N. (eds.). *Clinical Studies in Childhood Psychoses.* New York: Brunner/Mazel, 1973.

Szurek, S. A., Berlin, I. N., and Boatman, J. *Inpatient Care for the Psychotic Child.* Langley Porter Child Psychiatry Series, Clinical Approaches to Problems of Childhood, no. 5. Palo Alto, Calif.: Science and Behavior Books, 1971.

Tardiff, K. *Concise Guide to Assessment and Management of Violent Patients.* Washington, D.C.: American Psychiatric Press, 1989.

Tardiff, K. (ed.). *The Psychiatric Uses of Seclusion and Restraint.* Washington, D.C.: American Psychiatric Press, 1984.

Trieschman, A. E., Whittaker, J. K., and Brendtro, L. K. *The Other 23 Hours: Child Care Work in a Therapeutic Milieu.* Hawthorne, N.Y.: Aldine de Gruyter, 1969.

Valentine, N. "Seclusion and Restraint: A Nursing Perspective."

Paper presented at a conference on Seclusion and Restraint, McLean Hospital, Belmont, Mass., 1984.

Ventura, M. S. "A Look at Restraining Practices and the Use of Psychotropic Drugs." *Journal of Psychiatric Nursing and Mental Health Services,* May-June 1974, pp. 3-9.

Vitiello, B., Ricciuti, A. J., and Behar, D. "P.R.N. Medications in Child State Hospital Inpatients." *Journal of Clinical Psychiatry,* 1987, *48,* 351-354.

Vorrath, H. H., and Brendtro, L. K. *Positive Peer Culture.* Hawthorne, N.Y.: Aldine de Gruyter, 1985.

Wagonseller, B. R., and McDowell, R. L. *You and Your Child.* Champaign, Ill.: Research Press, 1979.

Weinstein, S. R., and others. "Comparison of DISC with Clinicians' DSM-III Diagnoses in Psychiatric Inpatients." *Journal of the American Academy of Child and Adolescent Psychiatry,* 1989, *28,* 53-60.

Werry, J. S., and Wollersheim, J. P. "Behavior Therapy with Children and Adolescents: A Twenty-Year Overview." *Journal of the American Academy of Child and Adolescent Psychiatry,* 1989, *28,* 1-18.

Whittaker, J. K. *Caring for Troubled Children: Residential Treatment in a Community Context.* San Francisco: Jossey-Bass, 1979.

Wilson, D. R., and Lyman, R. D. "Time-Out in the Treatment of Childhood Behavior Problems: Implementation and Research Issues." *Child and Family Behavior Therapy,* 1982, *4,* 5-20.

Winnicott, D. W. *The Maturational Processes and the Facilitating Environment.* New York: International Universities Press, 1965.

World Health Organization. *Report of Expert Committee on Mental Health.* Geneva, Switzerland: World Health Organization, 1951.

Wyka, G. T. "Nonviolent Crisis Intervention: A Practical Approach for Managing Violent Behavior." In J. T. Turner (ed.), *Handbook of Security and Safety.* Aspen, Colo.: Aspen Publishers, 1988.

INDEX

307

Jim, 154
Jimmy: and communication, 90–91,
98, 101–102, 111–112; described,
283–284; and environment, 36;
in lion story, 275, 276–277; and
postcrisis, 251; and time-outs,
170–171, 172, 176, 178, 179, 180
Joan, 124
Joanne, 219–220
John, 155, 165
Johnny: and active containing, 187;
and communication, 93, 94–95,
110–111; described, 284–285; and
discipline, 150–151, 154; and empathy, 79–82; and environment,
32; and postcrisis, 235–237, 238,
242, 247–249, 250, 254, 257–258,
262; and time-outs, 164, 171
Jones, R. R., 72, 189
Joshi, P. T., 201
Joy, 75–76, 141, 142, 145–146, 164
Joyce, 251
Judy, 85
Julie, 99, 106–107

K

Kalogjera, I. J., 3, 83
Kashani, J. H., 18
Kathy, 55, 76, 106, 165
Keith, 98, 117–118, 147
Kendall, P. C., 17, 58
Kennedy, K., 21
Knesper, D. J., 83
Koman, S. L., 65, 183, 184

L

Laatsch, A., 66
Lavin, D., 58
Leach, P., 210, 211
Leaving phase, described, 11, 18
Leokum, A., 103
Leslie, 101–102, 120, 155
Letters. *See* Note writing
Levinson, D. J., 5
Lewis, M., 224–225
Lickona, T., 127
Life-space interviews, 89
Linn, D., 224

Lion, J. R., 192, 226
Lion metaphor, 1–2, 273–277
Lisa (child): and active containing,
197–199, 217; and communication, 116, 117, 124–126;
described, 6–8, 10, 17, 286–287;
and discipline, 141, 148, 154,
155; and empathy, 73, 83–84;
and environment, 32; and postcrisis, 231–232, 249; and time-
outs, 169, 172
Lisa (counselor), 109–110, 187
Listening: good, 87–88, 89–93; not
good, 93–95; reflective, 97–98
Locks: role of, 32; for seclusion,
213, 217–221
Love, in socialization, 72
Lyles, W. B., 224
Lyman, R. D., 170
Lynette, 171

M

Macaulay, D., 103
McCarter, E., 224
McDowell, R. L., 149, 152
McGoldrick, M., 45
Macht, L. B., 5
McKay, G., 71–72, 88
Mackinnon, R. A., 193
McMahon, R. J., 72, 189
Maggie: and active containing, 202;
and communication, 103–104,
110, 118–119; described,
287–288; and discipline, 134,
137, 138, 142–143, 151; and en-
vironment, 28–29; and postcrisis,
240; and time-outs, 171, 176, 177
Maier, G. J., 222, 223
Maltsberger, J., 166
Maria: and communication, 99,
100–101, 105–106, 107, 114;
described, 1, 284; and discipline,
147, 148, 150; and empathy, 73,
84; and time-outs, 171
Marohn, R. C., 224
Matson, J. L., 242
Mayer, M. F., 4
Mazlish, E., 72, 87, 88, 89, 93,
97–98, 108, 112, 238, 241